The Last Full Measure

The Last Full Measure

An American Family and How the United States Brought Home the Dead of World War II

Kim Clarke

STACKPOLE
BOOKS
Essex, Connecticut

STACKPOLE BOOKS
The Globe Pequot Publishing Group, Inc.
64 South Main Street
Essex, CT 06426
www.globepequot.com

British Library Cataloguing in Publication Information available

Library of Congress Cataloging-in-Publication Data available

ISBN 9780811777667 (cloth) | ISBN 9780811777674 (epub)

For my family

Contents

Preface

When it was lowered into the Austrian ground, my grandfather's body was broken and burned, wearing a bloodied Army Air Corps flying suit. His wooden coffin was placed atop another casket, which in turn was stacked on top of the first coffin to be lowered into the grave. Cpl. Delbert Wayne Trueman, twenty-seven years old, was buried with strangers in a foreign land.

He was killed in the fall of 1944 on his first combat mission in World War II. Like the men buried with him, Delbert spiraled to his death aboard a crippled bomber from the skies above Vienna.

His grave was carved out of an isolated section of a remarkably beautiful place: the Zentralfriedhof, Vienna's sprawling Central Cemetery. The park is home to the remains of famous residents such as Johann Strauss, Ludwig van Beethoven, Franz Schubert, and Johannes Brahms. Now, it held a dead airman whom the German soldiers recorded as Dellert N. Triebmann. They marked his crowded grave with a simple cross and moved on to the next plot and another three coffins.

It took the American military ten months to transform Delbert from husband and father to soldier, gunner, and casualty. It would take that same military more than four years to locate his grave, recover his body, and return him to his Indiana hometown.

He was first reported missing and then killed in action. The army could not say where he was, only that troops were searching for his remains. When they found him, they did not tell his family for months. The journey home took him through western Europe and the hands of soldiers and civilians tasked with returning the bodies of thousands of GIs, airmen, marines, and sailors to their families in the United States.

Over the years, my grandfather's body would be buried, disinterred, carried on an airplane, buried again, re-exhumed, stacked in storage, winched aboard a ship, placed on trains, ferried across a river, lifted into a hearse and, finally, buried alongside his younger brother Dale. It was Dale—a bomber pilot—who was killed first, in a wartime death that Delbert vowed to make right.

The night before Delbert died, as he prepared to sleep knowing his first taste of war was just hours away, he wrote a letter. Since enlisting and leaving Indiana, his letters home were bright and typically sent to his daughter—my mother—who was six years old at the time. He teased her, calling her "Bud," "Judy Poody," and "Honey Bunny Boo." He encouraged her to write letters and draw pictures of airplanes for him. He asked about school, her grades, and whether she was helping her mother. Please don't cry when I call home, he asked, because I want to talk to you.

He mailed Judy presents—cowboy boots, money, a toy pistol, a tiny airman's uniform complete with a jacket and service cap. She and her friends were already bounding through their neighborhood wearing hand grenade belts and helmets and playing "Army." Nazis and Japs were always the bad guys.

Delbert now scribbled a quick note from Europe. He said nothing of the next day's mission. He knew he was headed to Vienna, a place hated by American air crews because the antiaircraft flak was so accurate and so thick it turned the skies black. Instead, he wrote that he was feeling a bit down because no mail from home had caught up with him since arriving at his base a week earlier. Rather than Judy, this letter was only for his wife.

> *Gosh, there just isn't anything to write about tonite so I will quit. Say hello to all for me and have them write. Bye sweet and don't forget I still love you very much and always will. Write me now.*

Two weeks after my grandfather was buried in Vienna, a young man from Western Union bicycled to the front porch of my grandmother's house. It was a Tuesday morning, and she was inside washing her hair when he knocked on the front door. The boy's face alone conveyed terrible news as he handed her a telegram.

> *The Secretary of War desires me to express his deep regret that your husband Corporal Delbert W. Trueman has been reported missing in action since seventeen October over Austria. If further details or other information are received you will be promptly notified.*

* * *

More than thirty years later, I am holding that telegram. It is tucked into a yellow envelope with a cellophane window that displays my grandmother's Indiana address from 1944.

I am fifteen years old, and my sisters and I are sitting on the orange shag carpet that blankets our quad-level home in a new subdivision. The yard has no trees. Our brother is somewhere in the house, too young to care or understand what our mother is telling us.

She wants to show us her past, a chapter she's never shared. We are old enough now, she says. A wooden crate, worn smooth by time, rests at her feet. It is a box that was first held by my grandmother and then passed on to my mother, who is opening it for us. It holds pieces of a life.

When she lifts the lid, the air turns musty.

In a quiet voice, my mom says she was barely six when her dad left for the Army Air Corps in early 1944. She tells us that when he was away, she and Grandma would sing every night while washing the dishes: "Off we go, into the wild blue yonder!"

My mom reaches into the crate. She hands us a Western Union telegram. Its purple type is still glued in place, every letter capitalized as it announces her father is missing in action.

* * *

When my mom tells us her dad was killed in the war, we know this means World War II, even as images of helicopters and Vietnamese jungles fill our television.

I think back to a few years earlier, to a day when she kept us home from school. We didn't have fevers or runny noses, even for winter in Detroit. But it was a holiday of sorts, the twelfth day of February, 1973: The prisoners of war were coming home from Vietnam, and she wanted us to see them. My mom wanted us to watch the happy reunions with wives and children who had waited years to know their loved ones were still alive. We didn't know yet about her missing father, or how our grandmother had hoped for her soldier-husband to come home from another continent.

We squeezed around a portable black-and-white TV set up in the living room, where the only voice belonged to the announcer who, my memory assures me, was Walter Cronkite. I couldn't understand why we weren't in the basement family room, with the bigger, color TV, the couch, and blankets. Maybe that would have felt too much like hooky, like goofing off when we were supposed to be paying attention. This was serious.

To a twelve-year-old's eyes fixed on the screen, the POWs looked handsome as they stepped from the airplane. I'd never met these men, but I knew them: Jeremiah Denton, Everett Alvarez, Robinson Risner. I'd memorized their names and pictures, grainy men who stared back from the pages of a *Reader's Digest* I saved. I knew their faces as well as I did those of Al Kaline, Elton John, and Jack Lord, the other lights in my seventh-grade universe.

The POWs on television were all airmen, just like the navy officer whose name was stamped into the metal bracelet around my wrist: LT. CMDR. THOMAS H. PILKINGTON. He flew into oblivion after launching his fighter jet from the USS *Coral Sea* one night in 1966 and crashing somewhere in North Vietnam. When I sent a letter to his sister to learn more, she wrote back with hopes that the Viet Cong held Tom in a prison camp. She said she believed her brother was missing but alive, and would come home. I believed, too.

I twisted the bracelet around and around as the broadcast continued. My sister wore the name of an Air Force guy, CAPT. JAMES E. STEADMAN. We were not a military family. My dad had been an army sergeant during the Korean War, but his only weapon was a typewriter at Fort Sill, Oklahoma. Writing reports, he joked, was safer than firing a howitzer at people who would shoot back. Yet everyone in our family wore a bracelet for a soldier missing in Vietnam. Whenever we talked of our bracelets, it was of "my guy." My guy was from Illinois. My guy was not married. My guy was twenty-five.

It was only later, in newspaper interviews and autobiographies, that we learned of the degradation and beatings, the starvation and psychological torture endured by the POWs. How men blinked their eyes to convey coded words to their families, and how the Hanoi Hilton, with its filth and cruelty, was worse than any of us, child or parent, could have fathomed. And that Thomas Pilkington and James Steadman would never emerge from the jungles where their fighter jets disappeared.

But that winter day, the men were smiling and slender, in dark shoes, dark slacks, khaki jackets zipped to their collarbones. Their hair was short. In his left hand, each man carried a small travel bag; I tried to imagine what it held after years in prison, perhaps a toothbrush and comb to fill the emptiness. Once on the tarmac, each man raised his right hand, saluted an officer, and walked off the television screen.

* * *

My mom continues to unpack the crate and its layers. Here is a scrapbook bulging with newspaper clippings about high school basketball and football games. Tiny crumbs of yellowed newsprint fall from the pages. A strand of twine wraps around dozens of envelopes addressed to her in neat blue handwriting. "Tell all your grand-folks hello for me and then run over to Mother, grab her by the neck, pull her down and squeeze to beat the band. Put a big smacker on her kisser, will you?"

Next come typed letters from the War Department, enlistment papers, and a small case holding a pair of aviator glasses, an ugly crack spread across one lens. A slender blue box with a hinged lid reveals a Purple Heart strung on wide ribbon. A scuffed leather wallet contains Italian lira, an Indiana driver's license, and a black-and-white snapshot: my six-year-old mother, standing between my grandmother and a smiling man in uniform.

Delbert and Virginia Trueman, with their daughter, Judy, in June 1944. *Kim Clarke photo*

I do not yet know this man, the airmen he died with, or the others who formed a different army, one that fanned out across Europe after the war to bring home hundreds of thousands of men like him.

All I know is fascination. The letters, the photos, pieces of a past I don't know and a grandfather I've never heard of—a mystery sits boxed in front of me, with my mother and grandmother in roles that are foreign to me. I return the lid to the crate and carry it into my bedroom.

Chapter 1

War

It was the early morning of October 17, 1944, when Delbert Trueman approached a skinny, dark-haired kid alongside a hulking B-24 bomber on an Italian airfield. Bob Davis was all of nineteen years old but had something that Delbert, at age twenty-seven, did not: combat experience. Delbert was new to Italy, new to the dusty air base of the 450th Bomb Group, and new to the fear and nerves of a bomb run. Davis had survived more than two dozen flights over enemy territory from his position as a gunner in the plane's midsection. He'd flown over Munich, Budapest, Vienna, and sooty Romanian oil fields, the B-24 Liberator barreling through flak explosions as the crew unleashed bombs on factories and refineries.

Delbert had spent all of 1944 as an Army Air Corps recruit, flying aboard bombers in Texas, Georgia, and Massachusetts. When he wasn't in the air and over the Gulf of Mexico or the Eastern Seaboard, he was on the ground training. Small men were favorites as gunners, and Delbert was groomed to be a nose gunner in the fat-bellied craft often maligned by aircrews as a "flying boxcar." His size made him particularly suited for the cramped bubble that dotted the nose and tail of a B-24 bomber.

He was resigned to being a gunner. His first choice, like so many men joining the Air Corps, had been to be a pilot. It was the glamour job, the command position glorified in recruitment posters and magazine advertisements, and Delbert desperately wanted to be behind the controls of a bomber. When the army said his eyesight was too weak to be a pilot, he knew it was merely an excuse. His eyes were fine. "Evidently they had just filled their quota for pilots when they washed me out," he would tell his wife. "It sure is disgusting, to say the least."

But he marveled at what he saw from the sky. Flying out of a base from the southern tip of Texas, he soared over the Gulf of Mexico, flecked with tiny fishing boats and dark convoys of navy vessels. He wrote home:

> *Boy let me tell you that it gives a fellow a funny feeling when he goes out over that water for the first time. Of course we wear "Mae West" life belts and parachutes in case we would have the occasion to use them. I hope that time never comes, huh? It was an awful pretty sight to see, as you can imagine.*

Now Delbert was envisioning combat as he stood with Davis along a runway in Manduria, a centuries-old village of olive groves, almond trees, and peasants leading horse-drawn carts. Wedged into the heel of Italy's boot, Manduria was an airstrip abandoned in late 1943 by the Italian Air Force. By October 1944, it was an established American base with more than 2,200 men and hundreds of B-24 Liberator bombers. Men nicknamed the base "Frantic."

Local stonemasons had been hired to construct barracks. Each of the four squadrons that made up the 450th Bomb Group had erected a day room, a place where men could relax, write letters, and have a drink; the day rooms complemented an officers' club that served cognac for thirty lira, or thirty cents, and champagne for 110 lira. The squadrons took up sides in athletics, with basketball and baseball teams sprouting up. Boxing was a favorite among the men, who went crazy when boxing great Joe Louis and other fighters staged a few rounds at the air base. Other forms of entertainment included nightly movies and the occasional touring show. Song-and-dance man Jack Haley stopped by to deliver an evening of music and comedy, although the showgirls who joined him onstage were a bigger hit with the crews.

The laughs were welcome, and necessary. The 450th had been engaged in heavy combat since dropping its first bombs in January 1944.

The airmen were the Cottontails, so called when the radio propagandist Axis Sally singled out "the white-tail Liberators" after one of their missions; the group's planes bore white rudders. In turn, the men called her the "Berlin Bitch." Their B-24 bombers were lifting off regularly for marshaling yards and oil refineries across western and central Europe. The 450th and other groups from the Fifteenth Air Force took a particularly intense pounding whenever they flew to Ploesti, a Romanian city lined with giant oil tanks; flak from German antiaircraft guns was always fierce and accurate. Men lost friends who only hours earlier sat beside them at breakfast; officers learned to write compassionate letters to mothers and wives. "We have grown accustomed to missing faces at the group club bar," wrote an officer as he recorded the 450th's daily activities. "Is the group getting heartless? No! We are becoming reconciled to the realities of war and seasoned to the outcomes of combat."

This was the world Bob Davis knew. He had been in Manduria for four months and already six of the ten men from his original crew were dead. The churn of combat was relentless. Delbert met up with Davis at the rear of the B-24; looking up, he could see the tail gun turret he would soon occupy. Months earlier at gunnery school in Texas, when learning to handle and fire a bomber's weapons, Delbert's upper body had turned purple from the constant recoil of the .50-caliber machine-gun barrels slamming into his shoulders. He could barely lift his arms afterward. For weeks, the recruits practiced shooting, firing everything from twelve-gauge shotguns to mounted machine guns and unloading thousands of rounds of ammunition. They shot at clay plates and clay pigeons, and at fixed targets pulled by trucks. To the Air Corps, the mission of a gunner was clear and critical: "Find a way to hit the fighter before it destroyed the bomber." As his first combat mission approached, Delbert would be aiming to shoot down any German fighter planes that tried to intercept his B-24.

The airmen always got their assignment the night before a mission. For the first time since landing in Manduria a week earlier, Delbert learned he was going up, and he blanched when he heard the target: Vienna. It was the most heavily defended European city outside of Berlin. They were to bomb the Osterreichische Saurerwerke, a factory where workers produced engines for German tanks. Men hated flying to Vienna because the flak was so precise and so thick, it turned the day black. It didn't take much to bring down a B-24, or cause it to explode in midair; a shard of red-hot flak was the Nazis' stone for the Goliath-like Liberators. In the briefing room, Delbert turned to Charlie Ward, his best friend from gunnery school, and stared in disbelief. Ward took one look and thought he read Delbert's mind: *I'm not coming back.*

Bob Davis saw that same fear on Delbert's face as they huddled alongside the bomber. *What's it like? What's combat like?* Delbert had heard the other men talk about Vienna, the noise, the dirty bursts of flak that rattled the planes and sliced through fuselages, the stink of cordite. Outside of Germany, no city was better fortified, with guns trained on the American bombers that every day swarmed overhead with their deadly cargo.

The Fifteenth Air Force had been bombing Vienna and its suburbs since the spring of 1944, chipping away at airplane factories, armaments plants, and oil refineries on the city's outskirts. By early fall, the B-24s were unleashing their bombs on the center of the Austrian capital. The city, often thought of as the cultural heart of Europe, had become an increasingly important target. With the Allies' successful invasion at Normandy in June and the consequent liberation of Paris and Rome, Hitler's hold on Europe was failing. As Allied troops moved closer toward Germany, the Nazis withdrew to Europe's interior, shifting men and equipment to cities like Vienna. By the fall of 1944, the Germans had two hundred heavy flak units stationed in Austria, with more than a quarter of them in and around Vienna. Soldiers trained close to 450 guns of varying firepower on the skies above the city. Teenaged boys as young as fifteen handled the powerful flak guns, propelling grenade-like shells that exploded four and five miles above the earth.

Davis knew Delbert was anxious. Now was the time to talk, because once the bomber lifted off, the noise in the fuselage would be deafening. It was always quiet on the morning of a mission. Men were rousted at an ungodly hour, dressed, drank coffee and ate toast if they could stomach it, and made their way to the planes. Davis motioned Delbert away from the bomber, and the men walked over to a nearby fence along the airfield. They made small talk, and quickly found a common bond: Both were married. In fact, of the ten men who would climb into the bomber, they and the pilot were the only ones with wives, and Delbert alone was a father.

Davis was a newlywed. Four months earlier, before shipping out of southern Virginia for Europe, he had sent a telegram to his girlfriend, Kathleen, in Brooklyn. Come down to the base, he said, let's get married. They were both children of immigrants who had made New York their new home. Davis's father came from Russia; his girlfriend's parents had immigrated from Ireland. Davis wanted to be a married man before flying off to the war. Kathleen took a train to Langley Field, and Davis's crewmates pitched in to buy a wedding ring he would place on her finger. Davis's lieutenant gave him a night off, and while the rest of the crew made a training run to Bermuda and back, he and Kathleen made their way to nearby Hampton. A Baptist minister pronounced them married on June 23 at 10:30 at night. Six days later, Davis and his crewmates flew to Italy.

Delbert's wedding ring was not on his hand that October 1944 morning. The men had been warned to leave all personal belongings in the barracks. There was no reason to carry anything that, God forbid, the enemy could use against a flier if he was shot down and captured. Delbert followed orders. He abandoned the tiny Bible from his in-laws, the one designed to fit in his breast pocket, a brass cover to protect his heart if the plane could not. His wallet, its worn leather curved to his body, carried a tattered newspaper clipping about his brother. Slipped throughout were snapshots, black-and-white memories of his wife and daughter. Delbert's favorite, a photo of all three of them, was tucked behind a plastic sleeve along with a dried and faded four-leaf clover. He removed his gold wedding band, inscribed with the name of his bride. He left everything in a pile on his bunk, and told his pal Charlie Ward to make sure his stuff got to his wife, Virginia, if anything went wrong.

He had been in Italy for only seven days and would be flying with strangers like Davis. Officers always assigned new men like him to seasoned crews. Green crews were split up, sent off to orientation, and teamed up with instructors; they were then assigned to fly several missions with experienced crews. These were the veterans, even though some men were nearly a decade younger than Delbert. It would be suicide to send an inexperienced crew into combat; no amount of training could simulate the noise and smell and terror of the real thing. Seasoned crews didn't like flying with newcomers. Green fliers disrupted a bond that was forged in combat, a sense of reliance and trust that was now threatened by someone whose skills and reactions were unknown. Replacement crewmen like Delbert were also flesh-and-blood reminders of men who were gone.

Delbert wouldn't fly with his friend Charlie, at least not right away. They had trained together in the States and flown with each other across the Atlantic to Italy; now, despite sharing barracks, each was assigned to a veteran crew. Eventually, he and Ward and all the guys from his original crew would reassemble and fly together. Once a man was credited with fifty missions, he was eligible to go home.

Bob Davis was more than halfway there with twenty-eight missions to his credit. He'd been to Vienna, and tried to put Delbert at ease. "Don't worry," Davis assured him, "October 17 is my wife's birthday and nothing bad will happen on her big day." Delbert relaxed a bit, and as a green flare went up from the airfield control tower, the men climbed into the airplane. Plenty of B-24s in the 450th bore provocative nose art with painted names like "Booby Trap," "Bachelor's Bedlam" and "Ten Fighting Cocks." But as more and more bombers were rushed to the war, there was less and less time for fancy nose work. Davis liked to say the paint wasn't even dry before the planes were shot down. The B-24 he and Delbert boarded was anonymous, known only by its serial number of 42-51566. At 8:30 a.m. on October 17, the silver bomber and twenty-seven other Liberators rumbled down the runway, pulled away from the earth, and flew north toward Austria.

Seven hours later, planes returning from Vienna began landing in Manduria. It was shortly after 3:30 p.m. when the first bomber touched down. As always, women from the Red Cross greeted the returning crews with hot coffee and cake doughnuts. A few planes straggled in around five o'clock after stopping at other fields to refuel. Dinner came and went, and a final bomber landed at 6:35 p.m. Charlie Ward, Delbert's best friend, waited. His mission had been a rough one, with flak nicking his bomber's fuel tank. With gasoline pouring into the bomb bay, the nose gunner and bombardier bailed out over Vienna. But Ward and his crewmates made it back. Now, he scanned the skies for Delbert's aircraft.

In the offices of the 450th, clerks compiled reports of that day's mission. They recorded the route to Vienna, the assault on the city and its results ("a break in the clouds at bombs-away permitted a fleeting glimpse of the primary target area and it is believed that bombs struck in the vicinity of the city gas works, possibly carrying over into the Saurerwerke installations."). Twenty-eight planes took part in the run, with four turning back early and twenty-four making it all the way to Vienna. Twenty-three bombers, it was noted, returned safely to Manduria. A clerk typed: "One lost."

* * *

Delbert Trueman had enlisted in the Army Air Corps for one reason: Dale, his younger, brasher brother.

When Dale passed an early but critical phase of pilot training in late 1942, he celebrated with beer. Lots of beer. After two failed flights to qualify, including a near-collision in the sky with another plane, he faced his third and final attempt. Flying a PT-19 trainer alongside an instructor, Dale maneuvered the aircraft through a series of stalls. He made the plane climb and then banked it in sweeping, 180-degree curves. He performed lazy eights, crisscrossing the sky at differing speeds and changing horizons. Next came a spin and a forced landing. When the test was over, the flight instructor was direct: "Mr. Trueman, that was a remarkable ride compared to the first two you gave me." He told Dale to drink a few beers and relax.

Dale followed orders and rewarded himself with Schlitz: "I slopped up so damn much it. . . . I must have had 15 or 20 big glasses," he wrote. The next morning, he had a booming headache, but it was worth it. He was competitive, and the prospect of failing a qualifying flight was almost too much to bear. He knew how to fly an airplane well before enlisting. Even his lieutenant was baffled at the initial botched test flights and scolded Dale for wasting his time with sloppy flying, followed by the flawless third attempt.

"All I could think of," Dale wrote to his parents as he nursed his hangover, "was what you and some others back there would think if I washed out. I wouldn't like it myself either, and you don't know how much you want to stay in this air corps until you get so close to being out of it." He would go on to become a second lieutenant and the pilot of a B-24—the very job his older brother would one day covet.

Delbert and Dale were born twenty-six months apart in Danville, Illinois, the first children of Paul and Nellie Trueman. Delbert arrived first, on Valentine's Day of 1917, almost nine months to the day that Paul and Nellie wed. Dale was born in the spring of 1919. Between the boys' births, Danville and the rest of the nation found themselves at war in Europe. Paul registered for the military draft—attesting that he was physically able, of medium height and build, with brown hair and dark brown eyes—but was never called up.

Men of Paul's generation did not have careers so much as they had jobs, and he was a workingman: a mechanic at the local service station, a clerk for the Chicago and Eastern Illinois Railroad, a delivery truck driver, a salesman. Nellie stayed home in the house they rented, raising the boys. When she and Paul celebrated their fifth wedding anniversary, Nellie was pregnant for the third time; a daughter, Virginia, was born in August 1921.

Nellie knew big families. She was one of nine children; her brothers, sisters, and their families were spread throughout Danville, and the three Trueman children had aunts, uncles, and cousins in the neighborhood, as well as their grandparents. But it was Paul's family—namely, a cousin—that prompted him and Nellie to leave Danville in 1926 and move 160 miles to the northeast, across the state line to Marion, Indiana. Paul would go to work with his cousin at Globe Mercantile, selling furniture and other home goods from a downtown Marion storefront. The Trueman family grew again in 1928 with the birth of Beverly, whom everyone affectionately called Babe.

Delbert and Dale established themselves as athletes in Marion by the time they were teenagers. Delbert made a name for himself in high school, appearing regularly on the sports pages as he steered the varsity basketball and football teams to victory in a town that entertained itself with the exploits of the Marion Giants. He was ramrod straight, both on and off the field. For all his popularity, from his pick as president of the junior class to receiving the high school's top athletic award, classmates still voted him "most bashful." No one would accuse Del Trueman of being wild.

Dale followed, starring on the basketball court and, like his brother, serving as president of his junior class. He was taller and lankier than Delbert and had a smile that looked to border on a laugh. By graduating from Marion High, each boy already had more education than his parents; Paul and Nellie had attended school as far as eighth grade as youngsters in Illinois. After high school and the basketball team, Dale suited up as a wing for the Idyl Wyld Roller Hockey Team, a group that would bring Marion a small measure of fame as state champions. His nickname was a far cry from his reserved, older brother. Dale Trueman was known as "Stud."

When the Japanese bombed the American military base at Pearl Harbor in 1941, there was a direct impact on Marion. Wendell Ray Hurley, who had been in the same high school class with Dale, was among the sailors to go down with the USS *Arizona*. He was twenty-two years old and, as in high school, he was a musician, performing in the navy. He had been aboard the *Arizona* for just three weeks before the attack that launched the nation into war.

Decisions faced the Trueman men.

Once again, Paul Trueman registered for the military draft. He was heavier than during World War I, his hair was gray, and his right forearm bore a tattoo: an American flag. He was forty-seven, and he and Nellie were still raising Babe at home. No one, including the military, expected men of his age to be called into combat. The real question of the government was what kind of skills older men could contribute on the home front.

The draft would also spare Delbert. He was married with a young daughter and, while eligible to be called, he and other fathers were passed over in favor of single men in town. Life went on in Marion amid the

Dale Trueman (left), with his older brother, Delbert, and their father, Paul. *Kim Clarke photo*

rationing of food and the collecting of rubber, tin, and grease. Delbert crisscrossed the city as a meter reader for the local electrical company, and his wife, Virginia, worked as a bookkeeper. They went out on Friday nights to watch the Marion High basketball team; Saturday nights were spent playing cards with friends.

It was Dale who took the biggest step. Living at home with his parents and working as a salesman, he decided to enlist with the Air Corps in March 1942. He traveled fifty miles north to Fort Wayne to volunteer at Baer Field, an air base that residents had watched materialize from cornfields in less than a year. Hundreds of men had worked around the clock to build an Army Air Corps base that would grow to house ten thousand airmen bound for overseas combat.

It would take just as long—one year—for Dale to be groomed for war, moving from the northern Indiana base to pilot training in Texas, Arizona, and California. In those twelve months, he would be commissioned an officer—2nd Lt. Dale J. Trueman—with gold bars on his uniform lapels. He also wore gold on his left hand, having married his Marion girlfriend, Leah Hayes, on Valentine's Day while stationed in Waco, Texas. They posed for photos amid cactus and barracks at Blackland Army Flying School in central Texas.

Together, the newlyweds moved to yet another base, this time in Salinas, California, where Dale would learn to handle a B-24 Liberator, a heavy bomber that carried a crew of ten and just as many five-hundred-pound bombs and .50-caliber machine guns. If the sleek B-17 Flying Fortress was the Air Corps' glamorous bomber, the B-24 was its workhorse. It was the biggest airplane Dale had ever flown.

"Dad, you sent me a clipping of the B-17 and the Lancaster. The 24 has both of them beat as to bomb load, amount of gas, rate of climb and speed, and better engines. Anything else? Oh yes—firepower is better," he wrote from Salinas. His letters to Paul and Nellie were long, detailed, and written in perfect script. He mailed home a sketch of a B-24 torn from a magazine, drawing a circle around the cartoonish pilot and scribbling "ME."

He was learning to handle the giant bomber at speeds of 225 miles per hour and faster, sometimes skimming just above the California ground at 500 feet. And the missions were longer, in preparation for the bombing runs he most likely would make from a base in England into France and Germany. "We're starting to fly eight-hour missions now," he told his father in late June, "and that's a long time to stay up in one stretch."

Dale had been at the controls nearly nine hours on July 5 when his B-24 slammed into the California countryside. It was 3:30 in the morning, and he had never flown so far or so long in the dark. He and his crew had covered the whole of Southern California throughout the night, from Salinas to Hunter-Liggett and south to Blythe, near the borders of Arizona and Mexico. They were returning north and trying to reach the airport in Bakersfield, and fell five miles short of the runway.

One of the plane's four engines—the No. 2 powerplant on the left wing—had a bad propeller, and Dale shut it down. Gauges indicated that the remaining three engines each held fifty gallons of gas, a trickle compared to the 2,900 gallons the plane was built to carry. From his seat

Newlyweds Dale and Leah Trueman in 1943. *Kim Clarke photo*

behind Dale, the radio operator's attempts to contact the ground for landing clearance went unheard, and no one in the Bakersfield tower saw the plane as it soared in the distant black sky. The No. 1 engine, the only thing keeping the left wing aloft, ran out of gas. The plane plunged to the ground and burst into flames, igniting the air and sparking a grass fire. One airman was thrown from the wreck and managed to pull another man from the plane. Seven men, including Dale Trueman, were burned beyond recognition; they joined the 40 percent of airmen who failed Air Corps training because of something so innocent as lousy eyesight or so unlucky as running out of fuel four thousand feet in the air.

The war suddenly came home to Delbert. He and his family were preparing to leave the house for a Sunday matinee when the phone rang.

He had just returned to Marion the day before from a trip to California to see Dale, joined by his mother and sister; the women had stayed behind for a longer visit. His father couldn't make the journey because there was too much to do at home. Dale had told his dad they would see each other later that summer when a furlough allowed for six days in Marion. ("Have your work pretty well caught up so you don't have to work all the time," he told his dad.) Delbert got back from Salinas on the Fourth of July, and the next day's phone call from the air base shattered all plans.

It was Delbert's job to tell his father. No one could find Paul at home; he was playing golf, and Delbert drove to the course. When he heard the news, Paul Trueman collapsed.

Nellie Trueman was now a Gold Star mother, with a gold-fringed banner to hang in her front window, telling everyone in Marion that her Air Corps pilot son was dead at age twenty-four. Leah Hayes Trueman was a widow coming home to Indiana after twenty weeks of marriage. Delbert became disillusioned and gripped by the desire to somehow fix the loss of his brother and the damage to his family. He would look for a way to take his brother's place.

Dale Trueman's commanding officer told the Truemans that the pilot died defending American ideals. "He would have rather given his life on the scene of battle, but to me he did," wrote Lt. Col. Harvey P. Barnard Jr., adding "he gave his life nobly, honorably and without hesitation."

Still, the Air Corps would blame Dale Trueman for the crash, saying he used poor judgment by trying to fly so far on not enough fuel. Officers also said he should have known how to land the B-24 safely with only two engines. The cause of the accident was clear: "Momentary lack of proficiency."

* * *

He was always Uncle Dale. I never met him, but when my mom spoke of Uncle Dale, it was matter-of-fact, as if he were alive and well and just in the next room. As a child, she loved watching him skate with the roller hockey team. He was fun and funny. He took her to the airport south of town, where he would lift her into a tiny Piper Cub, and together they would fly above the houses and streets of Marion.

On the day he died, when she was about to go to the movies and her dad received that terrible phone call, her reaction was like that of a five-year-old: *Are we still going to the show?* That's how she remembered that afternoon.

If there was a salve for the pain of Dale Trueman's death, it was that he died stateside. As his body was escorted home by a uniformed Air Corps lieutenant in 1943, the Trueman family was able to plan a funeral, meet his casket at the Marion train station, and bury Dale within a mile of where he grew up. Less than two weeks passed between his death and funeral, where members of the old roller hockey team reunited to serve as pallbearers.

For families of soldiers dying overseas, in places like Tunisia and Sicily, the wait was much longer. The military had no plan for bringing home the dead from battlefields.

Chapter 2

"His Duty"

No one had wanted Delbert Trueman to enlist in the military, particularly his wife. They had a six-year-old daughter to think of. He was now his parents' only son.

But someone, he argued, had to carry on for his brother, Dale. Someone, he said, had to bear the burden of his family's pain. "He didn't seem to be angry. He was hurt more than anything," my grandmother would recall. "He was just hurt, like he felt he had to do something to take Dale's place."

Delbert and Virginia Vey met in high school. He was a year behind her in school, but Virginia knew who he was: the popular but shy boy from the basketball team. He was handsome. And he was dating one of Virginia's best friends, Mary Ann Lees. When he asked Virginia to go out with him, she said yes. "I did sort of take it on the sly," my grandmother told me. "I really shouldn't have."

Virginia had had her own share of boyfriends throughout high school. She knew Delbert was a ladies' man and they secretly dated for a while before becoming known as a couple by the end of his senior year in 1935. "Finally, he broke up with Mary Ann. It almost broke us up as friends," she said.

Delbert's play with the basketball team earned him a scholarship to Butler University in Indianapolis. When he left Marion for college, Virginia was prepared to wait for him. She lived with her parents and younger sister, working as a bookkeeper; she had attended Indiana Business College in Marion when Delbert was a high school senior.

At Butler, Delbert pledged a fraternity along with a teammate from the Marion team, and declared he would major in physical education. But college life did not suit him. He quit school after less than a semester, but told no one and hitchhiked back home to Marion.

"One day I was downtown and here he came, walking downtown," Virginia said. She was angry with his decision, and so were Delbert's parents; they all expected his scholarship to lead to a diploma and a career as a teacher and coach.

Delbert shrugged it off. He took a job with the electric company and became a meter reader. He also proposed to Virginia, and they married in the living room of her parents' home in November 1936. It was a small gathering on a Saturday afternoon, with immediate family and two friends present as witnesses. For whatever reason, no one took photos, something Virginia would regret in the coming years. The bride and groom enjoyed a honeymoon of one night in Indianapolis, paying $4.50 for their room at the Hotel Lincoln.

There was a time many years later when my grandmother joined me in the car for a drive around Marion. We traveled to different neighborhoods to see where she had lived, both as a young girl and as a young wife with Delbert. As we sat outside the couple's first home, it was hard to see the house behind overgrown shrubs that crowded much of the front walk and yard. Two larger Victorian houses sat on either side of the small white building, which she explained had been a duplex. Friends who stood up for them at their wedding lived on the opposite side.

As newlyweds, she and Delbert had a living room, bedroom, bath, and kitchen. They had no refrigerator. She had a job six blocks away, and walked each day to a place called American Security Company, where she managed the books. She made seven dollars a week.

The couple had never really talked about children, and Virginia thought they were too young to be parents when she became pregnant in early 1937. Delbert was nineteen, and she was twenty. They had moved out of their first home and were now renting a three-room apartment upstairs in a duplex. A box hanging outside their bedroom window served as a fridge in winter. (On our tour of Marion, parked outside this house, I teased my grandmother about her pregnancy and asked if she remembered where my mother was conceived. She answered immediately: "Well, I believe it was in the kitchen.")

They lived from one payday to the next, and Virginia worried about supporting a baby. They were forced to move in with her parents when they couldn't make ends meet. While Delbert went to work, Virginia took care of the house and watched her younger sister. Throughout her pregnancy, she owned only two maternity dresses, which were all she had to wear. Delbert, however, was elated about becoming a father.

When a baby girl arrived on the night of November 9, 1937, they named her Judith Ann. Virginia's mother joined her in the hospital delivery room after she went into labor; Delbert waited outside. "My mother always said that I'd never called her 'Mommy' before, but when I was having Judy, I said, 'Oh, Mommy.' She'd never heard me call her that before."

It was that baby—now a six-year-old girl—who weighed on Virginia's mind in November 1943 when Delbert announced he was signing up for the war. She saw no reason for him to leave. She had loved Dale, too, and visited him and his new bride, Leah, when he earned his wings in Texas. She and Leah were the best of friends. Before the war, the two couples would get together and play cards or watch Dale's roller hockey games—anything that didn't cost money.

She saw how broken Delbert was by his brother's death. And yet.

"I didn't see any reason for it. He didn't have to go, because we had Judy," she recalled. "But he felt like it was his duty, so he did."

A week before Thanksgiving in 1943, Delbert drove north to Fort Wayne, to the same Baer Field where Dale had enlisted some twenty months earlier, and passed muster to volunteer as an aviation cadet. He said he wanted to be a pilot like his brother. The army noted Delbert was twenty-six years old, standing five feet eight inches tall, with blue eyes and brown hair. They offered him ten thousand dollars in life insurance and warned against any last-minute sexual flings before starting basic training. ("When the doctors went over you they looked for venereal disease," cautioned a pamphlet. "If you come back with either gonorrhea or syphilis they'll know you caught it since your examination.") When reporting for duty at Fort Benjamin Harrison in Indianapolis in the new year, the army said that Delbert should show up with the clothes on his back, an extra pair of underwear and socks, a razor, shaving cream, a toothbrush, and toothpaste. And be sober.

* * *

America was two years into its war with Germany and the Axis powers, with Europe as its primary combat theater. Since early 1943, American and British military leaders had made it clear that the destruction of Germany was a top priority. An air combat strategy known as the Combined Bomber Offensive directed U.S. and Royal Air Force fliers to go after the engine of Hitler's war machine. Their targets: factories producing aircraft for the Luftwaffe, ball-bearing plants, oil refineries, and fortresslike pens holding the German U-boats that routinely torpedoed Allied vessels in the Atlantic.

Essential to the offensive were heavy bombers, aircraft capable of carrying thousands of pounds of ordnance deep into Germany and the neighboring countries it occupied. The B-17 Flying Fortress and the B-24 Liberator led the attack. Each was heavily armed and could carry a crew of ten. While the sleek Forts flew higher and handled enemy flak better, the thick-set Liberators went faster, farther, and could carry more bombs. They were escorted into enemy territory by smaller P-51 Mustangs and P-38 Lightnings, nimble fighter planes that defended against Luftwaffe pilots trying to shoot down the bombers.

Delbert desperately wanted to be behind the controls of a bomber. If he couldn't become a pilot, he was told to choose between training as an airplane mechanic or a radio operator/gunner, handling both communications and a .50-caliber machine gun to protect the aircraft. "I chose the latter," he wrote to Virginia from basic training camp in Greensboro, North Carolina, in mid-January 1944. "It consists of 12 weeks radio school and then on to gunnery school. I certainly hope I don't have to take that, though. If I don't get through as pilot, bombardier or navigator, it (radio/gunner) will be satisfactory."

But before he became anything, he was sore. And tired. Day after day, he and his fellow recruits sprinted, squatted, pushed, and pulled themselves through body conditioning exercises.

"I probably won't be able to walk in the morning," he wrote to Judy. He also told her that if he couldn't qualify as a pilot, it "certainly will be a jab in my biscuits."

Equally important to the Army Air Forces was the mental and psychological condition of its potential airmen. Testing helped determine who was best suited for which crew position, and who could be trained quickly. Examinations were the norm, with day after day of questions and theories about subjects Delbert hadn't studied since high school. "It couldn't have been much harder," he wrote after a particularly frustrating battery of tests. "It was composed of geometry, algebra, history, physics, English, etc. Really was a tough one. I'll probably end up as a gunner. Ha!"

My grandmother urged him to become a mechanic. It's safer, she told him. Mechanics were part of ground crews, and ground crews stayed behind when gunners and their bombers took off for enemy targets.

"I would never make a mechanic, honey," he wrote back, "which is the reason (one of them) I chose gunner. I never did care for that kind of work. If I can't make a pilot, bombardier or navigator, gunnery is my next choice.

"It should be exciting and interesting and is one way of getting the b-----ds that started this and ended Dale's life," he wrote. "Understand? But don't let's talk of that now. I am not a gunner yet!"

He underlined the last sentence twice.

The Army Air Corps had too many men eager to become pilots, and not much else. When Delbert packed the few items he was allowed to take to basic training in December 1943, nearly three-quarters of a million men were training to be pilots. Yet someone had to navigate the bomber, spot a target from four miles above the earth as a bombardier, or sweat it out as a gunner in the cramped turrets that looked like blisters on a bomber's aluminum skin.

The Air Corps turned to novelist John Steinbeck to help promote the team spirit needed to recruit and man its heavy bombers. All airmen are equal, Steinbeck would write in *Bombs Away*, his detailed 1942 account of aircrew training.

"Not everyone on a football team insists on being quarterback," Steinbeck wrote. "He plays the position he is best fitted to play. The best football team is one where every member plays his own particular game as part of the team. The best bomber team is the one where each man plays for the success of the mission."

The Air Corps told former quarterback Delbert Trueman he had a weak eye, put him on a train, and shipped him halfway across the country from North Carolina to Texas and Harlingen Army Air Field. He would become an aerial gunner, the least prestigious of the Army Air Forces' "Four Horsemen," which also included pilots, bombardiers, and navigators.

Delbert was resigned.

He was also homesick. At twenty-seven, he'd never really been away from his family and friends; his days at Butler were the longest he'd been apart from them. Now, after just a few months of training, he was tired of the military routine, and didn't care much for the haircuts ("sure am glad that no one can see me with it this way") and the constant studying. And the injections—vaccine upon vaccine against smallpox, typhoid, yellow fever, cholera. He marveled that he could still move his arms.

He wrote letters almost daily to folks back home, and worried if he didn't see the same in return. He'd spent his birthday alone, in a base infirmary, sick with the flu. "I wish I were home so you could spank me 27 times," he wrote Judy. "I would probably have sore biscuits, wouldn't I?"

He had several rotten teeth pulled, leaving funny gaps in his mouth. Easter came and went. He ached for his family.

Life had its lonely moments for Virginia as well. None of the Marion couples they knew were split up by the war like she and Delbert; no other married men had enlisted. Friends didn't call as often; without her husband, she didn't seem to fit in with the old crowd.

Even so, Delbert rejected any idea of her going to a local tavern for fun. "I realize you have 'nothing' to look forward to but neither have I, at least during basic. I think we will make it through, don't you?" he wrote.

Virginia kept busy writing letters to him every day. She walked half a block from home to work for an electrical supply company; she had quit working after Judy's birth but started again after Delbert enlisted. As newlyweds, a second paycheck had helped when they struggled to pay the rent, and it helped now as she raised their daughter.

Delbert complained about the size of his army paycheck and how much was withheld for benefits such as life insurance and bonds. ("Judy, you get in your bank and send Daddy some money, will you?") But he objected to Virginia taking a job.

"I thought you were going to forget working unless you just had to. I still believe that you don't have to and would just as soon you quit," he wrote. "I never did believe in your working unless it was absolutely necessary, you know. I hate to always bring up the matter of working but, well, that's one of my sore spots."

It was trademark Delbert. Virginia knew he was not so much offended by her having a job as he was suspicious she might find someone new while he was away. She suspected it was the same reason he had quit Butler University and returned home to Marion.

If Delbert had a flaw as a husband, it was his jealous streak.

"I don't know why," my grandmother told me. "I never stepped out on him. But he always thought I might go out with somebody down where I worked or something like that. He wasn't accusing me, but he was just hinting at it. Protective—I guess that's it."

* * *

He did his best to shelter them from the world he was about to enter. A week before he graduated from gunnery school in Texas, several fellow airmen died in training like Dale, a loss that had triggered Delbert's decision to enlist.

> *I wasn't going to tell any of you this but you will probably see it in the paper anyway, so—. They lost a B-26 and 4 crew members in the Gulf yesterday. It was towing a target for some of our students to shoot at & they don't know whether it was accidentally shot down or*

> *developed trouble of its own. Anyway, I guess all they found so far is the nose gear & a big greasy spot in the water. That's sure tough on someone, isn't it? <u>Now don't let this put any ideas into your heads, anybody</u>. In the first place we don't ever tow targets and therefore are not in any position to be shot down, so think nothing of it.*

It was clear that Judy missed him. She wrote letters and shared the highlights of a six-year-old's life ("I can almost stand on my head. I'll be down to see you some time.") When her father called home, she would cry and have trouble talking to him. She also picked at her meals, which worried Delbert from afar. "You eat lots now and be big when Daddy comes home. Will you? Do that and then we can have a big wrestling match, can't we?" he wrote her. He started printing his letters instead of writing in cursive, hoping she could read them.

Delbert graduated as a gunner, earned his silver wings as an airman, and shipped from Texas to Westover Field in western Massachusetts. The train passed through Washington, D.C., where he could drop a postcard in the mail to Judy. "Daddy is still on the train. . . . Am *very* tired and *dirty*." He ended letters to her with XXs and OOs, adding, "You can let Mama have ½ of these if you wish."

The real preparation started at Westover. It was there that gunners and bombardiers, pilots, and navigators, all coming from their separate training schools, joined together as crews—men who would come to depend on each other for their lives in the sky. When the air war started, these groups of men were known as Overseas Training Units. By the time Delbert reached Westover in mid-1944, the groups were called RTUs—Replacement Training Units. The Air Corps was sending up a staggering number of planes in Europe and the Mediterranean; in June 1944 alone, it flew 130,000 sorties, nearly half of what was done in all of 1943. Original crews had either been blown out of the skies or rotated home, as the army realized that a fixed tour of duty was best for boosting morale and preventing airmen from breaking down under the strain of combat.

Replacement Training Units and men like Delbert would fill in the missing rosters of overseas squadrons.

At Westover, Delbert teamed up with airmen from across the country: a navigator from Connecticut, an engineer from North Carolina, gunners from Seattle and upstate New York, and a bombardier from Wisconsin. They became Crew 272. He especially liked his pilot, a solid six-footer named Lloyd White from a burg called Hornbeak in rural Tennessee. Like Delbert, he was a little older than the other men.

"He is about 7 months older than me, I think. He is a pretty big fellow and seems to be the kind of a guy who will handle these Liberators with ease," Delbert wrote. He particularly appreciated that White had been a flight instructor before moving on to the B-24.

Along with new crewmates, Delbert received his flight gear. It was the cusp of summer, but he and his crew needed clothing and equipment that would protect them from temperatures that plunged to fifty degrees below zero. At 20,000 feet, the uninsulated and unpressurized B-24s became flying freezers. Guarding the men against frostbite and hypothermia were ten-inch-high shearling boots with rubber soles, pants lined with sheep's wool and alpaca fleece, a leather flying jacket, goggles with eye cushions, leather flying helmets, and goatskin gloves lined with camel hair. Oxygen masks were also essential for keeping the men alive above 10,000 feet. It was just short of amazing to expect gunners to be able to move, let alone accurately shoot down enemy fighters screaming toward them at 400 mph.

Delbert and Crew 272 did their most serious training at Chatham Field in Savannah, Georgia, where they were shipped by troop trains to spend the summer of 1944. For two months, they flew together: Delbert logged eighty-one hours of daytime flying, twenty-two at night, and twenty-six hours at 4 miles or higher, all while practicing shooting from a gun turret. He found that a head cold was brutal at 10,000 feet, and your guts blew up like a balloon as the plane climbed higher.

But what really wore him down was the Georgia sun. The place felt like a swamp.

"Here it is the 11th of June, just five months to the day for the Army and myself. And here I sit with the sweat just running off me. Ha! It's really warm down here and I don't mean maybe. I hate to think of the next two months. Boy oh Boy!" he wrote just days after arriving in Savannah.

But Chatham Field became more like home to the Trueman family than any other base. Virginia and Judy spent the summer with Delbert in military housing, where other airmen and their families set up tiny apartments and tried to find some normalcy in their rote lives. Virginia and Judy boarded a train from Marion to Savannah and then, lugging their lone suitcase, hitchhiked the last few miles to the base.

Another gunner from his crew, Charlie Ward, moved in next door with his wife, Myrta, and their one-year-old, Carol. The families quickly became close friends, with Judy playing the role of big sister to Carol. It was hot and unbearably humid, but Virginia enjoyed watching Judy play in the Georgia sun with the children of other airmen.

Chatham Field was the only base that Virginia and Judy visited. Ice was delivered daily, and people took their showers in the evening using water warmed by the day's sun. Low-flying Liberators droned overhead, with gunners standing in the plane's waist and waving white handkerchiefs to their children on the ground. Pilots dipped their plane's wings to say hello to their wives. Training missions took crews to Cuba and back.

Crew 272 gelled. They left Savannah in August 1944 and headed to Langley Field in Virginia; four years earlier, Langley had housed the 34th Bomb Group—Dale Trueman's outfit. Now, his older brother was touching down long enough to receive a full set of clothing and equipment before heading to Europe and, finally, the damn war.

Delbert made one last trip home to Marion before heading overseas. Virginia was sitting on the front porch of her parents' house when a car pulled up and her husband stepped out. He bounded up the front steps to her. He had hitchhiked from Savannah—after his family went back to Marion and before he left for Langley—and, just like when he quit college, he told no one he was coming home.

Crew 272 took nearly a month to make its way across the Atlantic, following the convoluted route the Army Air Force laid out for aircrews heading to Italy. Their stops read like a fever chart on the atlas: Bangor, Maine; Goose Bay, Newfoundland; Lajes Field in the Azores, where

Delbert and Virginia Trueman with their daughter, Judy, at Chatham Field in Savannah, Georgia. It was the only time the family lived together during his training. *Kim Clarke photo*

Lloyd White put the plane down on a runway made of steel planking, almost scaring his crew to death; Marrakech, French Morocco, where Delbert slipped some local money into his wallet; and El Aouina, Tunisia. About seventy years after his journey, I sat in a commercial plane landing on the same airstrip in the Azores, trying to imagine what he saw as the pilot struggled with their bomber.

North Africa was where the airmen stopped in late September and waited to hear where they were headed next. Combat was still a continent away, but it was close in other ways. The men were instructed to write home and tell their mothers or wives to set aside important paperwork such as birth certificates and marriage licenses. "Now make sure you have those things," Delbert wrote Virginia. "If you don't have them, get them immediately. There is nothing like being prepared, you know." He had completed his will before departing the States, bequeathing everything he owned to his wife.

Along the way to Europe, Delbert kept writing home. No letters came his way; it was impossible to send mail to the moving target that was Crew 272. He started ending his letters with a postscript: "Still love me?" It was an echo, perhaps, of the jealousy he felt when apart from Virginia, and he was more distant than ever. His correspondence was now being censored by his pilot, as was all of the crew's mail. Writing from "somewhere in N. Africa," he was stumped for what to say, knowing anything of interest to his family would fall under Lloyd White's black marker or, worse, penknife. He was a meterman from Indiana who was seeing the world and could tell no one.

"Warner, Greene, Charlie, and myself are now sitting here throwing the bull, etc., and figuring out just how far we all are from home. Quite a ways, let me tell you. Further than I ever dreamed I would be," he wrote. "I sure wish you could be along, too, and see everything we have seen. Really interesting. I'll tell you about it when I get back."

While Delbert wrote from North Africa, Virginia headed to the Marion post office carrying a box addressed to her husband. She had filled it with playing cards and poker chips, shaving cream, bars of soap, lip balm, Kleenex, and hard candy. If she mailed it now from Indiana, in late September, the package would reach Delbert in Europe in time for Christmas.

Chapter 3
Colonel Harbold

Life insurance policies, Replacement Training Units, wills—all were inescapable evidence that the War Department was preparing for men in combat to die. What the military was unprepared for was how to manage the dead.

The military needed to ensure that every airman, soldier, or sailor who died overseas in the war received the same dignity and closure as families like the Truemans, who had lost Dale stateside: A body, a funeral, and a burial. If America were to have a quiet champion for those soldiers who could no longer speak and whose families were left with the questions, emptiness, and confusion that came with a Western Union telegram, it would be Col. Robert Pattison Harbold.

Harbold spent five decades wearing an army uniform. A 1904 graduate of West Point, the Pennsylvania native served at bases in places as remote and crumbling as Fort Niobrara, Nebraska, and as lush as the Hawaiian island of Oahu. He was stationed at a state university and managed winning baseball teams made up of African American soldiers. In World War I, posted in Paris, he oversaw the handling of thousands of dead doughboys and established U.S. military cemeteries in France. He managed the selection of America's first unknown soldier, a combat casualty from the world's bloodiest war, setting in motion a tradition of reverence honoring the nation's war dead that continued through the Vietnam War. He helped select a gravesite for William Jennings

Bryan, the distinguished statesman who said he wanted to be buried at Arlington National Cemetery because he knew no more beautiful place.

Harbold never engaged in combat, but he witnessed its destructive effects on soldiers and their grieving families. He read the letters from heartbroken parents and despairing wives. When he retired from active duty in 1934, he did so with the rank of lieutenant colonel and a thirty-year career. He was fifty-three years old. At the time, one of his sons was a West Point graduate serving with the Army Air Corps, and a second was a newly minted second lieutenant from the U.S. Naval Academy at Annapolis. His experiences with death and loss would prompt military leaders to recall him to service for the challenges of World War II.

That Robert Harbold had been an army officer at all was a fluke, thanks to a boy named Leo Faller.

* * *

Robert Harbold and Leo Faller grew up ten miles apart in south-central Pennsylvania, Harbold in the tiny borough of Dillsburg, and Faller in the larger community of Carlisle. Harbold lived with his parents and seven brothers and sisters in one of Dillsburg's original houses, dating to 1800. The borough had a railroad, a post office, one newspaper, and four churches, all Protestant.

Harbold began teaching school at age seventeen. When he and the nineteen-year-old Faller sat down in a classroom at Gettysburg High School with sixteen other young men in May 1898, both wanted to attend the U.S. Military Academy at West Point, New York. After two days of written and physical examinations, Harbold and Faller had passed, along with six others. They were West Point material and would compete for an open seat at the prestigious military academy. Six weeks later, Faller won out when his congressman, U.S. Representative George Brenner, selected him to attend the military academy. Faller prepared for army life, and Harbold, a West Point alternate, returned to teaching.

The boys' joint interest in the army may have been encouraged by their veteran fathers: John Faller and William Harbold both served in the Civil War, representing Pennsylvania and defending the Union against any Confederate incursions into their home state. The two soldiers could not have had more divergent wartime experiences that would come to shape their sons.

John Faller served alongside his younger brother, a nineteen-year-old named Leo, who was killed in the 1862 carnage that became known as the Battle of Antietam. John buried his brother and pressed on. In 1864, Confederates captured him while fighting in Danville, Virginia. Faller survived the remainder of the war in the notorious Andersonville prison camp, and spent the rest of his life talking about the experience. After the war, Captain Faller gave his dead brother's name to his youngest child, Leo, who undoubtedly grew up hearing about the combined sacrifices of his uncle and father.

Robert Harbold would have heard his father tell of the war, too. Pvt. William Harbold was a Union musician whose company was at Gettysburg in 1863. In early 1865, after being ordered to "beat the cymbals" heading into battle in Lovettsville, Virginia, he said he experienced an excruciating headache—"from sunrise to sunset"—in and above his eyes. The pain flared for months and would plague him for decades. A Union doctor discharged him in June 1865. He would spend years fighting the government for a pension and full medical disability.

When Robert Harbold and Leo Faller, the sons of these Civil War veterans, competed for a seat at West Point in 1898, the United States was at war again. The three-month-long Spanish-American War would come and go before Faller became a cadet; his admission to the military academy was scheduled for June 1899. "His career is now settled," his hometown newspaper proclaimed, "and if he makes as good a soldier as his father did in the sixties, he will do well."

But Leo Faller was not cut out for military heroics like his father and uncle. After six months, he was discharged by West Point officials for being "deficient in study." The door was now open for Robert Harbold to become a cadet and a career soldier whose contributions would touch military families in the nation's next two wars. He would leave teaching and Dillsburg, and become a soldier.

* * *

Harbold graduated in 1904 near the very bottom of his West Point class, but he excelled in courses about discipline and efficiency. His early army career as a junior officer took him to places both exotic and mundane: Texas and Kansas, the Philippines and Hawaii. In the twenty-four months following his graduation from West Point, Harbold became an officer, a husband, and a father. His first posting was to Nebraska's Fort Niobrara, where he was a second lieutenant with the army's 25th Infantry, a segregated regiment of African American soldiers; he would work with Black servicemen for fourteen years. West Point graduates with less-than-stellar academic records were often assigned to oversee Black soldiers, and Harbold had graduated 113th among 124 cadets.

Nebraska also brought him into contact with Rosanne N. Brown, the daughter of the post's civilian surgeon. They married in the fort chapel in the spring of 1905, and a year later, she gave birth to a twelve-pound boy they named Norris. For nine years, the Harbolds lived the life of an itinerant military family, moving with the Buffalo Soldiers of the 25th Infantry Regiment to five states. Their transfers involved an expanding family with the births of sons Robert Jr. and Edward.

And one transfer came after a taste for alcohol and a serious misstep. In the summer of 1912, as head of the military science program at Kansas State Agricultural College, Harbold was caught up in a raid at a fraternity house, where students and townspeople were playing poker, gambling, and drinking. The lieutenant was arrested and, after being charged with gambling, pleaded guilty. The college president liked Harbold but wanted Secretary of War Henry L. Stimson to recall him. He was more upset about the drinking than the gambling, because Kansas was a dry state.

"Previous to this time and subsequent to this date, he has used intoxicating liquors to excess and has . . . not set a good example to the young men of the Institution," wrote President Henry J. Waters. "Otherwise he has been quite efficient as a military officer and is a young man of more than ordinary promise."

Harbold was relieved of duty, ordered back to his regiment, and took a leave of absence. When Kansas State couldn't find a suitable replacement to run its military science program after several months of searching, it asked the army to reinstate Harbold. But by then Harbold was headed to Hawaii with the 25th Infantry.

The family's move to the island of Oahu in 1913 marked their longest post, with Harbold serving as a first lieutenant with the 25th Infantry at Schofield Barracks. Not everyone on the island welcomed the Buffalo Soldiers—African American men in a segregated unit that was created in the wake of the Civil War. It was the first time Black soldiers had served in the territory, and many arrived with their wives and children. Officers of the 25th Infantry defended their men, and the local newspaper extended a welcome couched in stereotypes: "There are some things for which the negro is not yet suited, but he is a good, steady, trustworthy fighter under white leadership."

These were good days for the Harbold family. Bob and Rosanne often entertained other officers and their wives. They threw a dance party at the 25th Infantry Club to celebrate their tenth wedding anniversary. They played cards and hosted suppers on the beach. Rosanne opened a small tea shop; the boys were the center of elaborate birthday parties. And then there was baseball. Lieutenant Harbold had been working with Black players since Fort Niobrara, and his posting in Hawaii paired him with exceptional athletes. He was both a player and manager, competing with his fellow infantry officers against members of the First Field Artillery and coaching Black players to championships in Oahu's army league.

On the other side of the globe, men were competing for their lives. Baseball and beach parties would end for Robert Harbold in mid-1917. Known for his efficiency, Harbold spent nearly a year moving from stateside base to base, working as an army inspector to determine the proficiency, discipline, and readiness of troops headed for the Great War. His family stayed in Hawaii, where the Harbold boys—eleven-year-old Norris, seven-year-old Robert, and Edward, all of five—dressed up in army uniforms complete with puttees, mirroring the look of grown-up Americans on the ground in France. They posed for a photographer, staring glumly at the camera and appearing in the newspaper under a headline that declared, "Future Defenders of the Flag."

In the summer of 1918, with America fully involved in the war, their father boarded the troop ship *Mauretania* for France and his first exposure to the horrors of combat. It would be nearly twenty-six months before the family reunited when Rosanne and her sons moved to Paris.

* * *

World War I ended the lives of some 78,000 American soldiers, sailors, and marines. It was the greatest overseas conflict Americans had endured, which meant determining, for the first time, how to care for those who died on foreign soil. The War Department pledged that it would "fittingly and tenderly" care for the dead and return them to their families if they wished. Keeping track of their burials, the identification of unknown bodies, the wishes of families, and the return to America of 44,000 dead men became Robert Harbold's wartime portfolio.

The duties, at first, were antiseptic. Soldier deaths were names on paper—thousands and thousands of names. Harbold, now a captain, was stationed with six thousand troops at the army's Central Records Office in Bourges, France. It was a living machine of paperwork: documentation for some two million men serving with the American Expeditionary Forces; casualty reports from the field; lists of the dead and wounded to send to U.S. newspapers; records of battlefield burials; and thousands of letters from anxious families asking about their sons, brothers, and husbands.

"This work was a gruesome task," wrote a soldier supervised by Harbold. "Imagine sitting at a typewriter during hostilities from 8 a.m. until noon and from 1:15 p.m. until 5:20 p.m., and then coming back after supper and hammering the machine from 7 until 9 o'clock, all the while making out cards that meant death or some severe wounds to some fellow American!"

Still, while the soldiers of the Central Records Office conceded their assignment was critical, it was also terribly dry. They envied soldiers in trenches at the front, the doughboys going over the top to face the Germans. "There was little of that excitement to inspire the patriotism which the Yank on the battlefield possessed," one observed.

Soldiers in the field, however, were eyewitnesses to the deaths being tallied in the Central Records Office. Burials were often hasty, sloppy, and sometimes made under fire. Army Col. Harry F. Rethers offered a glimpse from the battlefield:

> *Temporary burials were sometimes marked by a rifle, a helmet on a stick or any convenient object which would attract the eye of a searcher. The grave might vary in depth from six feet to six inches, and many were the cases in which bodies were hardly buried at all. There were also trench burials of many bodies together, and such if not soon exhumed and separated became like charnel houses.*

Rethers oversaw the establishment of the new American Graves Registration Service in 1917, which was charged with managing the war dead and worked closely with the Central Records Office.

From the Central Records Office, Harbold was next placed in charge of all Graves Registration field operations in France. By 1919, with the war over, Harbold was overseeing units working in temporary cemeteries to exhume the dead, either for permanent reburial in new U.S. cemeteries being established in Europe or for shipment home. Much of the hard, sickening labor of handling decomposing bodies fell on African American soldiers. ("Strange that the value of such a task did not gather full significance in the minds of all American soldiers. Strange that when other hands refused it, swarthy hands received it!" observed Addie Waites Hunton, a Black civilian serving with the segregated American Expeditionary Forces troops.)

Harbold was also in charge of army operations at the French ports, where bodies would be stored in temporary morgues and loaded onto ships headed to the United States.

Harbold eventually would lead the Graves Registration Service as chief in 1922, as the army wound down its work in France. He continued with the service in Washington, D.C., connecting with the families of men whose bodies had yet to be located or identified. It was work that would last a decade, but when successful, he said, it was "very gratifying."

Lt. Robert P. Harbold, when he was stationed in Bourges, France, in 1919. *National Archives and Records Administration photo*

During and after the Great War, he managed the dead in a multitude of ways.

He signed off on exhumations and reburials: "6 ft. earthen grave, wooden box. Buried naked. Badly decomposed. Unrecognizable."

He wrote to mothers, telling them their sons' remains had yet to be found: "Many bodies have been recovered this spring from isolated graves in the vicinity of the original burial location of your son. It is the intention of this office to endeavor to identify as many of these unknown bodies as possible. It is hoped the body of your gallant son will be ultimately identified among them."

He told fathers their boys had been permanently buried in France with dignity: "Please be assured that in effecting removal of the dead, the utmost reverential care was exercised and more than willingly accorded by those who performed this sacred duty."

He reached out to siblings with details of corpses, in hopes they could confirm their brothers' bodies: "Above medium height, large bones, large high-bridged nose, sloping forehead, protruding above orbits, large deep orbits. Very high arched feet as shoes were apparently too large [and] were slit over the instep. Teeth were large, strong and well cared for; many small gold and metal fillings."

And he sought out veterans for any combat memories that held clues to identifying human remains:

> *It is requested that you forward to this office any sketches or data which you may have, such as general direction of trenches, whether the men were buried separately or together, if the latter, the names of the men so buried if you recall them, any landmarks which you recall, or in fact any information you may have which can be forwarded to Europe to be used in a systematic search of the area for bodies. It is believed there is one entire trench of men whose bodies have not been found.*

Whether in France or Washington, Harbold encountered the detritus of war and the grief, anger, and love of widows, parents, and siblings of the dead. Emotions always ran high.

There were families like Joshua and Edna Barcus, desperate for the remains of their son to be returned to them in Indianapolis. Earl R. Barcus, a bugler with the 150th Field Artillery, died in 1918. Recovering from dental surgery, the twenty-year-old was killed when a German plane bombed the hospital where he was a patient. More than a year after the Armistice, the Barcuses were frustrated that the body of their only child remained overseas. At the time, the French government would not allow American bodies to be moved due to public health concerns and how it might affect the morale of its citizens, who were grieving far greater losses after four years of war. Hundreds of thousands of French soldiers remained where they had fallen, and the French government wanted their recovery to take priority.

Joshua Barcus would have none of it: "His life was sacrificed to America's call and the war-torn body of my son is ours absolutely and no one has any moral or legal right to question what we shall do with the remains." Barcus joined a movement called the Bring Home the Soldier Dead League. The United States eventually would negotiate for the return of its dead, arguing that while French families could visit their loved ones in local cemeteries, it was too much to expect American families to travel overseas to mourn their dead. The body of Earl Barcus came home in June 1921.

Other families were conflicted about what to do. August and Lydia Andelstedt grieved after learning their youngest child was killed in 1918. Raymond Andelstedt, a machine gunner with the 18th Infantry Regiment, had written from France about the exhilaration of combat and "going over the top." The scream of artillery shells was "the prettiest sound," although it was critical to dive for cover. And then there was the gunfire. "The rifle bullets are sharp and snappy, but I don't mind them so much," the private told his family. "Of course they are not pleasant to listen to, and make a whizzing sound over your head, but a man gets used to it, and gets so he don't mind it."

A screaming bullet fired by a German sniper pierced Andelstedt's head during the Meuse-Argonne offensive. He died instantly. Two days later, fellow soldiers recovered his body, dug a grave near the battlefield, and buried Andelstedt in his uniform near Fleville. It was October 1918, and the war would end in a month.

Lydia Andelstedt asked that her son's body be returned to San Bernardino, California, because "he would love his homeland the best." Graves Registration troops exhumed his body from its isolated grave in June 1919. They moved it to a temporary American cemetery constructed during the war, wrapping the remains in burlap and placing them in a wooden casket. But then the Andelstedts visited their son's grave in 1920 and saw, through their tears, that the temporary cemetery was more beautiful than they expected. *Please leave Raymond with his comrades*, his mother told Graves Registration leaders that fall.

A year later, with negotiations with France settled and bodies of American dead being exhumed and returned to the United States, the Andelstedts again changed their minds. "As so many of our local boys have been shipped home, we would like our son brought home also. When we requested that he should remain in France we were under the impression that all those who were in that cemetery were to remain there," Lydia wrote.

What the family did not realize was that the War Department had set a deadline for requests to return bodies, and it had passed months earlier. It was too late to bring home Raymond Andelstedt, who would remain buried with more than 14,000 soldiers in the Meuse Argonne American Cemetery. His badly decomposed body was exhumed, again, placed in a casket, and permanently interred.

And still, his rest was incomplete. In the spring of 1923, Lydia Andelstedt wrote to Harbold in Paris asking that someone place flowers on her son's grave. It was at the cemetery where a soldier noticed a misspelling on the granite cross marking his burial: ANDELSTADT. Harbold ordered a new, accurate inscription. Raymond Andelstedt's burial was complete.

* * *

America's entry into the war had come with a new, mandatory piece of equipment for soldiers: an identification tag. Since the Civil War, soldiers had been recording their names onto pieces of wood, metal, or paper and affixing them to their uniforms; if they fell in combat, they wanted their identities known to those collecting and burying the dead. At the turn of the century, so-called identity discs were a requirement. By 1916, the army mandated that soldiers wear two identical metal tags around the neck. Regardless of the war or era, the objective of an identity tag was to reduce the number of unknown dead.

Still, the violence of combat in France left hundreds of bodies unidentified, indistinguishable, or simply vaporized. Maj. Gen.

John A. LeJeune, the commandant of the Marine Corps who led troops in several critical battles, said the impact of high-explosive shells obliterated soldiers "so that in many instances only small bits or pieces or fragments of a body could be found."

The recognition of soldiers who had given their lives but would never be identified became Robert Harbold's most notable contribution in France. It would come to symbolize America's care for its war dead.

The concept of honoring an unknown soldier as a tribute to the nation's war dead was not an American one. On Armistice Day in 1920, England buried an "unknown warrior" inside Westminster Abbey, and France placed the remains of an unknown soldier at the base of the Arc de Triomphe in Paris.

In March 1921, Congress authorized the ceremonial burial of an unknown soldier, removed from the fields of France, at Arlington National Cemetery. Leading the legislation was newly elected Congressman Hamilton Fish Jr. of New York, a veteran who had seen combat and now wanted the country "to bring home the body of an unknown American warrior who in himself represents no section, creed, or race in the late war and who typifies, moreover, the soul of America and the supreme sacrifice of her heroic dead." Plans called for the body to lie in state at the U.S. Capitol and then be interred at Arlington's amphitheater during a ceremony on November 11, 1921, the third anniversary of the war's end.

But first: Identify an unidentifiable victim of combat.

At the time, there were some 1,200 unidentified dead in France. The Graves Registration Service combed through its records for unknown American soldiers buried in four cemeteries: Aisne-Marne, Meuse-Argonne, Somme, and St. Mihiel. The paperwork needed to show zero signs of identifying a body: no death date, no rank, no skin color, no uniform patches, and no name. These were anonymous men forever lost to combat. At each cemetery, on the same fall day of October 22, troops exhumed a body and placed it in a new casket; they repeated the process and collected four more unknowns as alternates, should anyone from the original somehow be identified. Orders called for the bodies to be delivered by trucks the next day, at three o'clock in the afternoon, to Major Harbold at the Hotel de Ville, or city hall, of Chalons-sur-Marne.

It was at the city hall where Harbold, as the officer in charge, prepared an elaborate ceremony to honor the nameless fighter who would be selected as America's Unknown Soldier.

When the officers who accompanied the four bodies arrived at Chalons-sur-Marne, they handed Harbold the scant records related to each man, including details about their original burial locations in the four cemeteries. Joined by a lieutenant colonel, Harbold did something anathema to his world of recordkeeping: They set fire to the paperwork. There would be no evidence whatsoever of the unknowns and their journey to Chalons-sur-Marne.

Inside city hall, American flags shrouded the caskets; the next morning, Harbold returned and, with a handful of soldiers, reshuffled the coffins and how they were arranged.

Harbold now turned to select a doughboy who would pick one of the four caskets. Sgt. Edward F. Younger, who was twenty-three years old, was a veteran of every major campaign in France and had twice been wounded. He was among six enlisted men designated as pallbearers for the ceremony at Chalons-sur-Marne, and was caught off guard when Harbold said one of them would choose the body to be honored. When Younger's name was called, he froze. "I had gone over the top many times, had known the agony of waiting for the charge," he said later. "But nothing had paralyzed me as that simple announcement did."

Cradling a spray of white roses, Younger entered the small chapel that held the four bodies. He circled the caskets. Did he ever serve with one of these men? Had one of them died near him? Did they share a meal? His mind raced as he made three slow, deliberate marches around the coffins, unable to decide. He stopped when he felt the sudden pull of one. "It seemed as if God raised my hand and guided me as I placed the roses on the casket," he remembered.

Younger stepped backward and saluted the casket. It was October 24, 1921, and the United States had a new symbol of wartime sacrifice. The remains were moved to a new coffin, which was sealed and inscribed: "An Unknown American who gave his life in the World War."

The doors to the city hall were opened to the public, and local citizens streamed past the casket in quiet tribute. A mile-long procession to the train station followed, with the casket bearing the nameless soldier placed atop a horse-drawn caisson and drawn past French army units, firefighters, bands, local Boy Scouts, veterans, and schoolchildren. The anonymous soldier was sent off amid a barrage of flowers and gratitude.

Harbold's work was done.

The Unknown Soldier was carried by ship to the United States for burial on November 11, which Congress had designated a national holiday. Church bells pealed for fifteen minutes before noon, when the nation observed two minutes of silence. President Warren G. Harding, speaking at the Arlington amphitheater, acknowledged the power of paying tribute to an anonymous soldier. The man, he said, was unknown but not unhonored.

> *He might have come from any one of millions of American homes. Some mother gave him in her love and tenderness, and with him her most cherished hopes. Hundreds of mothers are wondering today, finding a touch of solace in the possibility that the nation bows in grief over the body of one she bore to live and die, if need be, for the Republic. . . . We do not know the eminence of his birth, but we do know the glory of his death. He died for his country, and greater devotion hath no man than this.*

Harding, who had taken office eight months earlier, also called for an end to war. "With all my heart, I wish we might say to the defenders who survive, to mothers who sorrow, to widows and children who mourn, that no such sacrifice shall be asked again," he said.

Back in France, Robert Harbold continued on with the Graves Registration Service and the ramifications of the Great War. When his work was done in early 1924, he and his sons, Robert Jr. and Edward, boarded a ship in Cherbourg and sailed to the United States and a new posting in Maryland. His oldest boy, Norris, had departed France months earlier to attend a military prep academy. Rosanne stayed behind in Paris.

* * *

When the anonymous soldier recovered in France was buried at Arlington, near the cemetery's new Memorial Amphitheater, his grave was covered by a thick slab of white marble. It became a solemn tourist attraction, with thousands of people visiting every month afterward to pay homage to the unknown man. That included my grandmother, who, at age ten, was on a family vacation exploring the sights of Washington, D.C. In a photograph, she is in a summer dress, standing with her younger sister, just steps from the tomb and an honor guard with a rifle over his shoulder.

Two decades later, the man who helped with selecting and honoring the dead soldier would play a significant role in her life and the lives of thousands of other military families.

The Unknown Soldier was Harbold's most public work during World War I. But the private letters from families demanding answers, the spectacle of exhuming and identifying—or not—the dead, and the angst of parents like Joshua and Edna Barcus, desperate to be reunited with their sons, would carry far more weight for Harbold in America's next war, where the magnitude of death and the obligation to families was much greater.

Chapter 4
"Overawing"

After eight Christmases together, Virginia Trueman prepared to spend December 25 apart from her husband, undone by an ocean and a global war. Over three weeks in the early fall of 1944, she mailed seven holiday packages to his Air Corps address, hoping they would be forwarded to Delbert wherever he was stationed.

She made certain to label two packages as coming from Judy, who was starting first grade. I can imagine my mom and grandmother shopping together in downtown Marion for small items to fill the boxes, tiny gestures to connect him to home and family. With each mailing, my grandmother used a pencil to record the contents and shipping date. September 22: poker chips, two bars of Lux soap, a package of tissues. September 30: cigarettes, two boxes of Cheez-Its, and a packet of peanuts. October 5: fruitcake, Chuckles candy, and a paperback novel. October 11: razor blades, film, handkerchiefs, chewing gum.

Delbert was preparing for combat and facing the German war machine for the first time. Nine months of drills, training, and test flights stateside would soon be put to the test in the most realistic way in the skies above central Europe. Evading Luftwaffe fighters in the air and flak bursts hurled from massive guns on the ground meant life or death. Taking on the enemy was the mission Dale had signed up for, and one my grandfather was determined to complete. Fifty successful bombing runs would allow him to return home to Indiana.

In Washington, Col. Robert Harbold looked to the months ahead and saw a darker reality: bodies. As the new head of an obscure army office called the Memorial Division, he was responsible for a bureaucracy charged with finding and returning the war dead once the fighting stopped. His office was woefully understaffed for the rising casualties, bodies that by military edict were to remain overseas until the war was over.

During the Great War, when Harbold helped manage the remains of doughboys, the casualties were far fewer and, for the most part, mostly confined to one front. Now, fighting both Germany and Japan, America's war dead were scattered across places like Algiers, Normandy, Saipan, Casablanca, Tarawa, and Anzio. Harbold's Memorial Division had far fewer workers than he had supervised in Paris after the Great War, and he didn't like what he saw looming ahead. "I can emphatically state that my visualization based on personal estimates of present and future battle fronts and areas, probable casualties, length of the duration and complexity of transportation problems," he said, "is stupendous and overawing."

* * *

Hundreds of thousands of American families received wartime news of a son, husband, or brother who had died, but were not given any bodies to mourn and bury.

Two days after the United States declared war on Germany, Secretary of War Henry L. Stimson issued a one-sentence order that would leave grieving families in limbo for years. "During the period that the United States is at war," he said, "the shipment home of remains from foreign possessions and other stations outside the continental limits of the United States is suspended."

Instead, when men died in combat or from wounds, their remains were left in makeshift cemeteries and isolated graves in Sardinia and Yugoslavia, Holland and Luxembourg, Algeria and Malta. Thousands were interred on German soil. The war dead in the Pacific Theater were laid to rest in shallow graves on islands and archipelagos that stretched for thousands of watery miles.

Graves were marked and locations recorded for Army Graves Registration units, which would retrieve bodies only after the shooting stopped and if the dead could be quickly located. Bodies were then reburied in temporary military cemeteries, where they would stay until the war was over.

Managing the war dead was the job of the U.S. Army Quartermaster Corps. This was Harbold's world, one he had called home since immediately after World War I, when he was stationed in Paris. From the days of the Continental Army, the quartermaster has been responsible for supplies and logistics: providing tents and blankets, washing uniforms, baking bread and storing dry goods, delivering water and fuel, disposing of trash and old equipment. The quartermaster's role was to keep soldiers clean, clothed, fed, and on the move. When Harbold retired from the army in 1934, he was the quartermaster at Fort Ethan Allen in Vermont.

In 1941, as the country teetered on the edge of global conflict, the Quartermaster Corps lacked enough experienced officers and turned to retirees like Harbold. He was recalled from retirement and his Maryland home, found physically qualified, and sent to Fort Snelling along the upper Mississippi River in Minnesota.

A lot had changed since he left the army seven years earlier. Harbold was now sixty years old—the maximum age for being called back to service—and a grandfather to five. His oldest son, Norris, was a major in the Army Air Corps, training pilots and navigators at a base in Georgia. Robert Jr., a graduate of the U.S. Naval Academy, was a lieutenant in the reserves and teaching at a prep academy for boys interested in navy careers. Edward was with the Merchant Marines.

By the time the senior Harbold was back in uniform and on his way to Fort Snelling, he was raising a second family. Divorced from Rosanne, he remarried in 1936 to Florence Murphy, a law firm secretary nearly thirty years his junior. He and Florence were parents to a two-year-old girl, also named Florence, with another baby on the way. And they had experienced the loss of a daughter, a twin to baby Florence named Mary, who was stillborn. They buried the infant near their Maryland home, at the post cemetery at Fort George G. Meade.

Harbold, colleagues said, had a lot of energy. At Fort Snelling, he oversaw construction contracts for what would become a sprawling induction center for army recruits. In the fall of 1942, he was promoted to lieutenant colonel. His oldest son, thirty-five-year-old Norris, was already a lieutenant colonel in the Army Air Corps and pinned the emblem of a colonel—a pair of eagles—onto his father's chest. "Inasmuch as Lt. Col. R. P. Harbold is my father, it is safe to say that he is the ranking lieutenant colonel in the Harbold family," Norris said.

Robert Harbold's energy was tested in mid-1943 when he was ordered to Washington to lead the army's Memorial Division.

The office he was handed was lost. The Memorial Division was one of several administrative offices within the Quartermaster's Office that had become a bureaucratic dumping ground since before Pearl Harbor. He worked with other officers in charge of a mishmash of army work: training horses for ceremonial duty and dogs for combat; operating laundries; disposing of outdated equipment, vehicles, and gear; and managing the country's war dead.

Harbold focused solely on the war's casualties. Managing the dead was something he knew well from France and the Great War, and now he faced more bodies than the American military had seen since the first shots on Fort Sumter.

It was during the Civil War that the army quartermaster was first tasked with the bodies of Americans killed in uniform. In 1862, recovering and burying Union dead became one more extension of army life for the quartermaster to manage.

Regardless of the war, dealing with the dead is ugly, stomach-turning, physical work, with troops gathering up shattered and decaying bodies in the aftermath of combat, disease, or accidents.

Consider the words of one soldier who collected the dead after the Allies invaded France in 1944: "One develops a strong stomach quickly; the gas escaping is the worst you will ever encounter. We also learned that mass graves were necessary when a shell exploded inside a tank. As gruesome as it may sound, a mess kit cup and spoon were the tools of the trade."

Remains must be collected, identified, and disposed of with honor; graves must be marked and documented. Caskets and headstones are required. Creating and maintaining national cemeteries also fell to the quartermaster. Logistically, managing the war dead is an administrative maze of policies, records, notifications, forms, and regulations—one to be navigated by both the military and grieving families. As chief of the Quartermaster Corps' Memorial Division, Harbold was responsible for the burial records of all soldiers, marines, sailors, and airmen killed overseas.

His mission was, in the detached terms of the military, "determination of a method of disposal of the dead."

Families were waiting.

* * *

Early in his military career, when he was still a junior officer, Robert Harbold took on a role he was familiar with from his civilian days in Pennsylvania classrooms: teaching. As a first lieutenant in 1911, married with two young sons, he was appointed commandant of the military science department at the Kansas State Agricultural School. In charge of around four hundred young men, he drilled the cadets relentlessly. For periods of three and four days, he would march them into the hillside outside Manhattan, set up camp, and then return to campus.

Observers described the thirty-year-old Harbold as "a rigid disciplinarian." The commandant's appearance reflected his demeanor: a long face, pursed lips, and a hawk nose. He did not smile. He was a methodical man who believed in completing a mission. Even when the Kansas State president was calling for Harbold to be relieved from duty for drinking, he noted the lieutenant's skills of efficiency.

When Harbold's five-year-old son Norris contracted scarlet fever, the commandant was forced to separate from his cadets and quarantine at home for three weeks with his wife and family. He bristled at the absence, which threatened the rigor and rote of drills. But he had a solution, and it was right there in his house, along with his sick child.

"I can keep track of things by the use of the telephone," he told the student newspaper. "I might have an announcer up there, and I could give the commands over the phone." The strict disciplinarian would use technology to relay his commands. He had a plan.

Some thirty years after his drilling days in Kansas, Harbold once again had to manage logistics amid obstacles. This time, matters were far more serious than college boys mastering their field drills. Since his first days in the office, Harbold saw that the Memorial Division was overrun with paperwork from two war fronts and severely understaffed, lost in an army system that failed to plan effectively for handling the inevitable casualties of armed combat.

He had been given a mandate but not the tools to succeed. Not even close.

The army had grown to a force of eight million; Harbold had all of fifty-four civilians working in his office, and casualties continued to mount. The Memorial Division did not have enough people to write letters to families, confirm serial numbers and fingerprints, plan and map new cemeteries, and keep track of all the bodies. Staffing levels were so low, he told his superiors, that it was as if the army refused to believe the country was at war. It was, he said, "a critical situation."

Families wanted details and the remains of their loved ones; of four thousand letters mailed to the Memorial Division, only one family asked that their son's body remain overseas. A backlog of paperwork was growing: hundreds of letters to the wives and parents of the dead and thousands upon thousands of reports about burial sites were waiting to be processed.

Harbold was blunt: "This work, unless actively pursued at this time, will pile up and become an almost insurmountable task upon the cessation of hostilities."

Consider: In the early months of the war, thousands of men died fighting in North Africa and Sicily. Families were informed of the deaths but received no further details. No one knew where their sons, brothers, and husbands were buried, or if they were buried at all. Once those regions were secured and the army was comfortable disclosing the locations of graves in temporary cemeteries, the Quartermaster's Office was ordered to draft 12,000 letters sharing the details with families. Harbold had only a few workers, and the notifications took weeks.

Harbold also cringed when he realized that two different army branches were sharing burial details with families. Because bodies often were moved—from a combat zone to a temporary cemetery—and paperwork lagged, families were receiving bad information about one body being buried in two locations. "Unless some uniform policy is established and installed, embarrassment and confusion will result and much grief will be brought upon the relatives after cessation of hostilities," he said.

Harbold was particularly worried about the delay in identifying unknown bodies overseas due to poor staffing in Washington. He did not have enough personnel to compare burial reports from the field with dental records, fingerprints, serial numbers, and other clues that could aid in identifying a body. He knew that the longer the delays, the more families would doubt that the correct body had been sent home.

Returning the dead to the United States was a given for Harbold. He believed that after the war, all families should be surveyed; if at least 70 percent wanted their loved ones back, all of the deceased would be shipped home.

So he begged for more bodies—living, breathing ones, committed to accuracy—to fill the desks of the Memorial Division. Mistakes and missteps could mean heartbreak for parents and spouses of the war's victims. He believed his superiors did not appreciate the volatility of managing the war dead, nor what the mission of the Memorial Division meant for both the war effort and anxious families.

"Its relationship to the morale of the home front (and in this case the home front consists definitely of mothers, fathers and wives who have loved ones overseas)," Harbold wrote in a memo, "is direct, intimate and filled with explosives."

* * *

At no point in his long career did Robert Harbold reveal why he was so committed to serving the families of fallen soldiers.

It might have been ingrained in him at West Point that a soldier has a duty to honor those who had died. He could have been captivated by and skilled in the logistics of collecting, managing, and returning the dead.

Or it might have been because of his father-in-law, army surgeon Dr. Ira C. Brown. Besides being the father of Harbold's first wife, Rosanne, and grandfather to their three sons, Brown was stationed with his son-in-law at four different posts across the United States and the Philippines. Over the years, there would have been opportunities for them to talk about army life—including Brown's service caring for sick, dying, and dead soldiers at a field hospital during the Spanish-American War. That conflict claimed more men from disease than combat, and Brown's experience highlighted what could go wrong.

After the Spanish surrendered in Cuba in 1898, American officers and surgeons on the ground begged their commander, Maj. Gen. W. R. Shafter, to withdraw troops from the island. It was late summer, and the army was plagued by malaria "to such an extent that its efficiency is destroyed." The looming threat of yellow fever would all but decimate the troops.

Soldiers boarded ships headed for Camp Wikoff, a detention center under construction on Long Island's Montauk Point. Brown, then a thirty-six-year-old major, was the camp's executive officer and surgeon in charge. "I was the first man at Montauk and the last man," he said later. He arrived on Long Island after working at an army hospital in Florida, where he had contracted yellow fever and lost sixty pounds.

Hundreds of tents dotted the grounds at Montauk. The influx of thousands of sick men overwhelmed camp leaders, who were still working to establish the place. Visitors swarmed the camp, hoping to see their husbands and sons. For a month, there was no laundry; soiled clothing and bedding were burned. Some 40,000 troops passed through Camp Wikoff in August and September, and nearly 260 died. There were not enough doctors; several nurses died from exhaustion. Bodies were sent to a makeshift morgue, wrapped in nightshirts, and placed into pine coffins with a block of wood under their heads, despite protocol that a deceased soldier be embalmed and dressed in uniform.

A regular visitor to the morgue was the Rev. Henry B. Bryan, a Long Island Episcopalian who stayed at the camp to conduct Sunday services and minister to the sick. He stopped by the deadhouse to see who had died in the past twenty-four hours. He was appalled by the treatment of bodies.

"They gave the least possible time to each dead man, pushing the filled coffin out into the hot sun, where the dead wagon, after a delay of sometimes as much as six hours, came and got them. The men who nailed the coffins up sat on the lids and told indecent stories, swore, and spat tobacco juice in all directions," Bryan told a congressional committee after the war. "These poor Montauk boys had no flag and no taps." The morgue workers were not soldiers but laborers from New York City's Bowery. Another witness said some caskets leaked and smelled.

Brown angrily denied all but one of the accusations. He said he visited the morgue several times a day and never saw a problem. No soldier was buried naked. He went so far as to obtain affidavits from morgue workers who handled the bodies. He claimed that within twenty-four hours of a soldier's death, families were contacted and asked how to dispose of the body. If there was no response, the body was buried at the camp cemetery in a grave Brown himself selected. Ministers always said prayers as bodies were interred; Brown himself prayed over the body of the first man to die in camp, before there was a chaplain on-site. Those bodies being returned to their families were dressed in military uniforms, sealed into caskets, and shipped home at government expense.

He praised the morgue workers. "I never saw men work more carefully than those there."

His lone concession about the charges made by Bryan and others was that wood, rather than pillows, was used in coffins. It was for good reason, he said: "There is less liability of a stench by making a bad matter worse by having a lot of decomposed feathers under their heads."

Brown was backed by other physicians, who commended the care as exceptional, particularly given the rushed conditions. Complaints leveled at Camp Wikoff and its treatment of the dying and dead, Brown said, were the opinions of naive civilians. "They came here, never having seen a hospital and never seen a sick soldier or anything of the kind," he said.

"It was not a condition that would inspire a poet, but it was nothing unusual except as to the numbers."

Forty-six years later, bodies and numbers would weigh on his son-in-law.

* * *

On the morning of August 25, 1944, a disparate group of bureaucrats made their way into what was known as Temporary Building B in southwest Washington. Here were representatives from the Marine Corps, the American Red Cross, the Army Chaplain Corps, the U.S. Maritime Commission, the Army Transportation Corps, and the Navy Bureau of Medicine and Surgery, which was responsible for deceased sailors, marines, and Coast Guardsmen.

They filed into Room 2055 to discuss one main topic: how to manage the return of the war dead.

The navy, the State Department, the marines, the army—each was responsible for its war casualties overseas. But none had a plan for handling those bodies once the war was over.

Questions arose. Would bodies stay overseas? If the dead were being brought home, who would do the heavy lifting? How would a repatriation program be constructed? The Army Quartermaster General and Harbold had managed such matters after World War I. But this ongoing conflict was of an entirely different scope and scale, and no definitive answer had yet been given.

Robert Harbold believed he had the solution. For nearly a year, he had been lobbying for more staff. He made his personnel arguments to achieve the larger mission he had been assigned a year earlier: develop a plan for bringing home dead soldiers, airmen, sailors, and marines. For that to happen, and for such a mission to succeed, he believed the work needed to be placed in the hands of just one office: the Quartermaster General.

Evacuating bodies from hundreds of cemeteries, ordering thousands of caskets, hiring civilian embalmers, moving the dead by airplanes, ships, and trains, and managing the shipment of bodies to hundreds of thousands of towns and cities across the United States—Harbold wanted all of this work to be coordinated, efficient, and empathetic to grieving families. He and his Quartermaster colleagues knew the war was turning and was likely to end sooner rather than later. Families would want their loved ones brought home.

Harbold needed to persuade every government agency with a stake in the war and its casualties, and all their representatives were seated in Room 2055 at the Office of the Quartermaster General. Cooperation was essential.

The arguments were straightforward: "To have each department or agency responsible for the return of its dead would not only lead to confusion but would also lead to these activities competing with one another for labor, supplies, and equipment incident to disinterment, preparation, casketing, and shipment."

Soldiers and airmen were buried in the same cemeteries in Europe and the Pacific; it would be chaos to have different branches of the service removing their dead. Mistakes would be unavoidable "in this delicate task." And what of those families who had lost more than one boy, with one in the army and the other in the marines. They deserved consistent communication and care. Finally, there were the cost savings in both military and civilian employees needed, as well as the cascade of supplies (caskets, shipping cases, embalming materials, trucks, train cars, fuel, and more) required to bring the dead home.

Harbold's boss, Quartermaster General Edmund B. Gregory, led the discussion; he had graduated a year ahead of Harbold at West Point. There were charts and draft policies to review. The navy, coast guard, and marines all deferred to the army to return the war dead. The navy's Bureau of Medicine and Surgery, which managed bodies for the navy, coast guard, and marines, would give the army access to all its overseas burial records. They only asked that their men be the ones to communicate with families and accompany bodies upon return to the United States. The navy wanted families to see a sailor in dress blues escorting their dead.

As bureaucratic discussions go, the August 25 meeting was painfully uneventful. But the conversations, the questions asked, and the fact that everyone in the room agreed upon the need for a detailed, coordinated effort to return the war dead confirmed what Harbold had been saying for more than a year. It validated every critical, pleading memo he had typed.

Years after the war, an analyst pointed to the meeting's significance: "It marked the beginning of concrete operational planning for return of the dead."

* * *

For weeks after the meeting in Room 2055, Harbold dealt with questions and issues raised by those who, like him, were responsible for servicemen who had died abroad. The meeting had made real to the military what families already knew: The dead could no longer be ignored.

Harbold now had the momentum and support to finalize the mission he had been assigned in 1943: to create a global program, the so-called method of disposal, for the best way to return America's dead after the war was over.

No detail was too small. When the head of the army's Transportation Corps asked about the dimensions of caskets to be used—his men, after all, would be responsible for moving thousands of bodies by boat and rail, and oceangoing ships would need to be retrofitted to provide adequate storage—Harbold assured him that those details were being finessed. He would soon meet with leaders of the Casket Manufacturers Association of America to ask for their cooperation in producing a standard coffin for storing and shipping America's war dead.

The navy had the most questions and, after the losses of the army, the most casualties. Its leaders wanted Harbold to explain how the Quartermaster and its Graves Registration troops would locate isolated burials in far-flung places like Newfoundland and Brazil. Bodies of sailors had washed ashore on Pacific islands and were buried by local residents—would the army recover them? And then there were mass burials containing only fragments of marines—how would families learn the fates of their loved ones?

Harbold had answers to every question. His responses to the navy were so detailed that the letter became a blueprint of sorts for the army's extensive plan—drafted by Harbold—for how the dead would be repatriated once the war was over. Harbold dated his memo October 16, 1944.

On the other side of the world, Delbert Trueman was writing a quick letter to his wife. Another dull day had passed at his temporary home in Italy, and no mail had arrived from the United States. He and a buddy had enjoyed mixing cherry brandy and grapefruit juice at the base bar. But he discouraged Virginia from drinking alcohol or visiting any taverns in Marion. "Bye bye sweet & don't forget I still love you very much & always will. Write me now."

In a few short hours, he and the 450th Bomb Group would be in the air, rumbling toward Vienna.

Chapter 5

October 17

There is a restaurant in our Michigan town called The Bomber. While diners plow through orders of eggs and bacon, grits or French toast, model aircraft tethered to fishing line sway overhead. Here is a blue P-38 Lightning with its twin tails; nearby is a B-17 Flying Fortress, its giant wings spread like a hawk. Aircraft from different eras crowd the restaurant's skies: A B-52 Stratofortress from the Cold War noses its way eastward, on a direct path with a Luftwaffe Me 110 and a futuristic B-2 stealth bomber.

The restaurant walls are coated with photographs of airmen and flight crews, as well as *Life* magazine covers, images of factory women in coveralls and bandanas, olive-drab Air Corps uniforms, and other wartime memorabilia.

But the true star of The Bomber is the B-24 Liberator.

In World War II, the Liberator rolled off the assembly line at Ford Motor Company's behemoth Willow Run factory, just five miles from the restaurant. Willow Run was massive: an assembly plant in Ypsilanti, Michigan, that covered fifty football fields for building bombers, an airport with six runways, and an army air base housing 3,700 personnel. Construction began in 1941, and by 1944, when it was running at full bore, the factory produced one Liberator every fifty-nine minutes.

It was a titan of manufacturing.

All those shiny new Liberators required welders, millwrights, electricians, mechanics, and pilots. There were doctors and nurses on the plant grounds, cooks and janitors, plumbers and typists. Ford hired ten little people to help install parts in a plane's tiniest, narrowest spaces.

Ypsilanti was a town of about 12,000 people, now with an industrial neighbor that employed more than 42,000 men and women. A small government-run housing project on the grounds could hold only around three thousand. Ypsilantians began carving up their residences, converting single-family homes to duplexes, triples, and boardinghouses. Workers packed the rooms and apartments, and before and after their shifts, they flooded local diners like the newly named Bomber.

One of those cobbled-up houses belonged to a middle-aged man named Adam Loeffler. He had sold Buicks in Ypsilanti, but once the war started and Willow Run sprang up, he joined thousands of other men and women who signed on at the factory. And like many others, Loeffler turned his two-story home into an apartment house. Where one family had lived, there were now three in the Loeffler house.

In June 1944, when Loeffler was fifty-one years old and in his second year at Willow Run, a silver B-24J—serial number 42-51566—rolled away from the factory. It was among the 453 bombers produced by workers that month, and the one that ferried Delbert and his crewmates into the skies over Vienna.

Adam Loeffler's home is now our home. Where he had partitioned the house into three apartments, my husband and I live in a fully restored home that dates to 1858. Every night, I go to sleep in the same house as the man who helped build the B-24 that carried my grandfather to his death.

* * *

After Delbert Trueman, Bob Davis, and the rest of the crew took off that October morning for Austria, they climbed into a sky crowded with other Liberators.

Cottontails from the 450th Bomb Group rendezvoused above Manduria with the 376th Bomb Group and headed north to San Vito D'Normanni, where they joined two more Fifteenth Air Force units, the 98th and 449th Bomb Groups. All four bomber groups were based in Italy's boot.

More than three hundred planes droned above San Vito. The 450th would lead the attack on Vienna, which would take four hours to reach. From San Vito they headed north, out over the Adriatic Sea, and toward the Yugoslavian coast. Once at 10,000 feet, pilots told their men to put on oxygen. It was also the time to test guns. Men fired off rounds to guarantee the Brownings were working and to release their growing anxiety.

Some men on Delbert's plane were undoubtedly more nervous than others.

Like Delbert, Cpl. Charles Kleinhenz was on his first mission. He was a nineteen-year-old from western New York, and everyone called him Junior. He and Delbert had trained together since Greensboro and Harlingen, and stayed together in Westover and Savannah as Crew 272. Today, they were in reverse roles in the ship: Delbert, a nose gunner, was assigned to the tail turret's twin guns, while Kleinhenz left the familiar confines of the tail for the nose turret.

But there was plenty of experience aboard the ship, too.

Delbert's pilot was 1st Lt. Leonard Mojica, a twenty-one-year-old Californian who was joined at the controls by his co-pilot, 2nd Lt. Marvin G. Niederjohn. Together, the two officers had flown more than seventy combat missions. Joining them were waist gunners with dozens of missions to their credit: Elvin Killingsworth, a baby-faced staff sergeant they called "Killer," and T.Sgt. Bob Davis, who doubled as a radio operator and had befriended Delbert before leaving Manduria.

The four men had been flying together for months, bombing Munich, Budapest, and Marseilles, and felt a certain camaraderie. Mojica, Niederjohn, and Killingsworth had pooled their money to help Davis buy the wedding ring for his new bride back in the States.

Rounding out the crew were 2nd Lt. George Webb, who would decide when the bombs should be dropped; T.Sgt. Joe Marallo, an engineer and top turret gunner three missions away from a ticket home; S.Sgt. Dick Conkle, a gunner with thirty-seven missions to his credit; and Cpl. Richard Pinardi, a photographer who had flown twenty-two missions jumping from crew to crew to record the damage caused by the bomb drops.

"You'll never see it again and you only saw it once: the camaraderie of those ten men," Bob Davis told me years later. "The infantry wasn't even like that. We were close together. We slept in the same barracks and every day we saw each other. A guy in the infantry, he might be in a squad and have thirty or forty people there. But with us we only had ten men."

* * *

The skies were thick with clouds as the Mojica crew flew north along the Yugoslavian coast, and visibility didn't improve once the bombers crossed into Yugoslavia and Hungary. Three hours into the mission, P-38 Lightnings from a fighter base in Italy joined the bombers above Durdevac, Hungary. Pilots like Mojica always welcomed the sight of fighters, which the bomber crews called "little friends."

Protection against any German fighters that might be lurking was reassuring. The 450th had already lost four of its twenty-eight planes on this mission due to malfunctions.

The planes were at 25,000 feet, with the crews wrapped in freezing air. Gunners were always the coldest: The man in the nose was hit with blasts as the ship pushed forward, waist gunners stood exposed in the plane's side openings, and the tail gunner felt the rush of all the cold pulled through the 67-foot-long fuselage and out of the aircraft. Bob Davis would wear three pairs of gloves and struggle to fire his gun. As a waist gunner, he could at least jump up and down to get the blood flowing. In their heated flight suits, all of the men were bathed in cold sweat.

Heading north to Vienna, the twenty-four Cottontail bombers from the 450th veered toward an Austrian village called Turnitz. This would be the IP—the Initial Point, a visible spot on the ground from which the B-24s would follow a straight line to the target. Once at the IP, no plane veered off course, no matter how thick the flak or furious the Luftwaffe fighter attack.

Bombardiers like Webb were automatically placed in control of the aircraft and remained in charge until they spotted the target and ordered "bombs away." On this day, however, it quickly became clear to Webb,

Mojica, and the other bombardiers and pilots of the 450th that they couldn't see their target. Clouds formed a dense blanket between them and Vienna. Bombardiers told their pilots it would be impossible to sight the Saurerwerke factory. They would be bombing blindly.

The target was quickly changed: They would strike Vienna's industrial center in the city's southeast corner and rely on radar rather than bombardiers' eyes.

As the B-24s barreled toward their target, air raid sirens blared in Vienna; German radar had been tracking the American planes since they crossed the Adriatic. Citizens rushed into bunkers, and German army ground units moved to their flak guns.

Liberator gunners like Delbert rotated in their turrets and scanned the skies but saw nothing. No Luftwaffe fighters would challenge the Americans that day. Instead, the skies above Vienna were quickly pockmarked with the dirty bursts airmen called "ack-ack"—antiaircraft fire.

The Austrian capital's reputation as a monster for American bombers was baring its teeth.

"This is Vienna," Leonard Mojica radioed to his new men as they neared the target. It was one of the few exchanges during the flight. The noise and oxygen masks made talking nearly impossible. Half an hour earlier, Mojica told all the men to put on their flak vests and helmets, and to snap their parachutes to the harnesses they wore; it was standard procedure thirty miles from the target.

But in the plane's turrets, Delbert and the other gunners went without parachutes; there simply wasn't enough room for the bulky packs. The chutes could be snapped on once the gunners squeezed out of their Plexiglas bubbles.

Amid the flak bursts and the heavy cloud cover, the tightly formed attack formations of the 450th started to break apart. Pilots held tight to the controls as explosions shook their aircraft; the planes pushed forward at 160 miles per hour as flying metal tore through them. Bob Davis had flown more than two dozen missions, and always believed he was catching a glimpse of hell on a bomb run—the inky smoke, the stink of cordite, exploding aircraft, men falling to their deaths.

As the Liberators crossed Vienna's industrial center, bombardiers released bombs just before 12:30 p.m. More than forty-six tons of 500-pound bombs struck the earth. Crews on every plane shared the same thought after a bomb drop: Let's get the hell out of here.

Leonard Mojica's plane was in the first of two waves of bombers attacking Vienna, and was peeling away from the target when flak sliced into the empty bomb bay. Richard Conkle was the first to jump. Within seconds of flak hitting the B-24 and exploding an engine on the left wing, he threw himself out of the ship's bomb bay into the sooty skies some 20,000 feet above Vienna. Joe Marallo was right behind him, abandoning his top turret and snapping on a parachute before bailing out. Overhead, the wounded Liberator struggled, still carrying Delbert and seven other men.

All hell was breaking loose.

One of the plane's four engines burst into flames. Elvin Killingsworth rushed from the plane's waist to the back of the ship, where the escape hatch was located, and struggled to open it. Bob Davis radioed to the cockpit and his pilot.

"Don't jump," Mojica ordered, "I'll get you back."

Davis waved his arms at Killingsworth, signaling him to stay with the plane. No sooner had he yelled than the ship was hit again, harder, with flak tearing away the right wing. The plane spiraled into a flat spin, rotating like a corkscrew as it drove eight men toward the ground.

Chaos erupted inside the ship. As the pilots struggled to control the plane from the cockpit, men and gear were flung toward the tail, hurled by centrifugal forces they couldn't fight. Delbert pulled himself out of the tail turret and fought to keep the escape hatch open before being thrown back to the tail. Guns, parachutes, and ammunition collided with men, who struggled to free themselves from each other and the plane; Elvin Killingsworth was crushed at the bottom of a human pile near the hatch. At the other end of the ship, Junior Kleinhenz and George Webb dove to open an escape hatch in the nose.

As the plane whorled and plummeted, Bob Davis didn't jump as much as he was spat out, wounded by flak and unconscious after his oxygen mask was ripped away in the madness. When he regained

1st Lt. Leonard Mojica tried to fly his B-24 Liberator out of the flak attack on his crew.
Kim Clarke photo

consciousness, he was hurtling toward the ground wearing an unopened parachute; he managed to yank the ripcord before passing out again.

Richard Pinardi felt himself sucked out of the ship and opened his chute; falling, he believed he saw his life flash before him, with a vision of his mother cooking in their Massachusetts kitchen.

Half a mile away in the sky, Joe Marallo was drifting in his parachute and cursing. This was all Pinardi's fault. Itinerant photographers were known to be lousy luck for crews, and sure enough, here he was, floating into enemy territory when he should be just two missions shy of going home. Marallo twisted in his chute and looked overhead for his plane, but saw nothing. And he thought about photos taken at gunnery school—of men wearing their combat gear—and how he knew these would be the pictures that newspapers printed when men were killed.

Dick Conkle tumbled downward, and surely hated what he saw below: a knot of German soldiers waiting for him on the ground. He had flown nearly forty missions, including two over the inferno of the Ploesti oil refinery in Romania. He had been shot down twice, once over North Africa and again off the coast of Italy. But his knack for making his way back to Manduria was about to evaporate.

As the Fifteenth Air Force's planes pulled away from Vienna, men in other ships watched the Mojica plane spiral out of control; their job was to scan the sky for bodies. They knew that parachutes meant possible survivors. They also understood what a flat spin meant.

Curtains for most of the crew, thought a navigator from the 450th who watched the plane as it fell. He saw three men bail out in a scene he would replay in his mind for decades to come.

The co-pilot of another plane thought he spotted five men jumping. A tail gunner from a third ship who saw the Mojica plane get hit counted two chutes. No one really knew how many men escaped the doomed ship.

A nose gunner with the 450th, who was on his ninth mission, had never seen a B-24 fall from the sky. He later confided in his diary that it was "the most sickening sight of my life."

Elsewhere in the sky, a B-24 carrying Delbert's friend Charlie Ward was rocked by flak seconds after unleashing its bombs. Everyone on board reported they were okay. And then a second burst of flak tore into the aircraft, rupturing a fuel tank and sending gasoline pouring into the bomb bay. When the pilot checked on his men a second time, there were no answers from the nose gunner and bombardier. He made his way into the nose and found it empty. The river of fuel and the threat of fire had forced the two men to fling themselves through the nose wheel door. Men in other planes counted two parachutes opening. But Ward stayed with the plane.

Mojica's crippled aircraft with its trapped men plunged east of Vienna and the Danube River, toward the hamlets of Rutzendorf and Leopoldsdorf. The B-24 slammed into a field; amazingly, it remained largely intact despite the impact. When Richard Pinardi touched down, it was within yards of the ship that minutes earlier had carried him five miles above the earth. Hobbled by flak wounds to his waist and ankle, he ran to the burning plane and tried to pull men from it, only to be driven back by flames and exploding ammunition.

It was then that he saw a crumpled Delbert Trueman, dog tag No. 35900811, burned and bleeding on the ground alongside the ship. "There was no doubt," Pinardi would tell me years later. "I think every bone in his body was broken. There was blood coming out of his mouth."

Residents who rushed to the crash site snatched up Pinardi. "For you," someone said, "the war is over."

Joe Marallo floated into a different group of civilians and was whisked to the home of the local burgermeister, who offered him cigarettes and soup. The two men communicated as best they could with hand gestures. Marallo took Kraft caramels from his emergency kit and offered them to his captor's children, but not before the Austrian made him eat one first to prove it was safe.

Bob Davis and Dick Conkle, the first men to abandon the ship, landed in a potato field. German soldiers grabbed them while also holding off angry civilians rushing toward the airmen with shovels and pitchforks. A soldier slammed Conkle's head with a rifle butt, cracking the airman's jaw. Davis, his back and leg twisted by an awkward landing, was carried away on a stretcher.

* * *

Whenever I take a commercial flight and hear the pilot announce our cruising altitude—often 32,000 feet or so—I look out the window and think of Delbert Trueman.

What is it like to fall that far from so high up? What level of terror and panic would take over? And what kind of blessing would it be to black out from lack of oxygen, not knowing whether you would live or die?

Joe Marallo assured me that my grandfather would have felt nothing. Between losing his tether to an oxygen tank and being pinned in a flat spin, Delbert would have been unconscious as the plane plunged downward.

"He never knew what hit him," Marallo said. "Never knew."

Bob Davis wanted my mother to know this, too. "He was unconscious. I know, because I was," he said. "And he never knew."

We met Davis at a reunion of the 450th Bomb Group in 1995. The group's attendance was shrinking: Veterans were aging and dying. But I wanted my mom to meet the man who was the last person to talk with her father.

Davis told us about life inside a noisy bomber and about being an airman flying into combat. He described falling from a plane that is five miles above the earth, the last moments for my mom's father, and a day that would change everything.

"When they woke you up," he said of a mission day, "you never spoke to anybody. You were in your own thoughts. And it was only until you get out to the aircraft that you started to loosen up. That's when everything started—you got on the airplane, you knew what you had to do, and you did it."

* * *

That night in Manduria, Italy, at the home of the 450th Bomb Group, Lloyd White wrote in his diary as he always did. He had been Delbert's pilot since their training days as Crew 272 at Westover, and the Vienna mission had rattled him.

"Raid on tank factory at Vienna. My nose gunner, Trueman, and tail gunner Kleinhenz were killed," he wrote. "It was hell."

Cpl. William L. Waldrop, an airman who had trained with White's men but did not fly that day, scribbled in his journal that Trueman and

Kleinhenz had not returned from the mission. Trueman, he added, had a daughter.

In Vienna, Luftwaffe officers filled out paperwork recording the downing of six B-24s in fifteen minutes that afternoon. Broken planes and men were scattered throughout Vienna and its neighboring villages.

When German soldiers reached the wreckage of 42-51566, they could only identify three of the six men found in or near the plane: pilot Leonard Mojica, bombardier George Webb, and gunner Delbert Trueman. All six deceased airmen from the bomber would join more than 225 men, women, and children listed by local undertakers as killed in the October 17 bombing in Vienna, including residents such as Hugo and Monika Klimberg; Konrad Schützenhofer, who lived near the Danube Canal north of the Saurerwerke; and six members of the Schuster family—two adults and four youngsters. Another 6,200 Viennese people were left homeless by bombs and flames.

The residents' bodies were taken to morgues and church cemeteries. The remains of American airmen were moved to a wooded and weedy corner of Vienna's historic Central Cemetery.

A week later, Luftwaffe officers based in Vienna ordered the bodies buried, along with dozens of American fliers whose bodies had been collected over the past fourteen days. At the rear of the Viennese cemetery, in a section called Plot 88, German soldiers placed the airmen into simple wooden coffins and stacked three in each grave.

It was more than most of America's combat casualties received in Europe, where their fellow soldiers often buried them in ponchos, mattress covers, or pieces of field tents. General George S. Patton, who was fighting the German army in France, was known to say that one thing German soldiers did well was give proper burials to both their own dead and enemy dead.

After covering Delbert's coffin with dirt, a German soldier set a white wooden cross on the grave.

Chapter 6

The Waiting

No gray-faced men in uniform stood in my grandmother's doorway. No gleaming sedan idled at the curb. That might have happened in the movies, she told me years later, but not in her small Indiana town in 1944. Virginia Trueman was washing her hair when a Western Union boy on a bicycle rolled up to her front porch carrying the telegram every military wife feared.

Delbert was reported missing somewhere over Austria.

She learned about his disappearance on Halloween morning but had sensed it for days. She usually received a letter from Delbert every other day, and ten days had passed with no mail from Italy.

My mother remembered walking home from Horace Mann Elementary School for lunch that day, giddy because she was going to change into her costume for an afternoon party with her second-grade classmates. As Judy turned the corner and looked up the street, an odd sight struck her. Her grandfather was standing on the front porch of her house. That didn't make sense, she thought, because he should be at work.

"Something's wrong," her mind raced. "Something's wrong with Daddy."

She returned to school at her grandfather's urging; he did not betray what he and Virginia knew. Later that night, after the costume party, Judy learned her father was lost. Virginia wasn't sure her daughter truly understood what it meant to be missing in action.

Absorbing the telegram's message, Virginia's first thought—one she held tightly for months—was that Delbert had been captured and was being held in a German prisoner-of-war camp. Her second thought—one she acted on that afternoon—was to write Lloyd White, the pilot whom Delbert had trained with and admired. She had come to know White when she and Judy stayed in Savannah. He was based in Manduria and surely would have more details than the thin government telegram she had been handed.

Marion residents woke up the next day to read a newspaper report that Delbert Trueman was missing in action, along with two other local men: an infantryman lost in southern France and a pilot who had disappeared somewhere over Yugoslavia. The paper erroneously stated that Corporal Trueman was missing over Australia. No one in Marion knew that Delbert had been buried and his grave marked a week earlier.

In 1944, one in four men assigned to combat with the 450th Bomb Group ended up missing in action; nearly half of the group's planes were lost in action. Three days after their fateful mission to Vienna, Delbert and five crewmates were struck from the rolls of the 450th and listed missing in action.

Telegram messages about the other airmen began to arrive at homes across the country.

Three messages went to California: In San Bernardino, Mary Mojica learned that her pilot husband Len, a man who loved to build model airplanes, was missing. Three hundred miles to the north in Madera, Earl and Mabel Killingsworth heard the same news about their twenty-year-old son, Elvin; his mother had just mailed a camera to him in Italy. Arthur and Nina Webb received the news about their red-haired boy, George, at their home in Palo Alto.

Co-pilot Marvin Niederjohn's parents were notified in Laramie, Wyoming; two weeks earlier, another of their sons had enlisted in the navy. In Nunda, New York, Charles K. Kleinhenz was stunned to read that his namesake and only child seemed to be gone before his twentieth birthday.

* * *

After learning that her husband was missing, Virginia went to see her in-laws, Paul and Nellie Trueman, to share the news. She next drove to the local American Red Cross office to ask for help finding Delbert. It was not unusual for Italian-based aircrews to bail out of disabled planes and parachute into the safety of Yugoslavian partisans; the 450th saw it happen all the time, with men returning to the base months after disappearing in the sky. They would walk into camp, longhaired, unshaven, and grinning. The Red Cross also helped with tracking down men captured by the Germans and taken as prisoners of war.

Virginia was confident that Delbert had safely escaped before his plane vanished; he had gone through too much preparation not to survive. He was too young and too active to be anything but alive. "I just thought he'd be all right," she told me. "He'd had pretty good training, although it seemed to me it'd been an awful short training."

The Air Corps assured Virginia that her husband was well prepared to survive anything that went wrong in the sky. "Delbert has participated throughout a grueling aerial campaign constantly attended by extreme physical hardships and requiring the utmost in individual courage and sacrifice," wrote Maj. Gen. Nathan F. Twining, commander of the Fifteenth Air Force, weeks after Delbert was reported missing.

As the weeks passed, she regularly received letters from different branches of the War Department, each delivering slivers of information about Delbert and indicating that a search for the missing men was underway. All expressed regret and sympathy. None offered the details she needed.

Her faith was reinforced by a letter from pilot Lloyd White. Three weeks earlier, on the day Delbert's plane went down, White had scribbled in his diary that Delbert had been killed in the raid on Vienna. But he now wrote to encourage the gunner's wife about Delbert's chances of survival. It most likely was an act of compassion to keep up Virginia's spirits until the government could deliver any official news about Delbert's disappearance or death.

White recounted watching the plane go down carrying his two gunners, Delbert and Junior Kleinhenz. "It wasn't burning and not too much to get alarmed at except it was leaving the formation," he wrote.

Flak, he said, can damage a plane but not destroy it. His own Liberator had been hit forty-three times on the mission. "So getting hit never causes a ship to blow up or go into a spin," he wrote, "like some stories you hear back home."

When he last saw Delbert's plane, White told her, it was slowly drifting into the clouds below. A damaged plane could easily have glided a hundred miles.

"Ninety-six percent of the crews who were in conditions similar to this ship get out. Some of them return to base found by partisans, the others are picked up by the Germans and put in prison camp," he wrote. "Some are found by partisans and they have to stay in the mountains with them for months and no one hears from them for a long, long time and then when the allies capture the land, they show up."

It had just happened with another Marion man, 1st Lt. Charles D. Boxell, whose disappearance was reported on the same day as Delbert. Boxell was a B-17 pilot based in Italy. Eleven days after being listed as missing in action, he showed up at his Italian base. He and his men had bailed out of their Flying Fortress when it ran out of fuel over Yugoslavia. It was exactly as White described to Virginia.

"I sincerely believe that they are both alive in Yugoslavia or in a prison camp. I told my mother if they ever sent her word of missing in action, just figure I am in Switzerland or with the partisans in Yugo for that is where we would go," White wrote. "Del was one of the best boys I have ever been connected with and so was Junior."

(White also apologized profusely for not writing sooner. He wanted to contact her right after Delbert's plane failed to return to Manduria from Vienna. But that would have meant breaking the news before the Western Union telegram and official War Department notification. And the letter never would have passed the Air Corps censors. "From the bottom of my heart I am sorry I couldn't have written but my hands were tied.")

The War Department also urged Virginia to hold on to hope for her husband. Missing-in-action status indicated neither a closed case nor a death; in fact, she was told, men often became prisoners of war without

Germany or Japan notifying the American government. There was no way to compel the enemy to produce details.

"I wish to emphasize that every effort is exerted continuously to clear up the status of our personnel," wrote Maj. Gen. James A. Ulio several weeks after Delbert's disappearance. Unless new details came to light sooner, Ulio promised Virginia he would write again after three months. Twenty-five years earlier, during World War I, Ulio had worked with Robert Harbold in the Central Records Office to notify families about their missing and deceased husbands, sons, and brothers.

While assuring Virginia that a search was underway for the missing men, the War Department also confirmed she would continue to receive her husband's twenty-five-dollar monthly paycheck. Despite her requests, officials citing military security refused to reveal the names of the other men on the plane or their families. A month after Delbert's disappearance, the International Red Cross said it still had no word that he was a prisoner of war.

At school in Marion, Judy kept up her grades, particularly with high marks in spelling. She was in second grade and didn't miss a day of class in the first weeks of her father's absence. Her teacher told Virginia she was "one of my superior students."

Yet none of Judy's playmates had fathers in the service. A classmate gave her a sympathy note, using a crayon to print: *I am sarre about your father.*

Virginia started going to church. She and Delbert had visited the local Methodist church a few times during their marriage, but now she was a regular worshipper. Along with struggling with the uncertainty of her missing husband, she was losing the other man in her life to cancer. Her father, Charles, a fifty-one-year-old insurance salesman, had battled the disease since spring, including losing an eye. When it spread to his spine and liver, death came quickly. He was buried one week before Christmas and two months after Delbert's disappearance.

The house was suddenly bereft of men: Virginia survived with her daughter, a newly widowed mother, and her pregnant sister, whose husband was overseas with the army. Even the family dog was female.

The new year arrived with no real news. The army organized a nationwide tour that brought airmen who had been released from POW camps—either by escaping or through repatriation—face-to-face with the families of men still reported missing. The goal was to answer families' questions about the conditions airmen faced in German and Japanese camps, and to offer encouragement and hope. One army officer on the tour mentioned that 70 percent of men listed as missing in action were actually prisoners.

Virginia and Judy kept busy: bridge games for Virginia, Girl Scouts and birthday parties for Judy, and church picnics and potlucks for both. Virginia joined with neighbors to help mail ten thousand gasoline rationing books to county residents. She also volunteered to raise money for a new YMCA in town; years earlier, Delbert had overseen a men's basketball league at the Y.

Virginia kept writing letters: to the Red Cross, the War Department, members of Congress, and the chaplain of Delbert's bomb group. She received a wisp of detail from the War Department in March 1945, five months after Delbert's disappearance. For the first time, she learned that four men had managed to bail out of Delbert's bomber and were being held in German prisoner-of-war camps. Delbert, however, was not among them and was still considered missing, as were five other airmen aboard his bomber.

"We shall not give up hope that Delbert was able to escape from the ship. Until we are in possession of more information than we are at the present time, we shall not abandon hope," assured Capt. John H. Keefe, a chaplain who ministered to the 450th Bomb Group. "May God give you the courage bravely to face each day." Keefe had arrived in Manduria days after Delbert.

Packages that Virginia had mailed to Delbert in the fall of 1944 started arriving back in Marion, sporadically and unopened. They held vanilla wafers, olives, cigarettes, a two-pound fruitcake, rolls of film, cheese, jars of peanut butter, and mystery novels, all intended as Christmas gifts he never saw.

* * *

And still, personal items were left behind, in Italy with Delbert's squadron, and around the world wherever service members died.

When men were killed or missing in action overseas, their belongings were collected by a local officer, inventoried, and shipped home to the United States—not to their families, but rather to an eleven-story building in downtown Kansas City, Missouri. They served as tactile, painful reminders of life and loss that were both cherished and rejected by parents, spouses, and siblings.

The personal property of soldiers arrived daily by train at the Army Effects Bureau. Like Robert Harbold's Memorial Division, the Army Effects Bureau was part of the Quartermaster Corps. With service members dying and disappearing throughout Europe and the Pacific, Kansas City and its Quartermaster depot served as a central U.S. location for depositing and processing belongings. The navy, marines, and coast guard had their own units for managing personal effects, but the army's was the largest. At its busiest, the Effects Bureau and its workers sorted through more than 55,000 cases of personal belongings in a single month.

It was a job that demanded accuracy, compassion, judgment and, sometimes, a strong stomach.

Upward of nine hundred civilian employees, many of them older women, spent their days examining, inventorying, cleaning, deodorizing, and packaging all manner of objects. Standing at examining tables and workbenches, they handled cigarette cases, fountain pens, cameras, pipes, silverware, diaries, baseball caps, postcards, chess sets, knives, pistols (some still loaded), currency, and more. Army leaders pointed out that 80 percent of the civilian workers had a family member serving in the war, adding a layer of empathy to how they handled the belongings of dead and missing men.

One worker was Rosemary Hanaway, who spent day after day drafting letters to families with details about their loved ones' possessions. She'd lost a friend in the war, and a girlfriend's brother had been killed in action. She believed her work was essential, and although she was a quick typist, she was careful about the tone and details of her letters because sensitivity was crucial. Still, she resigned after fifteen months. "It was a job that, eventually, it just got to you," she said years later.

The work was important but depressing, yet no one could complain when it involved someone was had been killed or was missing.

At times, the place reeked of death. Personal effects bags—which became known as graves bags—carried the stink of blood, sweat, and mildew trapped in clothes, wallets, and jewelry. Employees tried chemicals and powders to mask the stench, even considering chlorine gas. They piled the bags on pallets near open windows and turned on electric fans, hoping to force out the odor. Supervisors found that hiring employees with a weaker sense of smell helped reduce turnover.

It was inevitable that items being returned from combat zones were damaged by bullets and shrapnel or stained with blood. It was just as certain that not all the blood could be removed. Women wielded dental lathes and picks to remove dried blood and corrosion from the grooves and crevices of rings, necklaces, and watchbands.

"You couldn't hardly send a ring home with a piece of flesh or something," one woman said. Clothing was put through the laundry, but not before workers checked the linings for money a soldier may have tucked away.

Other items couldn't be salvaged, like the returned wallet of an army private shot in the back on the Philippine island of Luzon. It didn't get past an examiner at the Effects Bureau: "Blood stained. Bad odor. Grewsome. Removed."

In addition to sparing families ghastly sights and smells, workers shielded them from uncomfortable materials, like dirty pictures or letters from girlfriends to married men. Censors destroyed anything deemed embarrassing. Army officers also checked for any paperwork that might contain sensitive military details.

And still, there were harsh reminders of combat.

When Pvt. Everett V. Curtin was mortally wounded by shrapnel in his stomach in early 1944, he had two handkerchiefs tucked into his uniform. After the hankies arrived at the Effects Bureau from Italy, a captain wrote to Curtin's wife, Mildred, warning her that they were stained and asking if she wanted them. She didn't.

"I would like to have my husband's belongings, but don't think I could stand to get anything with bloodstains so please don't send anything with bloodstains on," she wrote. The army shipped her the rest of Everett Curtin's belongings, including a mechanical pencil, a pocket knife, his wallet, and the forty-three dollars it held.

Jahue Blevins felt differently. His nineteen-year-old son, James, was an infantryman killed in France in January 1945. Blood from a head wound seeped into a pocket holding papers, including James's Social Security card and religious tracts. A chain holding his rosary was broken.

A lieutenant at the Effects Bureau worried it was too much for a parent: "It is our desire to refrain from sending any article which would be distressing; at the same time, we do not feel justified in removing the items without consent."

James was one of eleven children and had lived with his parents until he enlisted. He sent money home to his family in rural Virginia to help them. His father wanted every bit of him returned. "I will say I had rather you would just send everything on together," Jahue Blevins said, "as it is not my desire to depart from anything he had."

Capt. Edward J. Hackett was a thirty-seven-year-old surgeon who was killed in France while trying to save a wounded soldier in the field. When a footlocker with his belongings arrived at his New Jersey home, it contained all parts of his army uniform. There was a field jacket, khaki shirts and trousers, neckties, side caps, wool socks, and more. While the army salvaged enlisted men's clothing and gear for reuse, the uniforms of missing or dead officers—who had paid for the clothing—were considered personal property to be sent on to family members. It was a protocol that upset Hackett's widow, Evelyn.

"I can't see why you return all that military equipment," she wrote to the Effects Bureau. "The agony of seeing all those army clothes without my fine stalwart husband was only exceeded by the shock and grief of the War Dept. telegram."

Workers at the Effects Bureau strove to spare families the shock and grief felt by Evelyn Hackett, but there was no way to predict what emotions would be triggered by the items they cleaned, sorted, and returned to parents and wives.

Nellie Seder flew into a rage after the bureau boxed up her younger brother's belongings and mailed them to her parents in Detroit. Pvt. Vittolh Seder was killed at St. Lo, France, a month after the Allies invaded France in 1944. He was twenty-five years old and Nellie's only sibling. Her letters to the Effects Bureau were filled with bitterness, anger, grief, and a deep desire to shield her parents from additional angst. She accused the army of stealing her brother's valuables. She hated the war, she said, and her brother did, too. She wrote:

> *How can you dare of sending the families of the deceased such articles as we found? It was nothing but plain junk! The wallet was a gift from me and was in shameful condition. We can understand this to the extent of the inhuman life a soldier leads, but where is just one piece of currency? My brother was never* BROKE *and by the condition of the wallet we are lead to believe he didn't have a dime. Who picked his pockets while he was lying dead? That we would like to know! . . .*
>
> *For the sake of those who are yet to experience our tragic incident I would suggest that you refrain from sending articles to the families such as we received. If you can't send property that they can look upon without their very hearts being torn out don't send them at all.*

When a second batch of Vittolh Seder's belongings from France arrived in Kansas City, it included letters and birthday cards from his parents, sister, and girlfriend. Nellie Seder rejected the package. "It will just be opening a heart-ache that will never heal," she wrote, "but each time we hear or get something that has anything to do with my brother, it's worse."

The toughest cases at the Effects Bureau landed on the desk of its leader, Col. John R. Murphy. A Kansas City lawyer, Murphy was an army reservist and a lawyer with the Judge Advocate General's Department in the 1930s; he enlisted in 1941. As the effects quartermaster, he tried to comfort relatives like Nellie Seder by explaining the difficulties of recovering personal items—including money and valuables—from battlefields and overseas bases, as well as the diligence of civilian workers in his building sorting through hundreds of thousands of belongings. "I am ever conscious that we here at the bureau are dealing with wives, mothers, and fathers who have made, through the loss of their husband or son, a tremendous sacrifice," he said.

Each family was different: One wanted every last scrap of a soldier, another desired only valuables, and yet another could not bear to open the carton sent from Kansas City.

"Therefore, it is difficult to know just what to send or what to discard. What will be done with a billfold containing a lock of hair, pictures of a wife and child, and of a father and mother, pierced by a bullet or piece of shrapnel?" Murphy wrote to Seder. "What will be done with the bloodstained pieces of paper on which a last letter of a dying son and brother is written? These are the representative problems which confront us daily. Unfortunately, a type of action which brings letters of commendation from some results in censure from others."

Writing about bloodstained pieces of paper surely took Murphy back to the nightmare of Lt. Hershel G. Horton and the trauma of those in Kansas City managing his possessions.

In the first year of America's involvement in the war, Horton and his unit came under fire from Japanese troops in a New Guinea jungle. As Horton tried to grab the dog tags of dead comrades, a sniper's bullets shattered his hip and fractured his leg. Horton dragged himself into a grass hut, with enemy soldiers all of fifteen yards away. He spent eleven days pinned down by the Japanese—when he tried to move, a sniper hit him again, this time in the neck and shoulder.

He considered using his pistol to kill himself but couldn't go through with it.

Through his hunger, thirst, and delirium, Horton recorded his dying days in a prayer book he carried.

"I sit and lie here in this terrible place, wondering not why God has forsaken me, but rather why He is making me suffer this terrible end," he wrote. "My life has been good, but I am so young and have so many things undone that a man of 29 should do—we may never know God's purpose in striking me down like this, but He must have one."

Horton died in the jungle. His comrades eventually recovered and buried his broken body.

Horton's parents had been notified of his death in early 1943, but never knew the details or that their son had essentially recorded his own death. Ten months later, Col. John Murphy did know, and had to decide what to do with the young lieutenant's diary.

He wrote to Horton's father, George, in Aurora, Illinois.

> *It will cause you heartache and grief, but at the same time will give you even greater pride in being the father of a son who could face death as he did. . . . I sent this letter to you, his father, because with you must rest the decision of whether Mrs. Horton and your daughter shall see it and read it. Please do not let Mrs. Horton feel that I have any desire to conceal or hide this letter. I simply feel that such a letter might be too shocking for many a mother to receive.*

George and Odessa Horton asked for their son's diary.

* * *

Delbert Trueman's belongings, left behind in Italy, were neither bloodstained nor damaged. They arrived in Marion in May 1945, shortly after Germany's surrender and the Allied victory in Europe. Victory in Europe Day—May 8—saw Marion and the entire country erupt in celebration. Mayor Edward Wert asked all city businesses to close for the day. Bars shut their doors, school was canceled, and churches held special services.

As of V-E Day, 154 men from Marion and surrounding Grant County had been killed in the war. Those missing in action, like Delbert, were not counted as casualties.

A letter from the Effects Bureau to Virginia assured her that he was still considered missing and asked her to take care of everything until her husband returned. She opened a carton shipped from Kansas City to find the Bible her parents had given him. A leather case held a pair of aviator sunglasses; one of the lenses was cracked. Delbert's wallet contained paper money from Morocco and Italy; the army had no interest in converting small amounts of foreign currency and instead treated it as souvenirs to be sent to families.

The billfold also held Delbert's Indiana driver's license and a worn newspaper clipping that paid tribute to his brother Dale. There were several black-and-white snapshots of Virginia and Judy. His favorite, a photo of all three of them, was protected behind plastic, along with a four-leaf clover preserved for good luck.

Holding my grandfather's wallet, I think about all the hands it passed through during the journey that started at Delbert's base in Italy.

Charlie Ward would have followed his friend's request to ensure everything he owned in Manduria made it to Indiana, gathering the billfold and other belongings once it was clear Delbert's bomber wasn't coming back. A thirty-one-year-old first lieutenant named Elbert Whitt was responsible for organizing the possessions of the missing men of the 450th Bomb Group, typing up a detailed inventory to be shipped to the United States. The wallet moved from southern Italy to an army effects depot in Folembray, France, where all belongings of dead and missing men across the continent were sent.

The wallet would have been placed on a ship crossing the Atlantic to New York, then transported by train to middle America. A civilian worker at the Effects Bureau might have rubbed saddle soap into the wallet to give it added luster before boxing it for my grandmother in Indiana. They would sometimes do that to improve appearances.

Weeks after getting Delbert's personal effects, she received the last of the packages she had mailed him eight months earlier as Christmas presents. Among the gifts was a small model airplane.

* * *

The fall of Germany in May 1945 boosted the hopes of American families for two main reasons: Prisoners of war would be released, ending the limbo for families of men listed as missing in action. And bodies buried across Europe could be located and brought home.

But the War Department had to remind families that no war dead would be returned home until all fighting was over, and the country was still at war with Japan. All personnel and supplies would shift to the

Pacific. Men buried in the European Theater, where the war had taken its highest toll, would remain untouched for now.

Within days of Germany's collapse, the men of the 450th Bomb Group—the Cottontails based in Italy—began packing up and leaving their base in Manduria for the United States. They would glide into Boston Harbor aboard a troop transport, the USS *Wakefield*, a week before Memorial Day. More than 1,500 men from the bomb group had been killed in action or were missing in action.

While the Effects Bureau tried to avoid sending packages during the Christmas season, packages and personal effects kept arriving at homes, often months after a soldier was killed or reported missing. Charles Kleinhenz's parents received a small box of personal clothing, including a mohair tie. Mary Mojica, whose husband piloted Delbert's doomed bomber, ended up with more than a hundred items, from bath towels and facecloths to forty pairs of socks, forty-two handkerchiefs, and a set of house slippers. Gunner Elvin Killingsworth's belongings included a ring inscribed with *Rome 1944*, most likely a souvenir purchased while on leave; it became the property of his mother.

The trinkets and treasures provided an emotional stopgap, a type of connective tissue linking families with missing or dead soldiers. The feeling was temporary. Soon, parents and widows would want more from the army: details about where their loved ones were buried overseas and when those bodies would return home.

"I am writing you to ask if there could be any more chance to hope for his safety and return," a mother wrote. Her son, an Army Air Corps gunner, had been reported killed after the B-17 bomber he was aboard crashed into the North Sea. "I am sure you can tell me something to encourage me if there really is any hopes for him. However, if you know there is no hopes and you know he is gone I would rather you would say that. Anything definite would be better than this awful suspense."

Her letter made its way to Washington, D.C., the Quartermaster General's Memorial Division, and the desk of Col. Robert Harbold.

Chapter 7

The Plan

In early 1945, Colonel Harbold had a new assistant in the Memorial Division to help him manage the return of the dead.

Col. Michael H. Zwicker had spent most of the war stationed in Europe, where he helped set up the Office of the Chief Quartermaster as the right-hand man to Brig. Gen. Robert M. Littlejohn. With an ever-growing number of troops in the European Theater, their office was responsible for ordering, storing, and supplying hundreds of thousands of items, ranging from fly swatters, fresh oranges, and razor blades to forklifts, snowshoes, tents, and stoves for warming field hospitals.

In addition to meeting the needs of the living, the chief quartermaster and his Graves Registration soldiers collected and buried bodies and processed the deceased's personal effects to send home.

The work had been a grind.

By late 1944, Littlejohn believed Zwicker needed a change. His loyal assistant "still had much good service" to offer, but it would be best to work stateside. So off he went to the Memorial Division and an office in the nation's capital. Within weeks of relocating to Washington and joining the Memorial Division as Robert Harbold's deputy, Zwicker typed a letter to his old boss in England.

"I am afraid that the size of the job which is to be done has not as yet been fully realized," he wrote, "and I am just beginning to feel the impact and realize what is yet to come."

Harbold, Zwicker, and their colleagues in the Memorial Division faced intense pressure to find a way to recover and return the nation's war dead quickly, accurately, efficiently, and with respect.

There were army superiors demanding plans to address a situation they had failed to properly prepare for at the start of the war. They said that work needed to be completed sooner rather than later, so "the War Department will not be subjected to criticism in undertaking a job which has been anticipated for years."

There were members of Congress fielding letters and calls from grieving constituents asking when the remains of their loved ones would be recovered and shipped home.

And there were the families.

"They have begged us to hurry up," a U.S. Coast Guard representative told Harbold. This plea came from the military branch with the smallest number of overseas casualties.

* * *

On the first day of June 1945, Colonel Harbold walked into the Pentagon and up to the outer ring of the fifth floor of the sprawling building. In his hand was a proposal that would affect every American family that had lost someone overseas in the war. He delivered it to the office of the Army Service Forces commander, who oversaw all army logistics.

This was a blueprint nearly two years in the making, and Harbold had still needed more time. Army leaders had set a deadline of April 1, 1945. Twice, Harbold requested one-month extensions. One reason was that his office was missing about 75,000 burial records despite reports of deaths from Europe and the Mediterranean. This gap made it impossible to finalize a method to locate and return the dead. Accurate, current paperwork was a must.

Harbold's right-hand support in finishing the plan came from a World War I colleague. Lt. Col. Earl Sechrest served with an army machine gun unit in France before joining the Graves Registration Service, where he worked for Harbold in the Central Records Office. As a lieutenant colonel in 1944, he was chief of the Quartermaster's Graves Registration and Effects Division in Europe. He joined Harbold in the

Memorial Division weeks before the final deadline to help complete the plan.

The typewritten pages presented a sobering scenario.

More than 190,000 American bodies were scattered across six continents, with soldiers still fighting in the Pacific. Most of the dead were buried in 454 temporary cemeteries set up by soldiers in the wake of combat. In Europe, the burials ranged from two bodies in Dolga Vas, Yugoslavia, and three at a cemetery on the island of Corsica, to more than 8,700 bodies at Nettuno, Italy, and 27,581 at Henri-Chapelle in Belgium.

Several thousand more men were believed to be buried in Germany, Austria, the Balkans, and the Low Countries. Plus, there were isolated burials in fields and on hillsides. Finding the graves would be painstaking, but once located, the bodies would be moved and centralized to temporary U.S. cemeteries on Allied ground.

Added to the known burials were more than 44,000 men like Delbert Trueman who were classified as missing in action in Europe. The Memorial Division said it was a "logical assumption" that up to 90 percent of them were dead.

The Pacific Theater posed unique challenges for burials across islands separated by thousands of miles. The war with Japan continued, resulting in more dead and missing soldiers, sailors, and marines.

There was also a particularly terrifying unknown: the number of combat deaths if the United States invaded Japan. Overall, the report said, the government should prepare to handle three hundred thousand bodies before the war finally ended.

The return plan would work like this: Graves Registration troops would sweep all the smaller cemeteries and isolated burials, disinter bodies, and move them to larger, temporary U.S. military cemeteries on Allied soil. The bodies would then be reburied. The Memorial Division would next notify families about the locations of loved ones and ask whether they wanted bodies returned or buried in permanent cemeteries that the United States would establish in Europe, Hawaii, and the Philippines.

Bodies bound for the United States would be transferred from cemeteries to ocean ports, loaded aboard converted Liberty ships, and delivered to ports in New York or San Francisco. From there, soldiers would place the casketed remains onto special trains that would fan out to fifteen distribution centers across the country.

The final step in the journey would involve taking bodies from distribution centers to cities, towns, and villages where local undertakers would meet military escorts for funerals and final burials.

The return program proposal that Harbold submitted in June 1945 reflected the ideas he had been suggesting for two years, drawing on real-time data and his experiences from World War I. There was one significant change in approach. For months, Harbold had been telling congressional leaders, newspaper reporters, and families that if 70 percent of families wanted the return of loved ones from a specific area, then all the bodies would be exhumed and shipped to the United States. That meant ignoring the sentiments of a minority of families—those who wanted to see their sons and husbands remain buried where they fell.

Now, the government would grant "all feasible wishes" of families. The army would return bodies for burial in hometown cemeteries or national cemeteries. Or families could ask that loved ones be buried in new, permanent American cemeteries overseas.

"Our objective," Harbold said, "is to do what the families want done."

Still, families had to live with their choices. They would have three months to decide the final resting place for their loved ones. The temporary cemeteries that held large concentrations of remains would be emptied once and completely. "Graves Registration Service personnel cannot, obviously, return to the same cemeteries repeatedly to exhume bodies, as occurred, in some instances, after the last war," the plan stated.

Harbold's plan called for the return program to start six months after the war officially ended, allowing time to hire an overseas workforce, convert ships and trains to carry bodies, ramp up manufacturing for caskets and shipping cases, and recruit and train civilian embalmers and military escorts. He expected the army would start shipping bodies to the United States in the late summer and fall of 1946. After that, it would take up to eighteen months for the military to return all the dead. By early 1948, all the bodies would be home.

He estimated it would cost the government $700 for each body it sent home. After the Great War, the bill was $400 for each dead man. Caskets now cost more, salaries were higher, and almost half of this war's dead would be shipped from distant places unheard of in World War I. Sentiment, not money, was at the heart of the plan, Harbold wrote. Still, families would only receive fifty dollars to pay for funerals—half the stipend given to grieving families who buried loved ones from the previous war.

The final proposed cost to return America's war dead was $210 million. After the army higher-ups approved the plan in September, Harbold faced his next significant step: winning approval and funding from Congress.

* * *

Weeks after Germany's surrender in May 1945, Harbold made the first of several appearances on Capitol Hill to explain how the army planned to reunite families with soldiers, sailors, and marines who had died. It was June 6, the first anniversary of the Allies' invasion at Normandy, and the first of several sessions where House and Senate members would hear the disturbing details of what happened to men cut down in combat.

Dying on a battlefield meant leaving men's bodies exposed. Once recovered by troops, a man received what Harbold called "a soldier's burial." Graves Registration troops wrapped a body in a bedsack, blanket, or a shelter-half—a piece of canvas usually used to make pup tents—and buried it in a temporary cemetery.

The army placed no priority on supplies for tending to the dead on the front lines. What mattered in the heat of fighting was ammunition, gasoline, and food, not the tools of an undertaker. There was nothing normal about caring for a man killed in the chaos of a battle.

Harbold told members of the House subcommittee on appropriations:

> *The truck trains, the engineer regiments and the medical units are constantly on duty, every effort being made to provide the vital needs*

> *of the forward line. It would be manifestly impossible to make any attempt to place caskets and mortuary supplies near the front lines or even in the theaters of operations without serious detriment to the vital supply problems.*

"In beach invasions, river crossings and attacks on strongly held positions," he continued, "the dead may not be recovered for hours and even days."

The purpose of the June 6 hearing was to discuss the War Department's annual funding for managing the remains of soldiers who died both within the United States and abroad, often in accidents. This task was one of Harbold's more routine duties as chief of the Memorial Division—yet members of Congress started asking questions about the war dead overseas. Harbold explained,

> *The wounded are removed as soon as possible, but the circumstances are frequently such that burials of the dead cannot be accomplished until the lines have advanced or positions are secured. The dead are buried as soon as it is humanly possible without jeopardizing more lives in effecting their removal or the success of the military operation.*

Earlier in the day, before Harbold's testimony, members of the appropriations committee listened to Gen. Henry H. "Hap" Arnold, commander of the Army Air Forces. Arnold had just returned from touring the destruction in Europe and the Mediterranean caused by hundreds of thousands of tons of bombs. American airmen flying B-17s and B-24s had destroyed the Luftwaffe, annihilated German oil and gasoline reserves, and wrecked armament factories, bridges, railroads, and cities.

"I think the Air Forces can fairly say regarding the German war: 'Mission fulfilled,'" Arnold said. "It was very difficult for anybody to appreciate the terrific damage done by our bombers without seeing what was done. One of our responsible officers came back and said it would take Germany a hundred years to rebuild what we have torn down."

He singled out the airmen who flew the missions—pilots, bombardiers, engineers, and gunners. Their flights were often "a trip into hell."

Airmen were now shifting their attention and weapons to bombing Japan. "I can't really tell you how I feel about these men," Arnold said. "They are just the best there are, we can say no more."

That included no mention by Arnold of the airmen who had died or were missing in action in Europe.

* * *

After receiving Delbert's personal belongings that spring, Virginia continued her letter-writing campaign.

Where was her husband? she asked the War Department. She pressed her congressman: Was his name on any list of liberated prisoners of war? She had recently heard from S.Sgt. Richard Conkle, a gunner aboard Delbert's bomber who became a prisoner of the Germans after surviving the crash. Free and back in the United States, he told Virginia how he had watched as her husband helped other crew members exit the plane safely as it spun out of control.

Just as pilot Lloyd White had told Virginia months earlier that he believed Delbert was alive, despite everything he knew about the crash, Conkle's note about Delbert's heroism most likely was a well-intentioned white lie to soften his belief that Delbert was killed when the plane crashed.

Still, Conkle said he had jumped from the plane while Delbert was still inside. Nothing was certain.

It only raised more questions for Virginia. Could Delbert be a patient in a hospital, injured and unaware of who he was or what had happened?

None of the answers she received that summer were comforting. No POW rosters contained his name. Americans who had been held captive by Nazi Germany were now on their way home, and the government had notified their families. Commanders of all overseas hospitals were required to report the names of patients who may have been listed as missing in action.

"Although our injured personnel occasionally lose their identification tags," Maj. Gen. Edward F. Witsell wrote Virginia, "in no case do they remain unknown in the hospital since, through comparison of fingerprints and other positive means, their identities are positively established and their families are advised, without delay, of their status."

He added, "my heartfelt sympathy during this trying period of uncertainty."

Virginia's limbo ended nine days later. Shortly before midnight on August 10, a Western Union telegram from Washington arrived in Marion with the news she had tried to avoid for ten months. The War Department had determined that Cpl. Delbert Trueman was killed in action on October 17, 1944.

Witsell wrote again: "I know the sorrow this message has brought you and it is my hope that in time the knowledge of his heroic sacrifice in the service of his country may be of sustaining comfort to you."

The War Department had based its decision on the words of the four airmen who had parachuted from the wounded bomber that also carried Delbert. German troops had captured Robert Davis, Joe Marallo, Richard Pinardi, and Richard Conkle and moved them to a civilian prison in Vienna. The new POWs compared notes on the crash, and learned from their captors that the other six men aboard their B-24 had been killed and were buried near the wreckage. German troops eventually moved the captured men to prison camps until the war's end.

After being liberated, the men provided the Air Corps with the details they could remember about the crash. Pinardi, the combat photographer, specifically recalled Delbert's struggles to escape the bomber. "As the ship went down, he was pinned there and couldn't get out. He must have been knocked out or fainted and later thrown out of the ship." Later, he saw Delbert's broken body on the ground near the burning bomber.

As it did with Delbert, the War Department changed the status of the five other men aboard his ship from missing to killed in action. Pilot Leonard Mojica, co-pilot Marvin Niederjohn, bombardier George Webb, and gunners Elvin Killingsworth and Charles Kleinhenz joined the list of airmen whose bodies needed to be located and recovered once the war ended.

Secretary of War Henry L. Stimson told Virginia she would soon receive the Purple Heart medal awarded on Delbert's behalf.

"The loss of a loved one is beyond man's repairing," Stimson wrote, "and the medal is of slight value; not so, however, the message it carries. We are all comrades in arms in this battle for our country, and those who have gone are not, and never will be, forgotten by those of us who remain."

Virginia was a widow at age twenty-eight. Her daughter, Judy, was seven years old and without a father. Paul and Nellie Trueman had lost both of their boys to the war. The War Department gave no further details about Delbert's death, and there was no information about his body.

* * *

It would take lawmakers eleven months to study, question, and discuss the plan Harbold and the Memorial Division offered, even though there was little question that the War Department would return bodies to families.

There were slight revisions to the proposal, including lowering the estimated overall costs from $210 million to $195 million. The legislation also gave the army until 1951 to complete the program. Memorial Division leaders felt confident the known dead would all be returned home within eighteen months, but a five-year timetable provided time to locate isolated burials.

Congress members were particularly curious about the state of bodies that troops would recover years after men had died.

Harbold patiently explained. A body buried in a cold climate, such as the Aleutian Islands, could be preserved and even recognizable to someone. But in places like Tunisia, Algeria, or islands in the Pacific, conditions were unforgiving. Harbold spared no details.

"In North Africa, every body taken up will be just bones in wrapping and uniform. In wet land, we run into a different situation, where the body is decomposed. It is off the bones, and the whole mass, if in a casket, would be contained right there. But if the body has been buried in a blanket, some of it will pass out into the ground. There will still be plenty of water in a grave in low and marshy ground."

Because most of the dead were hastily buried combat casualties, Harbold made it clear that bones, not bodies, would be coming home in caskets.

"Those bodies will become, in the course of time, what we call dry bodies," he said. "The flesh decomposes, passes off into the soil, and the skeleton will remain with the wrapping and the uniform on it."

He added: "I am well prepared on that, because I handled that work after the last war. I was in charge of those operations."

He reiterated his belief that an overwhelming number of families wanted the government to return their loved ones to the United States. There was no chance of repeating the experience of World War I, when the government shipped home just 61 percent of the dead. The Memorial Division had received more than 75,000 letters from families, and fewer than one hundred wrote to ask for remains to stay overseas.

He confidently predicted that upward of 95 percent of the war dead would come home. Once the Memorial Division formally asked families about their wishes, Harbold said he expected his estimates to be confirmed.

Congressman J. Leroy Johnson, a California Republican who had earned the Silver Star as a combat pilot in the Great War, was compelled to reiterate that a family's request—whether for a hometown burial or a plot in an American cemetery somewhere in Europe—was paramount. "Whatever their wishes are," he said, "that is what we want to do."

"Yes, sir," Harbold said. "We will bring home all that are desired."

Whether legislation to return the dead was in the House or Senate, there was no opposition. For several months, Harbold took turns with other officers from the Memorial Division appearing before legislators. There were questions about budgets (it would cost just as much to return all the bodies as it would to bury all in new overseas cemeteries); whether the government would pay for a pilgrimage of Gold Star mothers to overseas graves, as it had in World War I (it would not); the styles of caskets (there would be one design for all, regardless of military rank); and how quickly the work could begin (the fall of 1946) and when would it end (1951).

What mattered most to lawmakers was providing families with answers and the remains of their loved ones.

"Unless this is done, there is going to be many a heartbroken, dissatisfied wife, father, and mother of these boys, who want their bodies brought back here," said Congressman John Rankin of Mississippi.

Even so, a colleague, Congresswoman Frances P. Bolton, gently cautioned that families should think twice about asking for remains to be sent home.

"Understanding the tragic longing in the hearts of our people for the return to this country of the bodies of their beloved dead," she said, "I hope it will be possible to make it clear to them that there may be much heartbreak and tragedy in store for them if and when they make these requests."

* * *

While House and Senate appropriations committees held hearings, Harbold and his colleagues continued to work on a program they anticipated would be approved and funded. Of all the moving parts that had to fall into place for the return program to begin, one of the most critical was recruiting civilians to do much of the work required overseas. That meant hiring clerks, drivers, janitors, identification experts, and local laborers to help remove caskets from the earth. Military officers would supervise the work.

At the top of the hiring list were embalmers needed to prepare hundreds of thousands of bodies for casketing and the journey across the ocean.

By the end of 1945, Memorial Division officers visited two dozen mortuary schools nationwide, hoping to woo new morticians to work on the war dead. And Col. Earl Sechrest, who had helped Harbold put the finishing touches on the plan, encouraged quartermasters stationed in Europe to seek out civilians and soon-to-be-discharged soldiers as new hires. He noted,

> *One word of caution in this respect—don't be niggardly in the rates of pay offered, especially for embalmers and other professional men,*

> *or you won't get them. Every conceivable benefit must be publicized, dramatized and propagandized. Unmarried personnel and those who have wed overseas are particularly susceptible to the "sales talk" of the recruiting officer who really knows his business.*

Another officer cautioned about the gravity of working with human remains and the need for mature veterans to join Graves Registration teams. "They know better from experience where they are likely to find bodies. They know from experience that certain types of disasters do different things to a man's body," he said.

There were other challenges.

Despite the strong sense of goodwill from Congress and the earlier approval of the return program by army leadership, higher-ups pushed for quicker results. Where Memorial Division staff mapped out timetables for querying 250,000 families about their wishes, ordering hundreds of thousands of caskets, and exhuming just as many bodies from overseas cemeteries—all in hopes of beginning to return the dead that fall—their superiors scolded them for not working faster. Prepare the letters more quickly, they ordered. Don't wait to retrofit Liberty ships to carry caskets—use existing army freighters. There is no need to delay orders for caskets—cobble together money from existing budgets.

And where the Memorial Division projected returning bodies would begin in early September 1946, superiors insisted on a July 1 start. One can imagine the grumbling from Harbold and others who knew that shortcuts could lead to mistakes, particularly when verifying burial records and accurately identifying human remains.

"One publicized error will raise doubt in the minds of every next of kin and cause the War Department to be deluged with criticism," cautioned an officer in the Quartermaster's Office.

The highest-ranking officers picking at the plan were applying pressure both to appease grief-stricken families and to make the army look good. They did not want the War Department to be accused of moving too slowly.

"It is imperative that every step be taken to reduce to the minimum the time lag between passage of the repatriated bill and the date on which the initial bodies are repatriated to their final resting places in the United States," said Lt. Gen. LeRoy Lutes, commander of the Army Services Forces. "It is likewise imperative that this operation be continuous and that it be conducted in a manner to bring credit to the War Department."

For all their planning, testimony, memos, and job postings, leaders in the Office of the Quartermaster General were content to wait for Congress to sign off on the return program for one overwhelming reason: Returning the dead required caskets, and there were none to be had.

The demands of wartime weapons and machinery had exhausted steel and coal supplies. Mills were now ramping up to produce cars, trucks, washing machines, stoves, and other goods unavailable to consumers during the war. The steel industry also busied itself making tin for millions of cans to store and ship food to war-damaged Europe. The plywood needed to build the shipping cases for caskets was being gobbled up by the housing industry that was constructing new homes sought by veterans. Supplies of the cotton sheeting required to wrap bodies and the rayon needed to line caskets were low.

In short, raw materials for the needs of the living were a higher priority than transporting the war dead.

An executive at Goodyear Aircraft Corporation, which was prepared to manufacture caskets, was blunt with the Memorial Division: It would be impossible to have thousands of coffins ready for the return program by the summer of 1946, as hoped for. "This may sound a little pessimistic, but these are the facts as we see them after a careful study and survey of the situation. Any other picture would be painting blue sky, which I am sure you do not want."

The delay in caskets would force the Memorial Division to hold back on contacting families about their wishes for final burials. It would only create anxiety and raise hopes for the return of a body on a schedule that the War Department could not predict.

"The entire Repatriation Program is geared to the production of caskets and shipping cases," said Maj. Gen. Thomas B. Larkin. "It is recommended that the poll letters be held up until such time as this office can be assured of a steady flow of caskets and shipping cases."

Families knew nothing of the internal memos flying back and forth at the War Department. As Memorial Division officers finessed their plans, the army ratcheted up an extensive public relations program for sharing details about returning the dead. The "colossal task" of bringing home the dead demanded that PR officers stationed at army depots throughout the country—those distribution centers that eventually would help to store and ship bodies—work with newspaper editors, radio reporters, city officials, clergy, and other civic leaders to explain the return program.

This would be an emotional, costly, and complicated enterprise, and generating goodwill was essential. "Public misunderstanding about the War Department functions and, in particular, this program for the return and final burial of World War II dead, can seriously hamper its success," said Maj. Gen. Floyd L. Parks, the army's top PR man.

One unnamed PR officer was honest with a reporter. He fully understood the delicacy of working with families to honor their wishes. "It's a rough job, and any help you can give us will be appreciated," he said, "but the main thing is that your readers would be reassured that we are honestly trying to do this thing right and not upset the emotions of people who may not be too stable in regard to their dead."

* * *

Weeks before Congress signed off on returning the war dead, a soldier who was very much alive and anxious to be home arrived at the train station in Marion, Indiana.

This was my great-uncle, William Seibert, an army technical sergeant returning from England after serving for two years as a radio engineer. He was twenty-five years old and married to my grandmother's younger sister, Marge. Throughout the war, Marge and Virginia had lived together, with their mother and Judy, while their husbands served overseas. They had endured the decline and early death of their father, and were with each other for the awful telegrams about Delbert, first missing and now officially declared dead.

This would be a happy day.

As the train pulled into town, my grandmother and mom idled in a car, ready to take Bill home to his wife. Someone else was waiting for him at the house—Marsha Lynn, a thirteen-month-old daughter he had never held, who was born while he was in Europe.

My mom later told me about all the adults gathering in the living room, my great-uncle hugging and kissing everyone.

Everything stopped when he heard a baby crying on the second floor.

As he bounded up the stairs for the first look at his daughter, my grandmother and mom burst into tears. There would be no such reunion for them and Delbert.

"That's when I realized he wasn't coming home," my mother said. She was eight years old.

* * *

With little fanfare, Congress on May 16 approved the military's plan for the "evacuation and return" of America's dead, and President Harry S. Truman's signature made it law. Nearly two weeks later, on May 29, Congress voted to allocate an initial $92.5 million for the program.

Senator Everett Dirksen said the homecoming would be "sweet agony" for widows, mothers, fathers, and siblings. A veteran of World War I, Dirksen was one of the Senate's great orators. He observed that Memorial Day would arrive in less than twenty-four hours, when Americans would remember those who paid the ultimate price fighting for democracy:

> *Everywhere voices will be raised in reverent tribute, and I can only hope that when that rather tripping phrase will come to the tongues of speakers in churches, in cemeteries, in schools, on rostrums everywhere, "that those honored dead shall not have died in vain," that it becomes something more than a trite and vacuous phrase.*
>
> *I hope that by policy, by conduct, by our action here in this deliberative body, we can prove to our fellow countrymen, to the memory of the holy dead, and to the world that we will carry on the purposes and objectives for which GIs died everywhere and that their sacrifices will in truth and in fact not have been in vain. This becomes a solemn obligation as we prepare to observe the first Memorial Day since the*

> *termination of formal hostilities in a war that engulfed all mankind and threatened the very foundations of civilization.*

The United States would initiate a worldwide undertaking—literally and figuratively—that no country had ever attempted in the wake of war. In the months and years to come, many of the dead would be brought home, although not nearly at the levels projected by Colonel Harbold.

The entire return program would take far longer than planned. And despite the flood of letters arriving daily at the Memorial Division, not everyone—including families, returning veterans, and elected officials—was eager for the dead to return home.

Chapter 8
Zentralfriedhof

On Memorial Day 1946, American and British officers stationed in Vienna paid tribute to Delbert Trueman and other U.S. airmen buried in the city's magnificent and vast Zentralfriedhof, the Central Cemetery.

The city, still scarred from war, was divided and controlled by American, Soviet, British, and French forces. Just a year earlier, Russian troops had wrested Vienna from the Nazis after a bloody siege.

On the American holiday, generals placed a wreath on a grave. Soldiers in white gloves raised rifles and fired in salute. Tiny American flags fluttered beside simple white crosses, standing in perfect rows. Each cross bore a handwritten tag with the names of the dead.

A bugler sounded "Taps."

The Memorial Day ceremony was the first opportunity for the U.S. military to honor its war dead in Vienna. Just two hundred graves lay in this cemetery of hundreds of thousands. Months earlier, in late 1945, American officers in Vienna were ready to search for American airmen buried in the area, but were desperately shorthanded.

A frustrated brigadier general wrote to his boss, Gen. Robert M. Littlejohn, chief quartermaster for the European Theater. "Aid was promised, but none has been forthcoming," wrote Joseph P. Sullivan, the army quartermaster for Vienna. "The continued lack of attention on this matter may subject all of us to severe criticism, so I thought a letter to you would remedy this situation."

Littlejohn understood completely. He was already trying to persuade soldiers headed for discharge to stay on and join the Graves Registration

Service. In the meantime, he would assign a small team to Vienna to work with Sullivan on how best to search for graves when warmer weather arrived in a few months.

By early spring 1946, American troops combed through the Zentralfriedhof and located a plot toward the rear of the giant cemetery holding the remains of American fliers. *Kriegsgräber*—war graves. The airmen's graves were hardly the only evidence of the war. American bombs had obliterated thousands of graves and crypts, leaving the ground scalloped and pockmarked by hundreds of craters. Two hundred trees stood broken and splintered, with no chance of recovery. The majestic dome of the Karl Lueger Church, the cemetery's centerpiece, was no more. The devastation was repeated throughout Vienna's city center and neighborhoods, rained down by what residents referred to as *Terrorfliegern*—terrorist airmen.

A few days after the Memorial Day service—after the troops had marched out, the bugle had faded, and the wreaths began to wilt—Virginia Trueman sat down in her Indiana home and wrote a letter. She had no idea that her husband's grave had been visited by generals and saluted by soldiers. She addressed her note to the Veterans Administration office in Indianapolis. The VA had no real authority in dealing with soldiers missing or killed in action, but to her, it was the face of the federal government with an office less than ninety miles from Marion.

"Dear Sir," she began.

> *Could you please advise me if my husband's body was ever found and if so where he is buried? His body was seen beside the plane that crashed by some crew members who had parachuted to the ground but they did not know what became of it and I had never been notified of its disposition by the Government.*

She signed her name: Mrs. Delbert W. Trueman.

Despite honoring Delbert and other airmen in the Zentralfriedhof, the military did not tell families about the graves. Yes, there were Air Corps reports indicating that men and their planes had fallen in Vienna.

And, yes, there was German burial paperwork naming some of the fliers reported missing.

But records were incomplete, and no one could be certain whose remains were under the white crosses. No word for Virginia. No certainty for thousands of waiting wives, mothers, and fathers. Any notifications would have to wait—wait until the war dead were exhumed, sufficiently identified and moved to a central Allied location, and then reburied with dignity in an American military cemetery.

For now, there was work to do in Vienna.

* * *

When 2nd Lt. Michihiko Hayashida first entered Vienna's Zentralfriedhof in July 1946, he didn't see destruction or death. He saw beauty.

It was a giant park, a vast, remarkable space. Famous musicians rested here: Johann Strauss, the waltz king and composer of "Blue Danube Waltz," whose elaborate tombstone featured a cherub playing the violin while others danced. Ludwig von Beethoven was here. Johannes Brahms. Franz Schubert. There was a memorial to Mozart, but the man himself was buried elsewhere in Vienna. The famous composers were intentionally grouped between the cemetery's main entrance and the Karl Lueger Church, along with noted poets, politicians, artists, and more. These were the *Ehrengräber*, the honorary graves, created as a tourist attraction of sorts. For Hayashida and other American troops entering the cemetery, the *Ehrengräber* would have been impossible to miss.

The twenty-one-year-old officer had already seen so much since arriving in Europe in late 1945 with the 612th Company of the American Graves Registration Service. His troops were searching for small cemeteries, isolated burials, and anyplace else that might hold the remains of dead American soldiers—sunk in bogs, forgotten in remote village cemeteries, tangled in airplane wreckage after slamming into fields and mountainsides.

Whether buried in a rural cemetery or recovered from a shattered bomber, the body of every dead American needed to be recovered by the Graves Registration Service, identified if possible, and prepared for a temporary military cemetery until a final resting place could be chosen.

Of the 25,000 war dead still unaccounted for across postwar Europe, nearly half were listed as missing in action. Most of them, everyone understood, were dead. Only one in ten MIAs would be found alive.

The task fell to nearly seven thousand troops like Hayashida. Many were trained on the job, or by officers who had been hurried into Graves Registration training schools set up in France.

Their job spanned a swath of land equal to half the United States. Graves Registration units traveled from village to village, country to country, searching for unburied remains and unmarked graves. The Air Corps helped out, providing Graves Registration soldiers with firsthand knowledge of bombers and fighters, details that might provide clues specific to locating downed airmen.

Soldiers would scour deserted battlefields, plane crash sites, villages, and local cemeteries. Companies like the 612th had anywhere from sixty to one hundred men split into teams that each played a role in advancing the work of others.

A propaganda team papered towns with posters written in English, French, and German. *Are any soldiers buried in your town cemetery?* Soldiers made broadcasts on town radio stations and placed announcements in local newspapers. The soldiers in each investigating team became diplomats, seeking out elected officials, undertakers, and police for burial records, eyewitness accounts, gossip, or any nugget of detail about graves. *Do you know of any Americans buried here?*

In some places, locals greeted them with suspicion. In others, precious commodities like cigarettes, chocolate, and soap helped loosen tongues. Black market bribery or not, the mission came first.

"Certainly no wife or mother would hesitate from buying all the cigarettes and soap she could lay her hands on if she thought that would help in locating her son's or her husband's body," a Memorial Division leader said. "The public wants those bodies found by hook or crook without questions being asked."

Once a grave or cemetery was identified as possibly containing an American, a disinterring team started digging. Army troops often hired local laborers or used prisoners of war for the spadework, but only Americans were permitted to handle the bodies of their fellow soldiers. Finally, after remains were moved from the grave to a makeshift collecting point nearby, soldiers in an identification team tried to match a body with a name.

It could be exhausting.

In the first three months of 1946, Hayashida, the 612th Company, and other units with the Third Field Command visited almost 3,500 villages and towns in southern France and parts of Germany. They drove and walked more than 28,000 square miles. Through it all, they found only 152 bodies. (It was the same in northern France, where fellow soldiers with the Second Field Command searched nearly 38,000 square miles and recovered all of forty-four American bodies.)

Hayashida moved from Marseilles and Aix-en-Provence, up to Grenoble, Vesoul, and Besancon, and then east into Germany and Munich. Troops interviewed mayors, clerics, police chiefs, village doctors, and everyday citizens. Hayashida found the priests to be especially kind and helpful. In searching for Americans, Graves Registration troops also came upon dead German soldiers. Enemy remains were returned to German soil.

No other Graves Registration unit would cover more European territory than the Third Field Command did in the first six months of 1946—some 72,000 square miles.

From Munich, loaded into trucks and Jeeps, Hayashida's company headed south into the Alps. They made what he described as "a long, dangerous, tortuous journey" along the Brenner Pass and into Austria.

Their assignment narrowed: Search for dead airmen. Hundreds—some 1,700—had tumbled from the skies in their aircraft and crashed in places like Vienna, Türnitz, Graz, and Wiener Neustadt. Bodies needed to be located and recovered.

* * *

No soldier willingly signed up to work in Graves Registration. Recruits wanted to be fighting the enemy, not gathering up bodies. Handling the

Lt. Michihiko Hayashida served with the 612th Company of the American Graves Registration Service. *Frances Hayashida photo*

dead, one soldier said, "cracked some of us, darkened the spirits of others and numbed the rest."

Pvt. Thomas J. Dowling recalled how he and other new soldiers reacted after hearing they were assigned to a Graves Registration unit. They had been hoping "G.R." meant "Guerrilla Raiders."

"You could hear the sucking in of breaths and the gasps of disbelief and feel a sudden numbness," he wrote years later. "My own feelings were a sense of letdown mixed with a natural aversion. It was a job that had to be done in war; it was certainly no disgrace, but it was something you always thought about being done by someone else."

George Ciampa felt the same way when learning what he would do as a soldier after being drafted in late 1943. "I got extremely nervous and wanted to get out because our job was handling the dead," he recalled. As a boy, he'd had a bad experience at a funeral and had feared death ever since.

He landed on Utah Beach on June 6, 1944, with the 610th Graves Registration Company, and collected the dead for the next eleven months. "It was pretty bad because you got that stench and you're spitting all the time. Your mouth is dry," he recalled.

Men gagged from the smell and vomited at the sights—maimed, burned, rotting bodies. Soldiers wrapped their mouths and noses with cloth in failed attempts to avoid the odor. Training—which for some soldiers included witnessing hospital autopsies—could never prepare them for the reality of death. "There's really no way of describing what it's like to smell a dead, burnt body," one soldier said.

Dowling and his comrades arrived on Omaha Beach a few weeks after the Allies invaded Normandy. After troops swarmed the beaches, soldiers had gathered the dead and lined them in rows. The army always wanted bodies moved quickly and away from the battlefield, because the sight of men killed in battle was bad for troop morale. Dowling and his comrades found themselves looking at a hundred decomposing bodies. "We picked them up, began our burial details and vomited our insides out at times," he wrote.

Trucks and trailers used to haul exhumed bodies to temporary cemeteries perpetually smelled, no matter how often soldiers cleaned them. As drivers passed by troops on foot, soldiers waved them on and pinched their noses. ("We always had the right-of-way," a major wrote.)

There was one thing worse than the smell.

"It was the faces of these dead GIs. It was their faces that hurt the most," Dowling wrote. "Some stared wide-eyed; others had died in the middle of a scream, and their mouths hung open. Others had no face at all."

African American soldiers with segregated quartermaster service companies typically were assigned to exhume bodies, move them into trucks, and dig new graves for reburials. They worked alongside white soldiers doing the same work.

After serving two years stateside during the war, 2nd Lt. Ronald Croft volunteered for "repatriation service" in Europe in late 1945. He thought it sounded interesting, and found himself joining dozens of other lieutenants for special coursework at the Army Quartermaster School in Fort Lee, Virginia. "At our first meeting, a major started the class by announcing, 'I guess by now you all know you are going to be gravediggers.' It was quite a shock to some of the class, but taken in stride by most of us—after all, we had volunteered."

While Dowling and others who served during wartime were repelled by the bodies of men that had been dead for only a few days or weeks, Croft and his team from the 531st Quartermaster Group—who worked after the war—had to handle remains that had been buried for months or years. They toiled without masks or gloves as they removed putrefied bodies from isolated graves and prepared them for reburial in temporary cemeteries. Men worked shirtless to avoid the stink settling into their clothes.

"The only way to protect ourselves from the odor was to keep a lit cigarette under our noses; or to take a strong whiff of gasoline every few minutes," Croft said. "The only way we had to sanitize our hands was to wash them in the field with gasoline."

When an interviewer asked George Ciampa years after the war about the morale of soldiers in a Graves Registration unit, the veteran became indignant. "Well how do you think morale was? How would you like to be picking up dead bodies every day, American and German, with all the stench in the summer, then in the wintertime picking up frozen bodies. It was very, very tough," he said.

At his lowest point, Ciampa recalled, when he had become robotic and all but emotionally paralyzed, his commanding officer pointed a pistol at him. "You get your ass out there. Suck it up." Ciampa did as ordered.

* * *

If conditions had been ideal during the war, a dead man was removed from the battlefield and buried when the fighting ended. Ideally, he would wear an identification tag around his neck or wrist. Sometimes fellow soldiers had stuffed a small bottle into his uniform, with a slip of paper bearing his name.

But conditions were not always ideal.

Michihiko Hayashida and Graves Registration troops learned early, first in the antiseptic language of training manuals and then more directly in the fields and forests of France and Germany.

> *At best, a human body is not particularly conspicuous on a modern battlefield, among trenches, shell craters, and resulting debris, stretching beyond the limits of vision. The clothing which is intended to make a man inconspicuous in life does likewise in death. . . . Self preservation is the first law of nature, and these actions spring from no lack of bravery—rather they are the result of the calm courage of good judgment and training.*

American soldiers died hiding behind trees, in ditches, under rubble. And that instinct—the instinct to survive—became, in death, an obstacle to being found.

There was an abiding air of deference as troops uncovered remains. They had to pay close attention to detail as bodies—damaged, decomposed—were lifted from the earth. There could be no overlooking anything, because accurately identifying a soldier's body meant everything. Army regulations made it clear: "Graves registration is not an easy task at best. It is *not* a task to which troops are assigned for disciplinary purposes. Rather it is one for which the highest type of military personnel should be chosen."

Despite the pressure for perfection ("results must be exceptional") and expectations of reverence for the dead, there were mistakes. Bodies were left unattended, personal identification was lost, records were misplaced. "I have seen some things that would cause the lid to be blown sky-high if the public knew what was going on," said a lieutenant colonel from the Memorial Division.

But most soldiers treated the dead with profound care.

Despite the grind of travel and the grim assignment, Hayashida never tired. There was always a new village or town, different people to meet and interview, splendid old cathedrals, and natural scenery that was breathtaking at times.

Other soldiers felt the same way. Months earlier, when the 612th Company worked in Belgium, a soldier reflected on his assignment in the Meuse Valley. After a morning of grim recovery work, the men often took the long route home, lingering through scenic valleys and charming towns. "Aside from the half hour's unpleasant work," he said, "the chance for a day in the countryside and the satisfaction of helping another GI get a proper burial made the trips quite popular."

Bombs, bullets, and fire had ruined landscapes. But to Hayashida, there remained a sense of beauty and grace that touched him.

None of this, the beauty or the bodies, was what he expected after being drafted in the fall of 1944. He had imagined himself "a basic mud slogging rifleman who will take the place of one on the front lines, a casualty, immediately after my few weeks of training." He'd hoped to be assigned to the army's medical corps but was okay with the infantry—"the dirtiest, hardest and most unglamorous branch of the army." He was prepared to learn how to kill someone who was trying to kill him.

But then came Officer Candidate School and the opportunity for Private Hayashida to become a second lieutenant. He grabbed it, and prepared to lead other GIs.

By the time he graduated, the war in Europe—and hopes of commanding a combat platoon—had faded. It was July 1945. He could not imagine being shipped to the Pacific Theater to face the one remaining foe, the Japanese.

"The possibilities of misidentity are too great," he told a friend. "Even now a number of the enemy are fighting us with captured U.S. uniforms. That complicates matters a little for us, doesn't it?"

He knew what he looked like. And he knew how he'd been seen at the war's start.

* * *

I had been reluctant to ask about his ethnicity.

When I first found his name in my grandfather's military records—there in the Vienna cemetery files, neat handwriting atop his printed name and rank, it stood out: *MICHIHIKO HAYASHIDA, 2nd Lt. Infantry Operations*. I searched online for the same name. I found a Dr. Michihiko Hayashida living in Hawaii and wrote a letter to him. Are you, I asked, the same man who was an army officer working in the Vienna Central Cemetery after World War II?

"I am."

He was seventy-seven years old and replied by email. His hearing, he wrote, had evaporated, a loss he blamed on being exposed to heavy gunfire during military training. Phone conversations were all but impossible. Short of my buying a plane ticket from Michigan to Hawaii, an electronic conversation would have to suffice.

We shared emails, and he described his work with the Graves Registration Service: the training, the disinterment of remains, the daily business he described as "gruesome" but necessary. It was a function of war. "The military assigns personnel according to the needs of the moment," he wrote, "and locating deceased servicemen where possible had a high priority at the end of the war in Europe. . . . I don't have misgivings about the assignment. It was something that had to be done."

He repeatedly asked whether I knew anything of a fellow officer from Vienna named James House, a man he thought highly of but had lost contact with through the years. "I recall him as a fine fellow, solid, fair haired and with a moustache." I said I would try to find him.

After several lengthy email exchanges, I needed to ask whether his surname, one that is Japanese, had caused him trouble during the war.

That is when this man—who had helped recover hundreds of dead American soldiers throughout Europe—told me that he began the war forced to live in a horse stall.

* * *

The Hayashidas were Family No. 13598.

On the last day of April 1942—two months after President Roosevelt issued Order 9066 allowing the army to remove Japanese Americans from their West Coast homes—seventeen-year-old Michihiko, his parents, and siblings were forced from their home in Berkeley, California.

Berkeley was where Mich and his eleven brothers and sisters had been born and where their father, Suezo, supported his family with his hands—first with landscaping, then by installing hardwood floors. Along with thousands of others of Japanese ancestry in the Bay Area—the Kawasakis and Tanakas, the Yamamotos and Noboris—the Hayashidas boarded a bus outside a Berkeley church. They stared out the windows, numb as they traveled southward to San Bruno.

"It almost seemed as if I were a member of a funeral," Mich wrote to Beverlee Howe, a white classmate who remained behind at Berkeley High School. Mich knew her because they were always seated alphabetically, Hayashida and Howe. They were friendly, not particularly close, but Mich began sending her letters from behind barbed wire. "The other people in the bus were quiet, for they too must have had that feeling."

He was exhausted from staying up late the night before, his last in Berkeley, sorting and packing essential items to load onto a Bekins moving truck. His oldest sister, Matsuko, left with her eighteen-month-old daughter. Another sister, Mary, was weeks away from giving birth to her first child. Only one of the twelve Hayashida children escaped the forced bus ride: Twenty-four-year-old Tetsuo, Mich's oldest brother, was already serving in the army, enlisting months before Japan bombed Pearl Harbor.

The Hayashidas' bus and four others rolled into the Tanforan Racetrack. Just weeks earlier, jockeys on thoroughbreds had raced around the dirt oval. Tanforan was now an "assembly center," and stables that held horses were transformed into temporary homes for the Hayashidas and 7,700 others. Five people lived in a stall built for one racehorse. The army called the stalls "apartments."

Soldiers frisked everyone for contraband and physically examined them before assigning families to a stable. Michihiko was assigned Apartment 14, Barrack 10. "The place had only recently been disinfected and it still smelled," he wrote to Beverlee, "but after a while I got used to it."

He spent his first days stuffing straw into mattress sacks for others. He felt lucky because he managed to secure an honest-to-God cot with a mattress and springs. He was a strong, solid teenage boy who went to work unloading the trucks pouring into Tanforan. He worked fourteen-hour days, humping residents' belongings to their stalls: suitcases, blanket rolls, duffel bags, boxes tied tight with string. Armed soldiers monitored the people of Tanforan from watchtowers.

> *Another thousand persons arrived from Oakland and since there was so much baggage, much of it had not yet been delivered. Someone had to help deliver it to these unfortunate people (babies and other small children were no exception), so I volunteered.*
>
> *There are hardly any flashlights in camp so the baggage crew on which I worked had a terrible time identifying the goods. Many mistakes were made, but the anxiously awaiting people were grateful that they at least received their bedding. They figured that tomorrow would be another day and that they could straighten things out then.*

Hayashida filled his days with work because there was no school, at least not in the early weeks of Tanforan. He watched younger children play and run around the dusty complex, but missed the routine of classes and the simple act of opening a book. The only Berkeley classmates at Tanforan were those who looked like him: "Hiroshi, Saburo, Minoru, and all the rest are here." But no one was in school.

When Tanforan finally began providing classes for high school students, more than six weeks after the camp opened, nearly seven hundred students enrolled. Officials told students that course credits could, possibly, transfer back to their old high schools. Mich had been forced into Tanforan just as his junior year ended, and he wanted a diploma from Berkeley High School. He was determined to earn a college scholarship.

He still believed in his future.

His optimism stood out. One of his teachers at Tanforan was Shozo Tsuchida. Before internment, Tsuchida had supported a widowed older sister by working in a San Francisco hotel while putting himself through law school at the University of California–Berkeley. As an undergraduate, Tsuchida had been an honors student who earned a Phi Beta Kappa key. As a law student, he joined Boalt Hall's Lawyers Guild and registered for the draft.

But by the summer of 1942, he was held at Tanforan as a perceived threat to his country. So Tsuchida taught high school students like Hayashida.

He saw that some were despondent. "They think their hopes for the future have been wiped out," he wrote. "We must teach them that there is a future and try to keep up their morale, because they would be the ones to lose out the most."

For Mich Hayashida, that immediate future meant a train ride to the desolate Utah desert, where he, his teacher, and all Tanforan residents were sent in the fall of 1942. Mich's sister and brother-in-law, Mary and Richard Miyake, moved with their newborn daughter, Tamiko; she had arrived on June 15, one of fifty-two babies born amid the stalls and stables of the transformed racetrack.

* * *

The U.S. government shipped the Hayashida family by train to Abraham, Utah, where the nearest town was fifteen miles away. There were no trees. Just wind, dust, and thirty-eight identical "city blocks." So-called apartments were built using Sheetrock and Masonite. Armed guards watched over everyone.

Greeting the newcomers was an information sheet about their new surroundings: "You are now in Topaz. Here we say Dining Hall and not Mess Hall; Safety Council, not Internal Police; Residents, not Evacuees; and last but not least, Mental Climate, not Morale." By the time the final trains arrived, Topaz had grown to be the fifth-largest community in Utah.

During the next twelve months of captivity, Mich Hayashida devoted himself to being a senior at Topaz High School. He helped draft the school's constitution and bylaws, ran for student council president, and chaired the graduation committee. The Class of '43 had 196 graduates, and seniors voted Hayashida the most likely to succeed.

He disagreed. He felt his classmates had accomplished more than anyone could have anticipated. He wrote to Beverlee Howe:

> *The lighting was poor, the schoolrooms were bare barracks save for a lone stove and a few wooden benches and tables, on wet days the walks were slushy and slippery, there wasn't any auditorium, there was a shortage of books. But these students overlooked these inconveniences and made up for them in other ways. . . . At our exercises we had cap and gowns, a huge platform to seat all of the graduating students, printed programs, student speakers, a school hymn of our own, and an audience of about 3,000 persons. The first graduating class of Topaz High School certainly has a right to be proud of its achievements.*

In September 1943, with the government's permission, Hayashida left Topaz and his family to enroll at Boston University. He signed up for a full load of classes, focusing on premed coursework and determined to become a physician. His first weeks of freedom didn't last long. Before he could finish his first semester, the government lifted its ban on enlisting Nisei—young men like Hayashida who were born to Japanese immigrants. Hayashida was draft material.

"So it is," he wrote, "that for the second time for many of us, we are being uprooted."

His orders arrived on October 26, 1944—two days after German soldiers lowered the bodies of Delbert Trueman and thirty-six other airmen into graves at Vienna's Central Cemetery.

* * *

Plot 88 held the Americans.

It was a square tract at the rear of the Zentralfriedhof, past the famous musicians and poets and writers, and not far from railroad tracks. Here, in July 1946, Second Lieutenant Hayashida and his company made their way to the graves of pilots and navigators, gunners and flight engineers, along with dozens of POWs from France, Italy, Russia, Yugoslavia, Serbia, and Romania.

The company knew where to find the bodies because of German army paperwork left at the Zentralfriedhof by Vienna's burial commissioner, who had recorded fliers' names, their service numbers, and their gravesites. The plot held 341 bodies altogether, with 198 U.S. airmen. Fewer than half of the American fliers could be positively identified.

For the next month, Hayashida's company worked row by row, methodically unearthing the dead. Fourteen of the twenty-one rows were marked with white wooden crosses. Row 1, held eight bodies in eight graves. But names recorded in the caretaker's log were a tangle of languages and guesswork: "Ajans Harry" (Harry A. Yanz) . . . "Wilholm Mafill" (Magill) . . . "Martinhon?"

Men on the disinterring team used shovels to break the earth and grappling irons and ropes to raise the caskets. Once a coffin was freed, soldiers would open it. They tried not to look at the face of the man inside; they could not avoid the horrible stink. They sprayed the body with disinfectant before lifting it onto a stretcher resting alongside the grave. Soldiers checked the casket for rings, dog tags, coins—any items that might have slipped from a body as it decomposed. The dead were carried one by one to a nearby workstation, where soldiers wrapped them in blankets, placed them in a reburial box, and stored them in a temporary mausoleum until all of Plot 88 was emptied.

They excavated one row at a time, using the soil from one to fill the last. The farther they moved in Plot 88, the more crowded the rows of graves became. Bodies were stacked three, sometimes five, to a grave. Row 6 was a nightmare: forty-six bodies crammed into fifteen graves. There were unidentified Americans, unnamed POWs from Serbia, France, Yugoslavia, and Italy, and at least eleven known members of the Air Corps, men like Collin S. Chong, Rudolf Lunak, and Billy B. King.

Further back, Row 19's twenty graves held twenty bodies, each a nameless prisoner of war. No matter which row, it was rare to find a grave with what passed as complete records—a name and a military service number, both potentially invaluable information for identifying an airman. Even then, names were mangled. A sergeant named Joseph W. Burness became "W. Josef Brunner." Second Lt. Glenn H. Strom was "Strom, Genn H." First Lt. Adam J. Hrostowsky became "Adam Kroslovsky." It was all Hayashida and his men had to work with.

At the far edge of the plot, in a row with thirty-five graves, cemetery records told Mich Hayashida and his company that the last cavity held one "Dellert N. Treibmann," army serial no. 3590081. On August 9, 1946, soldiers opened the grave and retrieved a casket containing the body of Delbert Wayne Trueman. They made a tentative identification, using records from the cemetery, a missing air crew report filed after Delbert and his crew had failed to return from their October 1944 mission, and the dog tags on Delbert's body. An officer noted the limitations they faced: "Impossible to make a detailed investigation. German Military made burials; all records destroyed except cemetery records."

Delbert Trueman had not died alone, and he was not buried alone. Just as his fateful mission over Vienna had been flown with airmen he did not know, he shared his grave with strangers.

Before burying Delbert's body in 1944, the Germans had already lowered two other caskets into the same grave. The first held Sgt. Sam A. Holquin, the other Sgt. Kirk G. Mosher. Both were gunners with the 451st Bomb Group, killed four days before Delbert.

For Holquin, the Air Corps had been a fresh start. Before enlisting, the twenty-five-year-old led a troubled life in Los Angeles that began with his father's suicide when he was an infant and ended behind bars for stealing cars as a teenager. Sentenced to California's San Quentin Prison in 1939, he was nineteen and the youngest inmate admitted that day. His mug shot showed a short, slight boy with dark curly hair and a detached look. Elsewhere in the prison, Holquin's twenty-two-year-old cousin was serving a life sentence for murder; several years earlier, the boys had spent time at the same juvenile detention center for auto theft.

On the day Holquin was paroled—December 9, 1941—he also registered for the draft. He was called up eight months later and, after showing up for induction, the army rejected him. In March 1943, the army again called for him and, this time, accepted him into the Air Corps.

Kirk Mosher's coffin rested between Holquin and Delbert. Mosher came to the Air Corps from New Mexico and was one of three Mosher boys serving in the war; his younger brothers were marines. Mosher played guitar, banjo, bass, or mandolin when he wasn't sketching with pencils. Singing and performing had been his passion since Albuquerque High School, and he later traveled around the state with his father's dance band, playing bars and veterans clubs.

Just days before shipping out to Europe in August 1944, Mosher married his sweetheart, Carmie Smallridge, in an Air Corps chapel in Topeka, Kansas. He was twenty-one, she was eighteen, and their marriage would last forty-nine days.

Holquin and Mosher were gunners aboard a bomber named *Rabbit Habit*, with a buxom woman with floppy ears painted on the plane's nose. As with Delbert, their B-24 had rolled off the assembly line at the massive Willow Run factory in Michigan. It was barely three months old.

The downing of their plane four days before Delbert's death was eerily similar to the casualties of October 17. Like Delbert, Holquin was a tail gunner; he had flown a handful of missions, including to Munich and Vienna. Mosher, like Delbert, was a replacement crew member; his first combat mission was also his last. Their noontime target was a factory in Vienna. Repeated flak strikes caused fires to break out on the plane. Five men bailed out. Five trapped men, including Holquin and Mosher, perished when the bomber exploded in midair.

As with Delbert and his crewmates, German soldiers gathered the airmen's remains, placed them in wooden caskets, and buried them at the rear of the Zentralfriedhof.

The other men from Delbert's doomed bomber were scattered throughout Plot 88. The body of pilot Leonard Mojica ("Mojica Bernhard") was buried twelve sites away from Delbert. George Webb, the bombardier, was buried between them. The remains of three others—co-pilot Marvin Niederjohn and gunners Elvin Killingsworth and Charles Kleinhenz—were among those Hayashida and the Graves Registration Service could not identify, at least not in Vienna. Remains were labeled: Unknown X-7122, Unknown X-7111, and so on.

With all bodies removed and the empty graves filled with dirt, soldiers sprinkled lime over the rebuilt ground. They set fire to the discarded caskets. At the mausoleum, Delbert's body and all the others were loaded into trailers hitched to army trucks that would rumble toward Vienna's Aspern airfield and a waiting C-47 transport plane.

Nearly two years after being cut down in combat, the airmen were lifted into the skies again. Their destination: France, and burial in a temporary American military cemetery outside the village of St. Avold.

* * *

I wanted to make good on my pledge to Mich Hayashida: to find James House, the Graves Registration lieutenant he regularly asked about and clearly admired.

House was nearly a decade older than Hayashida and had outranked him by a grade. They each weighed 150 pounds, but House stood a good head above Hayashida. One man was blond with blue eyes; the other had brown eyes and pitch-black hair. They followed different paths to the war. House joined the army as a married man with a professional career, while Hayashida had barely started college. Hayashida grew up in a family of twelve children, while House was orphaned as a toddler when the 1918 influenza epidemic killed his father and pregnant mother; an aunt and uncle raised him.

What the two officers shared was an army uniform and the grim job of recovering dead soldiers from the soil of Europe.

Hayashida told me he believed House last lived in Denver. Phone directories pointed me to a James E. House on Zenobia Street. I wrote a letter much like the one I had sent to Hayashida, inquiring about serving with a Graves Registration unit in Vienna after the war.

When a reply came from Denver, it contained unexpected news. The writer was Margaret House, who shared that her husband, James, had died several years earlier. I would learn nothing from him about Vienna and would have to tell Mich Hayashida that his friend was gone.

But Margaret House herself could tell me about Vienna and the Central Cemetery.

She was there with her husband in the summer of 1946, working as a civilian employee for the Graves Registration Service. She was thirty-five at the time, six years older than her husband. She was witness to Vienna's destruction by American bombs, and saw the mangled wreckage of an Air Corps bomber near the Vienna Woods. A young Austrian girl, hoping to learn English, befriended Margaret—until her grandmother scolded her: *You should be ashamed for speaking with an American.*

Margaret's office job was in the city. But she sometimes boarded the No. 71 tram and traveled south of town to the Zentralfriedhof and the worksite of the Graves Registration soldiers. "I went to the cemetery to see the plot of ground where the American war dead were interred," she wrote. She had carried a camera and snapped two photographs of Plot 88.

Nearly sixty years later, she pried the pictures from an album, slipped them into an envelope, and mailed them to me. "I thought," she wrote, "perhaps you might like to have them."

Each photograph was the size of a playing card. Jagged black paper from the old photo album stuck to the edges and backs of the prints. The black-and-white photos were shiny and creased, with tiny rips. The arthritis that gave Margaret House's handwriting a wobble also made it difficult for her to pull the glued photos from her scrapbook. But they clearly showed rows of white crosses. The cemetery's grounds were not nearly as tidy as from the Memorial Day ceremony that had played out a few weeks earlier. This was a worksite. One photo captured empty graves, rectangular openings in the earth where Graves Registration soldiers had labored and excavated.

The photographs were the first time I had seen the Zentralfriedhof of 1946 and any evidence of where my grandfather was first buried. When I called Margaret House to thank her, she was gracious: "They mean more to you than they do to me."

Years later, I stood in the same place where Margaret House, James House, and Mich Hayashida had once stood. It was just after Christmas, quiet and cold. The Zentralfriedhof was beautiful, full of tall trees and deep shadows, nothing like the barren expanse shown in Margaret's photos from 1946.

Before traveling to Vienna, I had written to the cemetery to confirm whether the layout of graves had changed in the decades since the war. The reply was brief: "Nothing has changed."

The graves of American airmen buried in the Vienna Central Cemetery in 1946, as captured by Margaret House, a civilian worker with the American Graves Registration Command. *Kim Clarke photo*

But something had.

The ground that first held the body of Delbert Trueman, my grandfather, was now the final resting place for an Austrian family whose names were carved into a tall but simple headstone: *Familien Rajewsky Sladek Voglsinger*. The tombstone stretched well above my head. Thin layers of lichen crept along the mottled limestone. Someone had nestled holiday greenery at the base of the stone, where a red ribbon and pinecones were now yellowing. A Christian cross rose from the top of the headstone—the only visible echo of the wooden marker that once honored Delbert.

Just beyond Plot 88 stands a modern art sculpture that pays tribute to more than a thousand Yugoslavians who died in Austria during World War II. Nearby lie Polish soldiers and civilians, men killed in Vienna at the hands of Germany in the early years of the war. Stone crosses mark the burial places of Maj. Kazimierz Żmudziński, Cpl. Stefan Lobczk, Chaim Klieger, and others. In Polish and German, a large bronze marker memorializes them as victims of fascism.

There is no sign, anywhere, that American airmen ever rested here.

Chapter 9
Transitions

I'm seven or eight years old, weaving between adults holding cold beers and iced tea.

It's mid-1960s Detroit, and our backyard is filled with neighbors for a summer cookout. We live on a block brimming with kids, and our collective sets of parents—all young with growing families—constantly gather for parties, road rallies, birthdays, and cookouts. Our family station wagon is pulled up close to the garage, idle for the day. My dad is a white-collar manager with Chrysler, and we have a new car every year. The driveway is littered with bicycles and empty baby strollers.

My father is at the grill, spatula in hand, as meat sizzles over the coals. His other hand grips a sweaty bottle of Stroh's. His focus darts between hamburgers, hot dogs, and a neighbor who joins him at the grill. As the two men talk, my dad pokes at the meat and waves the spatula as if conducting an invisible orchestra.

I walk by just in time to hear, "Russ isn't Judy's real dad. Her father was killed in the war."

This is when everything stops: the party clatter, the sputtering grill, my breathing. Even though my Keds continue to carry me past my dad, I feel frozen. Russ means Russell, and Russell Smalley is my grandfather. Grandpa. And not just my grandfather, but my mom's dad: the man whom I adore, who calls me Kimbo, and who is somewhere in the backyard. He and my grandmother, Virginia, make regular visits from

Indiana, and every weekend stay means being spoiled for forty-eight hours.

We live three blocks from a dime store, a place simply called Joe's Department Store ("Joe's Saves You Dough!"). Grandpa always walks there with my sisters and me to pick out toys and candy. Fun stuff like Silly Putty, candy cigarettes, Super Balls, and Bazooka gum. Three Musketeers candy bars are a must. Grandpa himself is fond of malted milk balls.

He is handsome and loving and makes me happy. He smells like pipe tobacco and Mennen aftershave. And now my dad is saying this man is not my grandfather. It is outrageous and, above all, upsetting. At first, I am angry (who is this imposter?) and then confused. And then, with the fleeting attention span of a second-grader, I go back to playing in the yard.

But that moment—just a few overheard words—would return to me again and again in adulthood. Only later would I understand what my child's mind couldn't: the difference between the grandfather I adored, Russ Smalley, and the man he quietly stood in for—Delbert Trueman, killed in the war. How my grandmother found love again after a devastating loss. And how my mother came to be raised by two men equally devoted to her as fathers.

* * *

Virginia Trueman could not have known that in the same month she remarried, the body of her first husband was being unearthed from a Viennese cemetery and moved across Europe.

She met Russell Smalley in the spring of 1946 through mutual friends. One of them told her, "I know someone who's just home from the service, and we're going to fix you up a date with him." Virginia's thirtieth birthday was approaching. She was still living with her mother, working full-time, and raising Judy, who was in the third grade. There had been no word from the military for months about Delbert's body. Instead, the government started sending mail that focused on money: how to claim the $10,000 life insurance policy and the monthly Social

Security benefits that came with being a war widow. It was further proof that he was never coming home.

"After he was pronounced dead," my grandmother later told me, "I wasn't going out hunting for a man or anything like that." She was not looking for a relationship, but at the same time, "your life has to go on."

Russ Smalley, thirty-three years old, was a navy officer who grew up on a farm near a crossroads called Rigdon, some fifteen miles south of Marion. Born Joseph Russell Smalley, he was always Russell or Russ to his family and friends, and Joe to everyone else. Where Virginia had known only city life—even in a small town like Marion—Russ was a farm boy. His parents raised him and his four brothers and a sister in a house surrounded by hundreds of acres and cattle, corn, hogs, and chickens.

He did well as a student in his one-room schoolhouse, and liked to write poems about nature: the outdoors, hunting, the solar system, and wild animals. He signed his work "Lord Russell."

Like Delbert Trueman, Russ Smalley was the first in his family to go to college. In 1931, he left the farm and headed seventy miles west to Purdue University, where he pledged a fraternity, trained with the Reserve Officers Training Corps, and played basketball. Competing in sports left his nose broken more than once, and it came to look like a small mountain range on his face. He was not an athlete as much as a coach, both in the classroom and on the playing field, and was determined to be a teacher.

With a degree in physical education, he began teaching history, science, economics, and gym at small rural high schools across northern Indiana. He coached boys' basketball and track. He was the first of the Smalleys to hold a white-collar job.

He was also the first of his brothers to enlist after the Japanese attack on Pearl Harbor, joining the navy in 1942. He left behind five years of teaching, coaching, and a short-lived first marriage that had gone sour. He put his 1939 Plymouth coupe up for sale and left Indiana for a naval base in Norfolk, Virginia.

While his navy physicals always qualified him to serve at sea or abroad, his duties kept him on land. As a sailor and then an officer, he spent his war training recruits on the shores of New York's Seneca Lake, leading physical training for officer candidates in Chapel Hill, North Carolina, and pushing sailors through workouts at Oahu, just miles from the wreckage of Pearl Harbor.

He never saw combat but still witnessed the chaos others experienced in war zones. While stationed in Charlestown, Massachusetts, in late 1942, he was called to the scene of a horrific fire. The Cocoanut Grove supper club in Boston had been packed with sailors, soldiers, and local revelers when a flash fire ripped through it on November 28. Some people were trapped, some trampled, and still others were either choked by toxic fumes or burned by flames. Russell was among the sailors called from the Boston Navy Yard to help the injured and clear nearly five hundred bodies from the blackened scene.

Russ—back in Indiana and teaching—and Virginia dated for less than three months. He won over Judy quickly, taking her to the Smalley family farm to show her where he had grown up. She loved raw carrots, so he always brought her a sack of them when he visited. Before accepting Russell's proposal, Virginia talked with Delbert's parents about the prospect of Judy having a new father. Paul and Nellie Trueman liked him and gave their approval—Paul felt especially sure that Russ would be a good father. The Truemans also made it clear they wanted Judy—their first grandchild and a piece of Delbert—to remain in their lives. Virginia assured them they could be with their granddaughter as often as they wished.

On a Thursday afternoon, Virginia and Russ married in the parlor of Marion's First United Methodist Church. Judy was there, along with family members and a few close friends. Virginia's brother-in-law, Bill Seibert, gave her away. This time, Virginia made sure there were wedding photos. The new family moved to the northwest corner of Indiana, to the small town of Walkerton, where Russ had taken a job coaching and teaching at the high school. That fall, Judy would start fourth grade as Judith Smalley.

* * *

Russell Smalley and Virginia Trueman celebrate their wedding in 1946. *Kim Clarke photo*

Three months into her new marriage, my grandmother was frustrated and annoyed with the federal government.

She had just received a letter from the Veterans Administration demanding repayment of a $65 monthly pension check issued to her as Delbert Trueman's widow. Because she had remarried, my grandmother was not entitled to the money. Return the payment to the U.S. Treasury

Department, the VA told her, and the account would be reviewed for future payments, if any were due to her.

Virginia had already provided proof of her marriage months earlier, along with paperwork confirming that she was the legal custodian of her daughter, Judy. Now everything was a mess. Government checks were held back for some months but issued for others, and not in her new, legal name. VA benefits due to Judy as the child of a deceased serviceman had never been paid. Virginia had provided every detail requested by the government, but it was clear the various offices in Indianapolis, Chicago, and New York weren't sharing that information. The letters also lacked any sympathy or acknowledgment of her loss.

"You have requested that I return the pension check for August, which I will be glad to, as I understand that I am not entitled to the full amount of it," she wrote. "But in return I would appreciate your efforts in doing all you can to speed the adjustment of my account. . . . I believe you will agree that I have reason to be not a little disturbed at so much delay."

It was November 1946. My grandmother composed this letter with the help of her new husband. I have a thin, two-page draft of the correspondence written in pencil—in his handwriting, not hers. Words are crossed out and new ones scribbled in between lines. Tiny edits reflect my grandmother's penmanship.

When I think of them working together on the letter in a new home and new town, I see a husband—himself a veteran—supporting his new wife and child, and a mother fighting for everything she is due as a war widow. It is a faded, marked-up testament of both love and loss.

* * *

Grief, absence, and acceptance touched each family differently.

For Charles and Elsie Kleinhenz, the loss was shattering. Their only child, nineteen-year-old Charles Stanley Kleinhenz—the youngest airman aboard Delbert Trueman's doomed bomber—had died on his first mission. Named for his father, everyone knew him as Stanley. He would have graduated from high school in the spring of 1944, but instead, he trained with the Army Air Corps. His classmates dedicated that year's school yearbook to him and two other classmates serving in the war.

On that October 1944 run, Stanley was wedged in the bomber's nose. Just as Delbert was crammed into the plane's tail turret, Kleinhenz had eased himself behind Plexiglas and machine guns. He and Delbert had trained together at gunnery school in Harlingen, Texas, and were part of Lloyd White's crew that crossed the Atlantic for Italy in September 1944. When the plane spiraled out of control over Vienna, the teen was unable to make it to the escape hatch and went down with the ship.

His body—his stocky frame, wavy brown hair, blue eyes—was mangled so badly that Michihiko Hayashida and his Graves Registration troops could not identify him when removing bodies from the Vienna Central Cemetery. They labeled the remains simply "X-7111."

Kleinhenz's parents did not know this. All they knew was that Stanley was dead.

They had raised him in western New York, where Stanley helped out at his dad's gas station and auto garage in Nunda. It was a region of the state where Charles's and Elsie's families had lived for decades, and neither strayed from their roots or relatives. Elsie had grown up with two sisters; eight siblings had surrounded Charles. Now, as parents, their only child was gone, and the house was unspeakably quiet.

Charles Kleinhenz couldn't take it.

In the months following Stanley's loss, he had buried his mother, a sister, and a brother. He began carrying a gun. He intimidated strangers and chased customers from his garage. He threatened to kill a school principal, a Red Cross worker, and the head of the local draft board. He rewrote his will, scratching out his wife as his beneficiary and leaving everything to his dead boy.

Elsie Kleinhenz accepted her son's death but was terrified by her erratic husband. To keep him calm, she went along with his admonitions that Stanley was alive. She also worried about how she would let the War Department know how to proceed with Stanley's body if—and when—it was recovered.

The emptiness that came without knowing the fate of a body would haunt parents. Juanita Harding felt it every day. Her son Leonard Mojica had been at the controls of Delbert's bomber when it crashed. She had become pregnant at fourteen, married at fifteen, and divorced a year later. She raised Leonard on her own after her husband walked out when the boy was ten months old. He grew up never knowing his father.

"My boy was my and my mother's whole life and his loss is something that can't be put into words," she told the War Department. "And just to know that his remains are here where we can visit him will help us to find courage to go on." She offered to sell her house trailer to pay for the return of her son's body.

Ruth Mosher was tangled in grief and disbelief. Her firstborn, Kirk, had been buried in the same Viennese grave with Delbert Trueman.

"I cannot resign myself to the fact that my son has actually been killed," she wrote to the War Department. "I believe that if I could secure some tangible information or proof that he is actually deceased, that it would help both myself and my family. Can you give us any definite information to substantiate his death, and is there a record of a grave?"

The War Department understood that uncertainty was an open wound that wouldn't heal. It turned to veterans as emotional bulwarks for grieving families. Those who had survived combat were reminded of comrades left dead and dying on the battlefield. While families wrestled with the final decision about the burial place of their loved ones, they did so clouded by sadness, confusion, and anger. A returning vet could help.

Speaking to 16,000 veterans gathered at the Veterans of Foreign Wars convention in Boston in September 1946—the first VFW national meeting since the war began—Quartermaster General Thomas B. Larkin urged them to help:

> *In a major decision of this kind it is not easy to find an answer. When you ultimately assist these good people to the best of your ability, you will in some measure be making payment on the debt we all owe those who have passed on. I believe there is not one among you who will not give freely of your time and bring your best judgment to bear in helping the next of kin who might seek your assistance.*

That included warding off predators looking to scam grieving parents and widows with promises to help return bodies—for a price. Larkin condemned them as the "lowest examples of humanity." The solemn task of returning the dead belonged solely to the army. And it would not be rushed. Unlike the speed demanded in war, this mission was about individual attention, of one American caring for another, Larkin said. "Time is on our side now."

The conference's general chairman was a navy veteran who had returned home with a broken back and a Purple Heart. Lt. John F. Kennedy reminded those who crowded into Boston Arena that 43 percent of men in the country were veterans, dating back to the conflict with Spain in 1898.

"This is a large percentage, too large to permit ourselves to feel that we are a privileged minority, too large to feel that we have only rights, not duties," Kennedy said; "too large, indeed, to be indifferent to the future of the country."

* * *

For the Trueman family, the reality of a future without Delbert and Dale took hold. During the war, Paul Trueman had worked as a sales manager for auction houses in Marion. He later bought an empty bakery building as his own place to sell off other people's property: beds, rugs, lawn mowers, dressers, washing machines, and houses. He traveled to Kokomo, Elwood, and other small towns to sell bungalows, businesses, and everything they held. Wednesday nights were reserved for sales at the auction house, including on the first anniversary of Delbert's death. Paul was fifty years old.

He gained a son-in-law in 1946 when his daughter, Del's and Dale's sister—also named Virginia—married William Helbert, a navy veteran who had served as a medic on a torpedo boat in the Pacific. "Red" Helbert had played alongside Dale Trueman on their state champion roller hockey team before the war. But neither Red—nor anyone—could replace Paul's sons. His family had been forever scarred by the losses of Dale and Delbert.

One day, Paul Trueman drove to the auction house with his granddaughter Judy in the car. Sometimes they would go fishing together on the Mississinewa River that ran through Grant County. She also helped out at the refreshment stand at his auction house on Wednesday evenings. Now, driving through Marion, his sadness was palpable.

"He was down in the dumps," my mother recalled. "He'd always planned on both boys coming home and going into business with him. He said he'd never have that."

* * *

With the return program slowly becoming real, Col. Robert Harbold decided it was time to step away from the army—for a second and final time. He had started pulling back on his duties as director of the Memorial Division in the fall of 1945. Shifting to a role as special assistant to the director, he watched four different generals and colonels cycle in and out of the Memorial Division's top position over eight months.

Throughout the turnover, Harbold continued to represent the office, testifying before Congress, meeting with grieving families, and explaining the vast and delicate operation of bringing the war dead home.

His second tour of duty had lasted four years, and much of it was spent crafting a plan to honor those who died during the war. He built the framework that ensured hundreds of thousands of families would have a say in what happened to their loved ones' remains. He laid the groundwork for thousands of soldiers and civilians who would search for, disinter, identify, and rebury those Americans who made the ultimate sacrifice defending democracy.

For his contributions, Harbold received a final medal for his uniform: the Legion of Merit. The medal, created during the war, recognized "exceptionally meritorious conduct in the performance of outstanding services."

By the time of his retirement in mid-1946, Harbold had spent nearly forty years as an army officer. A phalanx of soldiers and officers would carry out the global strategy he had so meticulously drafted and detailed

Col. Robert Harbold, right, receives the Legion of Merit medal from Quartermaster General Lt. Gen. Edmund B. Gregory in December 1945. *National Archives and Records Administration photo*

while World War II still raged. He could lay claim to helping bring together families with loved ones who fell in two world wars.

He was sixty-five years old and a grandfather of seven. More importantly, he and his wife, Florence, had two young children to raise—a five-year-old girl and a boy who was not yet three. The war was over. It was time to go home.

Chapter 10

St. Avold

Before Graves Registration troops could move Delbert Trueman's remains into the cemetery at St. Avold for burial, the military first needed to confirm his identity.

When troops removed his coffin from the soil of Vienna, they had relied on German burial records, which matched up with a dog tag found on his body. Graves Registration troops then compared those details with an Air Corps report about the 1944 crash of his bomber. All indications were the body was Trueman's. But it wasn't enough detail for a positive identification.

As the army began collecting the dead after the war, Graves Registration troops were expected to identify bodies after exhuming them. That turned out to be a waste of time, with disinterment teams standing around while specially trained technicians tried to establish identities. By mid-1946, as the remains of the airmen buried in Vienna were being unearthed, the army opened a high-tech laboratory in northeastern France, in Strasbourg, not far from the St. Avold cemetery. The Central Identification Point operated out of an abandoned French cavalry barracks, where civilian technicians hired by the army—anthropologists, dentists, embalmers, chemists, photographers, and X-ray technicians—studied bones, hair, dried blood, clothing, and personal effects. A fluoroscope would sometimes reveal a dog tag embedded in a man's skin or clothing, driven in by a blast of ammunition.

The Memorial Division established the Central Identification Point after working with Harry L. Shapiro, the head of physical anthropology at the American Museum of Natural History. He spent the summer of 1946 alongside Graves Registration units in Europe as they recovered bodies and tried to identify them. Field identification, he determined, was horrible work, a "highly disagreeable job" in need of scientific rigor for positively identifying the dead.

"I cannot stress too strongly the fact that the task facing the AGRC [American Graves Registration Command] represents an undertaking without precedent," he said. He called for a lab, and the army responded with state-of-the-art equipment.

At Strasbourg, the processing of remains saw technicians work their way through bones and flesh, searching for anything that might reveal a dead man's identity. They measured and weighed femurs, tibias and skulls, which could yield details about gender and age, as well as old injuries. They studied and laundered pieces of uniforms—shirts, pants, gloves, boots—looking for a stenciled name. If a corpse still had hands, technicians would inject the shriveled fingers with water or hot paraffin to allow for making fingerprints. When scraps of letters or other papers were found on a body, techs applied ammonium sulfide to yield faded writing. They also used chemicals to burnish old photographs.

The work was both methodical and messy. Men processed up to eighty bodies a day. For the technicians handling human remains and soiled uniforms of dead men all day, Shapiro recommended powerful disinfectants, strong deodorants, and hot showers. Workers would bathe three and four times a day.

Delbert Trueman's body arrived in the lab's first week of operation, with the job of identifying the remains going to a team of technicians. There was little for them to work with. Unwrapping the body after its shipment from Vienna, team members recorded the state of the remains. There was no uniform, no boots, no underwear; no matter how torn or dirty, clothing could sometimes yield a printed serial number, but Delbert's had disintegrated. His hands were missing, making it impossible to study fingerprints. Technicians could not determine the body's age or weight. The common condition of the remains was UTD—"unable to determine."

Complexion: UTD.
Height: UTD.
Legs, feet: UTD.
Hair color: UTD.

The remains—badly fractured—were laid out on a processing table. In total, the bones weighed about twenty pounds. That is where one member of the identification team, Thomas W. Turner, worked. He held Delbert's cracked and charred skull in his hands. Turner was twenty-nine, a civilian employee, and no stranger to death. During the war, he served three years as a private with the 46th Quartermaster Graves Registration Company, a unit with an exceptional reputation for identifying unknown remains. He helped lay out cemeteries in Italy, including in Sicily, following the Allies' 1943 invasion. In Italy and later in France and Germany, Turner and his comrades dealt with the human detritus of combat. Working in a French cemetery in the bitter cold of Christmas 1944, the soldiers placed frozen, twisted bodies alongside small fires. Thawing the corpses made it easier to take fingerprints and search for personal effects.

Turner even watched an infantryman become a corpse when a twelve-man army firing squad killed a soldier for deserting. Pvt. Eddie Slovik was the first American soldier executed for desertion since the Civil War, and Turner was part of the Graves Registration team that gathered up his body in 1945. Slovik was riddled with eleven bullets when Turner and three comrades lowered him into a section of France's Oise-Aisne American Cemetery reserved for dishonorably discharged soldiers.

When the war ended, Turner signed on as a civilian with the army and the Central Identification Point. Instead of interring the dead, the Ohio native handled their unearthed remains in hopes of assigning identities to bodies. With the bones believed to be Delbert Trueman, Turner examined the skull, where several teeth remained embedded in the jaw, along with a partial dental plate. He noted which teeth were missing and which intact ones had fillings. A man's teeth could often lead to an identification, and the army constantly reminded technicians like Turner to record every detail about crowns, bridges, chips, and fillings. A manual for identifying the dead carried blunt instructions:

> *IN MAKING A TOOTH CHART, YOU CAN'T BE HALF RIGHT. EITHER YOU ARE 100% RIGHT OR 100% WRONG. ACCURACY IS OF THE UTMOST IMPORTANCE.*

Delbert had left a dental trail. During his first weeks of military training in 1944, with the goal of qualifying for the Air Corps, he was sent to the dentist by his officers. Then they sent him again and again. At base after base, dentists looked into his mouth and either pulled bad teeth or filled cavities with droplets of silver. He survived on soup as his mouth healed. He mailed home photos showing off the ugly gaps in his smile, and warned his daughter to brush her teeth every day. "If my age doesn't keep me out," he wrote to her, "my having no teeth will."

It was Delbert's fractured jawbone, with its absent teeth and repaired cavities, that gave Thomas Turner and his fellow technicians the confirmation they needed. They agreed that the badly burned teeth before them matched Delbert Trueman's dental records from boot camp. Officially identified, the body could be moved to the St. Avold Military Cemetery.

* * *

When I began researching the fate of my grandfather's body, I wrestled with whether to share the details with my mother.

In her mind, he was vibrant and strong. She remembered him as tall; her perspective as a child loomed larger than his actual frame of five feet and eight inches. When he was away in training, she and my grandmother would sing the jaunty Army Air Forces song about airmen soaring toward the sun. Reading about the charred condition of his remains made me wonder if they knew one verse boasted, "We live in fame or go down in flame."

From the military documents, I knew that what little remained from her father's flight suit was blackened at the edges. It was impossible to identify the color of his hair or the complexion of his naked body. His blue eyes were gone.

I asked my father about showing the documents to my mom. If nothing else, I wanted him nearby if I decided to share them. "It's fine," he said. "Go ahead."

My mother read the pages slowly. She had always known one lone detail about her dad's death on the outskirts of Vienna. A crew member who survived by parachuting from the plane landed near the wreckage. Alongside the burning aircraft, he reported after the war, was her father's crumpled body. German soldiers were rummaging through the corpse. It was a kernel of information that made my mom furious any time she spoke of it.

Now, silent and seated on the family room couch, she read the military's antiseptic burial reports, disinterment directives, tooth charts, cemetery sketches, and government forms labeled "disposition of remains."

"I don't want to upset you," I said at one point, hoping for a response. She continued, saying nothing. She gave an occasional sigh, and I tried to guess which page she was reading. I began to regret what I'd shared.

When she finally finished, she gathered the papers into a neat pile and handed them back. She sat still for a long moment, and then, softly, deliberately, she spoke.

"Don't ever show this to Grandma," she said.

* * *

A key element of Robert Harbold's strategy to repatriate the war dead was the relocation of remains from isolated graves and small, hastily built cemeteries into larger military burial grounds established by the army during the war. The small cemeteries were created in the wake of combat and were always intended to be temporary. By concentrating all remains in larger cemeteries, Graves Registration troops were essentially storing the dead until it was time to move them to the United States or permanently bury them in Europe and the Pacific.

The cemetery at St. Avold was one of dozens of temporary military cemeteries in Europe at the war's end. Established in March 1945, it would become one of the war's last and largest burial grounds, with the remains of 7,400 American soldiers killed while pushing eastward across the Rhine River and into Germany. More than 1,800 German dead were also buried there.

But the early conditions at St. Avold reflected the chaos of war's end. When an officer with the Seventh Army—whose soldiers made up the majority of St. Avold's dead—informally inspected the grounds in early June, two months after the cemetery opened, he called it "unsatisfactory." Clumps of dirt littered the pathways between rows of graves. A gate to the cemetery had only a thin, pale coat of white paint. There was no one on duty.

The situation didn't sit well with Maj. Gen. Robert M. Littlejohn, the chief quartermaster for Europe, who was responsible for caring for the dead. During the war, Gen. Dwight D. Eisenhower had expected all cemeteries to be cared for, an order that looked good on paper but was impractical with bullets flying and troops on the move. In the waning days of the fighting in Europe, St. Avold was one of several French cemeteries in poor shape. Littlejohn pledged to have them "put in apple pie order" by the Fourth of July of that year.

Improvements did not happen quite that fast, but Littlejohn pushed forward an extensive plan for landscaping and beautifying the cemeteries. The burial grounds may have been temporary, but Littlejohn wanted them to be reverent and immaculate, with a uniform appearance. He had always been impressed with the grounds at West Point, and recruited the military academy's chief horticulturalist to work in Europe.

Cemeteries would have flowers, shrubs, and trees. Blends of Kentucky bluegrass and Colonial bentgrass would blanket all gravesites. Visitors would cross narrow footpaths layered evenly with gravel. Edging would be clean and crisp. Soldiers were expected to give a fresh coat of paint to buildings, fences, and signs every six months. The beautification benchmarks were high: "Apperances generally considered satisfactory for Army installations will be considered sub-standard when applied to

The temporary military cemetery near St. Avold, France, in 1946. *Kim Clarke photo*

cemeteries." Even the florist industry got involved—FTD donated nearly 34,000 packets of flower seeds in red, white, and blue.

Although the repatriation plan called for eventually creating nine permanent military cemeteries in Europe, St. Avold was not one of them. It sat at the bottom of a list of ten possible locations; its soil was considered unsuitable for a permanent burial ground. Instead, by 1946, it would function as a temporary home for the remains of recovered soldiers, like Delbert Trueman, and a location where army chaplains like Howard Lee would oversee their reburials.

* * *

The Rev. Howard A. Lee visited St. Avold Military Cemetery for the first time to honor a fellow army chaplain he had never met.

Rabbi Frank Goldenberg had joined the Chaplain Corps in the spring of 1945, following in his father's footsteps. After college and seminary, Goldenberg served two years at an upstate New York synagogue before requesting a leave to join the army. After enlisting and attending chaplain school, he first cared for soldiers hospitalized at Fort Benning in Georgia, and then was shipped to Europe in March 1946. He joined the 42nd Infantry Division—the famed Rainbow Division. It had been a year since the division entered the Dachau concentration camp and witnessed all its atrocities, including more than 32,000 emaciated survivors. Soldiers were now in Vienna as part of the occupation forces. Goldenberg ministered to them, as well as to those who had outlasted the death camps.

Two months after arriving in Austria, Goldenberg was critically injured in a Jeep accident outside of Vienna. He could not be saved. He was twenty-six years old.

Just as Graves Registration soldiers would transfer the remains of American airmen like Delbert Trueman buried in Vienna to France and St. Avold, Goldenberg's body was moved to France. He would be laid to rest in a military cemetery on Allied soil until the government began asking families like his how to handle his remains.

Howard Lee, a Southern Baptist minister stationed some sixty miles away in eastern France, felt compelled to attend the young rabbi's funeral. Military chaplains were known for supporting and respecting each other, regardless of their faith and practices. They were united in the common calling of serving God and country.

Goldenberg's burial took place on May 29, the eve of Memorial Day. A Star of David would mark his plot.

The cemetery, home to more than 9,200 American dead, had been meticulously prepared for the next day's ceremonies. Army brass expected all military cemeteries in Europe to be in top condition for ceremonies honoring the dead of World War II.

At St. Avold, cemetery workers busied themselves, checking the wooden grave markers for any damage wrought by the snow and ice of winter and applying fresh coats of white paint. The cemetery was ready for thousands of visitors the next day, including American and French troops, local elected officials, Boy Scouts, and a French girls' choir.

There would be chaplains of all faiths and a bugler playing "Taps." Tiny American flags dotted all the graves.

For Howard Lee, the solitude of Goldenberg's funeral the day before the holiday would be his first and last quiet moment at St. Avold.

* * *

Lee knew what combat could do to a man. His brother-in-law was severely wounded by a land mine while fighting on Okinawa in 1945. The blast destroyed his right eye, heavily damaged the left, and put him in the hospital for seventeen months. Lee was torn about leaving home for the army, not knowing whether his wife's brother would survive his injuries.

But Lee had long felt the call to minister. Growing up with three brothers in rural Texas, he surrendered himself to God at age twenty, shortly after the birth of his second child in 1937. He began preaching part-time in small churches north of Houston while studying at Southwestern Baptist Seminary and then Sam Houston State Teachers College. With the blessing of Southern Baptist leaders, Lee applied to be an army chaplain in June 1945, only a month after earning his bachelor's degree. The war in Europe was over, but he still hoped to somehow serve in the field.

The Chaplain Corps rejected him.

Despite his college degree, seminary training, and glowing recommendations—including one from the president of Sam Houston State—Lee lacked one credential: a high school diploma. The Chaplain Corps suggested he find a way to serve on the home front.

Lee was undeterred. It was true—he had not graduated from high school. Sam Houston State had accepted him as a special student at age twenty-five because of his experience and maturity, and Lee knocked down his high school courses as a college freshman. He gently appealed the absurdity of his disqualification.

"It is such a small matter," he wrote to the Chief of Chaplains, "that it is difficult for me to understand how it would make too much difference after a person has gone full-time to college and has been granted a degree on the merit of his work." He added he was praying for a different decision.

Two weeks later, those prayers were answered; he would be accepted into the Chaplain Corps. It was early August, and he prepared to leave his wife and three young children for chaplain school and the Chaplain Overseas Replacement Pool.

During World War II, some nine thousand Catholic priests, Jewish rabbis, and Protestant ministers served in the Chaplain Corps, offering faith as a weapon for soldiers, sailors, and airmen. They saw themselves as soldiers of God, winning the war through spiritual power, said Maj. Gen. William R. Arnold, the chief of chaplains and a Catholic priest. After Roman Catholics and Methodists, Southern Baptist ministers—some twelve hundred—were the third-largest faith represented in the Chaplain Corps.

In 1944, when Col. Robert Harbold pulled together representatives from all service branches to talk about how the army would coordinate returning America's dead after the war, a member of the Office of the Chief of Chaplains was at the table. Chaplains would be needed to serve with quartermasters and Graves Registration outfits, providing graveside services for reburials, emotional support for soldiers handling the dead, and succor for grieving families abroad. Chaplains also counseled soldiers on matters ranging from girlfriends to God, faith to fear. They led weekly worship services, visited the sick and injured in hospitals, and performed marriages between soldiers and local civilians.

As with so many other branches of the army, the Chaplain Corps thinned after the war, just as Howard Lee was arriving. The army was smaller, but chaplains were still needed, including to oversee the reburials of hundreds of thousands of war dead.

As a newly commissioned first lieutenant, Lee underwent three months of schooling at the army's chaplain school at Fort Oglethorpe in Georgia. Most courses focused on practical duties and military drills. Graves registration was barely touched on in the curriculum—just a single short class—but Lee excelled in all areas. One of his instructors said Lee would make a fine chaplain.

Arriving in Europe just before Christmas 1945—he helped lead a service for soldiers aboard a transport ship crossing the Atlantic—Lee was deployed to the American Graves Registration Command in France. He received a Jeep and a chaplain's kit—a small suitcase holding candlesticks, bottles for water and wine, and a Latin cross, all for use on a makeshift altar.

Lee began the new year—one free of a worldwide war for the first time since 1939—by handing out Bibles, helping men write letters to send home, sitting at the bedsides of wounded soldiers, and devoting hours to one-on-one discussions with troops. He was immediately popular. When soldiers began carrying themselves higher and showing a new level of morale, Lee's superiors credited him.

Lee soon began officiating a small number of funerals—usually about a dozen a month—of pilots, airmen, and infantrymen killed fighting in 1944 and buried in isolated graves. After Graves Registration troops recovered the men's remains, Lee stood over their fresh graves at a temporary military cemetery set up in Luynes, in southern France. Once again, Lee's commanding officers noted his work, saying he was "very instrumental in the improvement of funeral services."

But the chaplain's grace would be tested in the summer of 1946. Graves Registration teams, including the one led by Michihiko Hayashida in Austria, had located thousands of bodies—upward of 90 percent of the war's dead—and were moving them to the larger, temporary military cemeteries. There seemed to be no end to the bodies arriving for burial and blessings at St. Avold.

* * *

Chaplain Lee experienced a rare moment of joy in a place usually steeped in sorrow when, in early June 1946, he performed a wedding ceremony. Second Lt. Madalyn D. McIntosh, with the Army Nurse Corps, and Pvt. Paul R. Garrison exchanged vows at a U.S. military hospital for German prisoners of war. The doctor who ran the hospital stood by as a witness.

The rest of the month brought death by the truckload. Lee oversaw the burials of nearly 450 men and women at St. Avold. July was worse—more than six hundred dead in need of graveside rites—and August closed out the summer with some three hundred bodies. A few were soldiers and American civilians who had died recently in car crashes and accidents, including two military police officers killed instantly when their truck ran off the road.

But the majority of the bodies were war casualties recovered and moved to the cemetery until their families could be notified and asked about their final wishes for permanent burial.

"War in the raw" was how one chaplain, a Catholic priest, described it: "With each succeeding burial service, instead of becoming accustomed to it, I shrank from it with greater dread."

Death came to men in countless ways. There was a first lieutenant who had died in a German POW camp after being wounded when mortar fire hit his tank; a twenty-year-old killed by a sniper while giving cover to comrades who came under fire; and a B-17 gunner who jumped from his damaged plane over Germany only for his parachute to fail. When townspeople found his body with a picture of Jesus tucked into his uniform, they assumed he was Catholic. A local priest offered a funeral mass before burying him in a civilian cemetery.

The burials at St. Avold occurred daily, with local laborers digging graves and soldiers interring them. Every six or seven days, Lee walked into the cemetery and performed a burial service for all those buried in the previous week. There was no required prayer, and he was free to say what he wanted. The army issued chaplains a song and service book, but most disliked it; they considered the hymns and prayers too limited. Lee most likely offered brief, solemn words—a few lines of Scripture, a short prayer, a quiet goodbye.

A soldier's dog tag was stamped with a lone initial indicating religious faiths: P for Protestant, C for Catholic, and H for Hebrew. But bodies recovered without any identification tags meant Lee and other chaplains performed graveside blessings that were universal in tone and respected all beliefs.

Lee never recorded his thoughts. But other chaplains did. Maj. Theodore R. Pfeiffer, a Presbyterian pastor from Wisconsin, visited cemetery upon cemetery, week after week, to pray over graves. The loneliest duty, he said, was the weekly committal service for the countless dead recovered and reburied after the war.

> *They have been brought from many places to rest among their own. The chaplains stand alone with the commanding officer of the cemetery, prayers and requiems are recited by the chaplains, and a final salute is given. There are no mourners. Only God knows that America is giving her final tribute to the heroic dead.*

The real emotions emerged after the burials, when Lee wrote to families of the newly buried, sharing details about their loved ones' graves and offering guidance about their next steps. His heart went out to parents and wives as he reflected on the agony his own family had experienced when his brother-in-law nearly died. In one letter to the parents of a Michigan soldier, Lee acknowledged what words could not do: "We know that mere words cannot assuage heavy and bereaved souls," he wrote. "But they do help us to carry our burdens and sorrows."

It had been an honor, he told them, to preside over their son's burial—a service conducted, he assured them, "in a most reverent and sacred manner."

* * *

From the Strasbourg identification lab, soldiers transferred the remains of Delbert Trueman and the five crew members he died with to St. Avold cemetery in mid-August—each arriving on different days. Delbert was laid to rest next to his pilot, 1st Lt. Leonard Mojica. Investigators had found a parachute ripcord mingled with the lieutenant's remains, which weighed all of ten pounds. The bodies were shrouded in cloth and lowered directly into the ground for temporary reburials.

On the other side of Mojica lay Sam Holquin, the gunner who had first been buried in the same Viennese grave with Delbert. Unlike the crowded cemetery in Vienna, where bodies were sometimes stacked in shared graves, each man at St. Avold had his own plot—five feet deep.

At the head of each grave, soldiers drove a Latin cross made of wood into the ground. Whether buried under a Christian cross or the Star of David, a soldier's name was stenciled on the front of the marker, and an ID tag bearing his name was attached to the back. No other decorations were allowed.

By the end of August, Graves Registration soldiers worldwide had located 92 percent of America's war dead. Nearly all were now concentrated in temporary military cemeteries like St. Avold. That meant more than 265,000 bodies were ready for the next phase of the return program, with another 25,000 still to be located, most of them in Europe. The military hoped to begin unearthing all the bodies for permanent burial, either in the United States or in new overseas military cemeteries, starting in July 1947.

For Chaplain Lee, the endless days of burying the war dead began to wear him down. He was twenty-nine years old and had presided over the burials of more than 1,400 men and women—soldiers both known and unknown, merchant mariners, American civilians working for the U.S. military, and even German prisoners of war. Years later, Lee would tell his family he wasn't sure he could have lasted much longer. His final burial services were performed in August 1946.

As he did every month, Lee reviewed lists filled with names, service numbers, death dates, burial dates, and grave locations.

Sgt. James T. Bourne
1/Lt. Leonard A. Kornblau
Cpl. Herman C. Blohme
2/Lt. Richard C. Winsor
T/Sgt. Maynard A. Latten

Too many burials on the list bore no names, only an X followed by a number, men still unidentified despite the efforts of technicians at the Central Identification Point. Lee often wished there was a stronger emphasis on the importance of wearing ID tags, unaware perhaps of how they could vanish in the mayhem of combat and makeshift burials.

Chaplain Lee offered rites and blessings at St. Avold Military Cemetery for the last time on August 21, praying over the graves of eighty-seven men. When he signed off on the paperwork, the last name on Lee's list of burials was Delbert W. Trueman.

Chapter 11

Debates

The Rev. Howard Lee sailed home in September 1946 after nine months in Europe with the Chaplain Corps. He made a point of standing watch for several shifts while aboard the troop ship, surrounded by 1,400 soldiers who were very much alive. He undoubtedly reflected on his time at Luynes, St. Avold, and the dead he had blessed and buried.

"My stay in the army as a chaplain has been of inestimable value to me," he wrote in his final report, "and I thank God for the opportunity and privilege of serving with you."

After Lee reunited with his family and resumed his preaching in Texas, another American minister was heading in the opposite direction—toward a temporary U.S. military cemetery in Europe.

The Rev. Edwin P. Booth, with his wife, Elizabeth, and their two teenage sons, traveled to see the grave of Bray Booth, the couple's firstborn.

Sgt. Bray Booth had been a paratrooper, killed in Germany in March 1945, just weeks before his twentieth birthday. His parents had been numb with grief ever since. They listened as well-meaning friends and congregation members stumbled through clumsy condolences, saying it was a blessing that their son was with God and did not have to witness the world's tragedies. His father, a widely published theologian, bristled.

"But he hadn't intended to be in heaven yet," Edwin Booth thought, "and he hadn't considered the world a vale of sorrow!"

The Booths made their journey to Margraten, a small village in the Netherlands, where the U.S. military had established a vast temporary cemetery. More than 17,000 Americans were buried there beneath white wooden markers. In October 1946, the military notified the Booths that Bray's remains had been found in an isolated grave in Germany and reinterred at Margraten. Within a month, the family set out for Europe.

Standing there, before the white wooden cross that marked his son's grave, Edwin Booth experienced a long-lost sense of peace. He felt reconnected, at last, with his child. Rows of white crosses stretched in perfect symmetry across the manicured cemetery, crowned by an American flag. He could not imagine disturbing the setting by having his son's body dug up and shipped to the United States. The idea horrified him.

Booth would soon learn that others—families, war veterans, politicians, and editorial writers—felt the same unease. Not everyone, it turned out, wanted America's war dead to come home.

* * *

In the early years of World War I, long before the United States became involved, a young poet from New York City enlisted with the Foreign Legion to fight for France. Alan Seeger had been living and writing in Paris after graduating from Harvard University. He loved France and wanted to defend his adopted country against German aggression. "Everyone should take part in this struggle which is to have so decisive an effect, not only on the nations engaged but on all humanity," he told his mother in 1915.

A fatalist at heart, Seeger wrote of "that rare privilege of dying well." In July 1916, while fighting during the Battle of the Somme, death found him.

Months after he fell, one of Seeger's poems appeared in print just as American troops were beginning to arrive in Europe. "I Have a Rendezvous with Death" immediately became a classic of wartime verse.

It may be he shall take my hand
And lead me into his dark land
And close my eyes and quench my breath—

It may be I shall pass him still.
I have a rendezvous with Death
On some scarred slope of battered hill,
When Spring comes round again this year
And the first meadow-flowers appear.

Had he survived, Seeger would have known his nephew, Pete, who would go on to make his own cultural impact as a songwriter and outspoken anti-war activist. Instead, Alan Seeger was buried in the Lihons French National Cemetery.

Seeger's fate and resting place were on his mother's mind as the United States emerged from another world war and began its global mission to recover and return the dead. Elsie Adams Seeger was eighty-six years old and a widow when the War Department started asking families about shipping home bodies from the European and Pacific theaters.

She was appalled. She could not comprehend how families would find any real comfort in uprooting the dead from well-manicured military cemeteries in France and elsewhere to move them across the ocean to the United States.

So when Edwin Booth, a Boston theologian, expressed his wish for the remains of his son, Bray, to stay buried in Europe, Elsie Seeger put pen to paper. "Give all the time you can," she urged him, "to stop the ghastly idea of moving those few bones!"

The government's plan to exhume and return the dead had always generated a low rumble of disapproval and discomfort. Episcopalians and Catholics opposed the exhumations on religious grounds; obsessing over mortal remains rather than immortal life bordered on paganism. Some African American families, particularly those in the South, questioned why they would want their loved ones returned to racially segregated communities, including cemeteries. Others felt taxpayer dollars should go toward the living, including wounded veterans and the children of dead soldiers and sailors.

After Congress signed off on the plan in 1946, a Washington correspondent wrote: "We are about to engage in a mass desecration of our war dead."

Among the most recognized of the war's fallen was Gen. George S. Patton. "Old Blood and Guts," as his men called him, did not die in combat but rather from a broken neck suffered in a car crash in December 1945. His widow asked the army to bury him in the American military cemetery in Hamm, Luxembourg, where many of his Third Army soldiers rested. A year after her husband's death, Beatrice Patton issued a sharp rebuke to those families contemplating moving the dead:

> *What do most of those graves overseas hold? Parts of men wrapped in blankets or mattress covers, without coffins—gone back to earth because they could no longer serve their purpose. What will come home to you isn't what you remember and love. Will it ease your grief, or make you happier to know that some young soldier, drafted to serve our country overseas, is digging up these poor bones?*

She went so far as to equate the character of those who had died with where they would rest for eternity. "Every good soldier I have ever known wanted to be buried where he fell. Mine did. Our dead have earned the right to rest in peace."

For all the punch of Beatrice Patton, however, it was Edwin Booth's quiet resolve that touched the deepest nerve with Americans when he told of wanting his firstborn son to remain buried with his comrades.

* * *

Like Alan Seeger in an earlier war, Bray Booth was a Harvard man when he crossed the Atlantic. He was drafted in 1943 after his freshman year, and life in the army left him confused. He began to doubt his faith.

He had always attended church—namely, Islington Community Church, a Congregational church outside of Boston where his father had been the pastor since before Bray was born. He loved the rituals, the sermons, the hymns. Studying at Harvard with plans to become a minister, he began exploring science. He felt his religious beliefs shift. The war challenged his thinking even more, and he started to question whether it was possible to live without God in his life.

After being wounded in January 1945 and hospitalized in Belgium to recover, he spilled out his fears in a letter home. "Now I have known bitter cold, hunger, exhaustion, and have seen death and destruction, have known fear as only the screaming shell can bring fear—and know that the human mind is not enough."

He realized he did need God—and his father. "Don't know whether it's just because you are my Dad, or because I can now see you also as the deeply human, understanding, religious person others have come to love and respect," he said.

Edwin Booth wrote back in a consoling tone, acknowledging his son's doubts and encouraging him to ask God for comfort and support. "At nineteen, my boy, you have looked on death and come to know the preciousness of life. To the Giver of Life and Death alike all men must turn."

But Bray Booth never read his father's words. He was killed in March 1945 after jumping into Wesel, Germany, with the 513th Parachute Infantry Regiment, as U.S. troops pushed across the Rhine into enemy territory. "Operation Varsity" saw paratroopers dropped into a nest of German gunners and "picked off like pigeons coming in for a landing."

British soldiers buried him in a civilian cemetery; a month later, Graves Registration troops moved his remains to a temporary military cemetery in Margraten, Holland. It was a cemetery overwhelmed with the dead of the Wesel attack.

"No one could better understand the terrible cost in human life of this operation than we who were on hand to pick up the dead and transport them back to Holland for burial," wrote the captain in charge of Margraten.

Bray Booth's death smothered his family in anguish. His mother stopped going to church; it was too painful to sit in a pew and not hear Bray's voice join hers during hymns. Alternately, Edwin Booth could not stay away. He believed his son had made the ultimate sacrifice for the good of a world loved by God.

"I feel that Bray died with the weight of centuries of sin upon his generation," he wrote, "and with the light from millions of people in a more abundant life falling backward from the future upon his grave."

The grave at Margraten mesmerized Booth. As he and his family approached the cemetery for the first time in 1946, the ground glowed with a thin, almost ethereal light. Booth quickly realized it was the sea of perfectly spaced white grave markers.

"Row upon row, they lie as they marched. Side by side, they sleep in death as they had slept in camp, no rank or honor sets one aside from the other," he wrote.

At home in Massachusetts, Edwin Booth had a bully pulpit larger than his village church. He was a professor and chairman of historical theology at Boston University's School of Theology, where he had earned a doctorate. He was also a frequent guest speaker at Boston-area churches, be they Episcopalian, Methodist, or Unitarian. Since arriving in Europe in the fall of 1946, Booth had visited several temporary military cemeteries. Each one, he believed, was perfect and peaceful.

Wanting to encourage families to leave their war dead in Europe, Booth wrote an essay from Paris that first appeared in February 1947 in the *Boston Globe* and *New York Herald Tribune.* Other papers followed, from the *Washington Post*, where it would be seen by officers in the War Department, to publications in Racine, Wisconsin; Buffalo, New York; Allentown, Pennsylvania; and Honolulu, Hawaii. His largest audience was still to come: *Reader's Digest*, the most popular magazine in the country, with some ten million subscribers.

"If my voice could be heard in America I would say to my government that we should do all in our power to keep the simplicity and naturalness of these surroundings unchanged," he wrote.

The military cemeteries in Europe are visually perfect, he argued, and residents often adopt the graves of American soldiers, gracing them with flowers and prayers. For grieving families like his, the burial grounds were a source of quiet contentment now threatened by the government's plans. "Nothing will restore what once has been. Those many thousands look so quiet—let them rest in that quietness!"

Sgt. Bray Booth was first buried at the temporary U.S. cemetery at Margraten, Holland.
National Archives and Records Administration photo

No other nation was bringing its war dead home. The British Embassy made clear that its soldiers "should remain buried together with their comrades who fought with them in life." That applied to all soldiers fighting for the Commonwealth, including Canada, India, Australia, and New Zealand. The British government also frowned upon requests from American families with British roots asking that a loved one be buried in the United Kingdom. It was too awkward to accept an American body for burial while leaving the UK's own war dead abroad.

As Booth's essay ran in publications throughout the country in the spring of 1947, letters poured into his office at Boston University. Mothers, fathers, widows, siblings—all were eager to share their family's loss and were desperate for details about the fate of their loved ones. *Did you see my precious boy's grave? How will we know if the right body is sent home? Our son is buried on Leyte Island—would you give the same advice?*

* * *

Booth's essay appeared just as thousands of bereaved families were receiving thick envelopes from the War Department. It was time to make a decision.

Inside was a twenty-page booklet explaining the government's burial program. Families had four choices. One option was for burial in a permanent American cemetery overseas. Another was for interment in a U.S. national cemetery. A third choice was for a body to be buried in a foreign country that was the native home of the soldier or his family. The final option was to have a body returned to the United States for a private, hometown burial, with the government providing a seventy-five-dollar stipend for funeral costs. The government would cover all other expenses—exhuming, casketing, shipping.

The mail also included a glossy foldout showing the locations of national cemeteries in the United States and American military cemeteries in Europe. Because not all national cemeteries had room for more burials, an additional document listed where space was available. Gravesites in those sixty-five locations would be filled on a first-come, first-served basis. The European military cemeteries featured in the brochure housed the remains of the World War I dead and were meant only as examples—new cemeteries for World War II dead would be created once enough families chose European burials.

Finally, there was the official "Request for Disposition of Remains," a two-page form that next of kin needed to complete and return to Washington. All of it made for an informative but confusing jumble of paperwork.

Families had thirty days to make their choices.

The letters were sent in the same order that the Army Quartermaster General planned to clear the temporary cemeteries. When the War Department started mailing questionnaires in March, questionnaires went to families with loved ones buried at Henri-Chapelle in Belgium; St. Laurent, France; Cambridge, England; and the Hawaiian Islands.

Booth's column brought clarity to some families making their decisions.

"Since reading it, a peace has come into our hearts that we have never had before," said Bessie Schwensen of Wichita, Kansas. She and her husband, Justin, had lost three sons to the war over fifteen months—two were with the Army Air Corps and one was an infantryman killed in Germany. "Our two pilots were never found, so you can understand that we were content to let our one rest in peace."

In Pennsylvania, Harry and Jane Woodin had five children, all serving in the war effort either with the military or as government translators. Four came home safely. Their youngest, Harry, was killed fighting in Italy's Po Valley in 1945. Jane Woodin said Booth's views about overseas cemeteries reassured her about leaving their son buried in Europe.

"When all my children returned we all got together to decide whether we would bring him back and the answer was no," she said. "I could never think of my son returning in a casket. I want to remember him as he left, with a smile saying, 'Don't cry, dearest mother—I will be back soon.'" The family later changed its mind and asked that Harry Woodin be buried in Arlington National Cemetery.

Others wrestled with what would cause the least harm to those still living. A widow worried that asking for her husband's remains to be returned from Guam would reopen wounds for their eight-year-old daughter. "Now that Molly accepts his death . . . and once more is a happy, normal child, it would seem cruel to thrust more grief upon her."

Another woman felt similarly about her husband's return. When he died at age twenty-seven, the soldier left behind an infant daughter; he was buried at Margraten, where Bray Booth rested. "After reading your article, I have decided to let Manfred remain near your son, and one day, when my daughter is old enough, we will stand in Margraten as you did—and we'll have a special hello for your son."

If Edwin Booth opposed repatriation, plenty of families opposed the reverend's views. They accused him of being pretentious and arrogant, of flaunting his financial ability to travel abroad. He was butting in where he wasn't wanted. He was behaving un-Christianly by not showing more sympathy for those who wished for the bodies of their sons, husbands, and brothers.

"It seems to me I can hardly wait for the ship to bring him home, him who was the light of my life, who now rests in a lonely, isolated Pacific island, resting in soil defiled by the feet of Japanese, soil completely foreign to our boys with its foul jungles and ugly lava islands," wrote Margaret McIntyre of Worcester, Massachusetts. Her son, Stephen, died fighting in Okinawa. "I resent you, as I resent Mrs. Patton, attempting to dissuade the bereaved of this land from having the consolation, however slight it is, of having their martyred sons rest with 'their own.'"

Others pointed out that even if Booth wanted his son to remain in Europe, the military planned to tear up all the temporary burial grounds and move bodies to new cemeteries. Some families could not imagine their child buried anywhere other than the United States, where they could keep watch over care and maintenance of the grave.

"My son is buried at the edge of an old stone quarry in Italy," a father wrote from Iowa. "The place is positively hellish and the natives there are filthy, scabby and godless." The same man wished that every soldier's body returned home could be paraded solemnly through hometowns to demonstrate the very personal cost of war.

Still others were frustrated, including the father of a boy who had failed to return from patrol after being shot by a German sniper. "Lucky the parents who are able to visit the cemetery of a dead son, even in a foreign land, where he is buried as a 'War Hero,'" he wrote. "But what shall we do, Sir, the parents of many ten thousand boys, killed and missing in action . . . whose corpses never have been found? Where shall we go? What shall we do?"

Among the most thoughtful letters to Booth came from a California father whose son, an infantryman, was killed in Germany and buried in Luxembourg. William R. Weill did not want to argue with Booth. The choice about where to bury one's child was too sacred to debate. Weill and his wife Nell wanted their son Charles brought home, in part because they could not afford to travel to Europe. Even if money were not an issue, the Weills still would not visit Charles's grave.

"Once having been there, I, for one, would never be content to leave," Weill wrote. Instead, the family believed Charles would want to rest near those who had loved him. They planned to ask the government to bury him in Golden Gate National Cemetery, nestled between San Francisco Bay and the Pacific Ocean.

"The sun rising in the early morning shines down on other rows of white crosses and as it sets in the West kisses them goodnight," the father wrote. "It is American soil, surrounded on all sides by American homes, American families, American churches and American might."

* * *

While families struggled with their decisions, America's funeral industry enthusiastically supported the return of the war dead. Owners of funeral homes and private cemeteries, along with manufacturers of coffins and mortuary supplies, all stood to benefit.

While the military prepared bodies, provided coffins and urns, and transported the dead from overseas, there still were funerals to plan, grave plots to purchase, and flowers to arrange. The government's seventy-five-dollar stipend given to families meant money in the pocket for funeral homes; still, it often did not cover all costs, with parents and widows dipping into their bank accounts for additional expenses.

Cemetery associations, eager to protect their market, successfully lobbied against efforts in Congress to expand the national cemetery system, arguing that most families—armed with their government checks—preferred private burials anyway.

The return program also opened the door to con artists eager to prey upon grief-stricken families. Swindlers asked for money to watch over foreign graves that already were under government care, told families they could return bodies faster than the government, or tried to sell caskets they claimed were nicer than the military's "plain wooden boxes."

FTD and foreign florists offered a new service of guaranteed delivery of wreaths for overseas graves for Memorial Day. FTD—which worked out the program with the Quartermaster's Memorial Division—called it a public service to families "because the boys themselves laid the foundation for overseas service by wiring flowers home from every combat theater."

* * *

While many bereaved parents and widows were angry at those like Beatrice Patton and Edwin Booth for calling to leave the dead where they fell, some in the military quietly applauded their views. Officially, the War Department maintained a neutral and respectful position: Families had a choice, and their wishes would be honored. Privately, many military officials wanted men to stay buried overseas.

Americans opposing repatriation often pointed to World War I and the example set by former President Theodore Roosevelt. His youngest son, Quentin, was a pilot who was shot down and died in 1918; he was buried in France. Roosevelt and his wife, Edith, lodged "a most respectful but most emphatic protest" when they learned the government would be exhuming the dead to ship home. "We have always believed that 'Where the tree falls, there let it lie.'"

Determined to let the next of kin of World War II know they had choices, the military produced a short educational film about the burial options and shipped it to veterans' organizations and churches for viewings around the country. In the dramatization, a war widow talks with her mother about how to manage the remains of her late husband. When a friend of the widow stops by her home, he explains her choices. There is heavy emphasis on the beauty and maintenance of the overseas cemeteries to be built: "Grass and trees and flowers, well, just like you'd see back home," the widow is told. By the end of the fifteen-minute film, she decides her husband should be buried abroad.

For many veterans who had watched their friends die in combat, an overseas burial was the only real choice. Their letters to Booth and opinion page editors were unanimous: Leave the dead with their buddies. An army chaplain who, like Howard Lee, had buried hundreds of dead in Europe, wrote admiringly of local townspeople who placed flowers on graves. "It will be a great mistake to bring our men back."

Even some managing the return program discreetly hoped for the dead to remain where they fell. Maj. Gen. Robert M. Littlejohn, the chief quartermaster for Europe, had been a pallbearer at General Patton's funeral in Luxembourg in December 1945. Afterward, he dashed off a candid note to the general's widow. At the time, Congress was early in its discussions to bring home the war dead. Littlejohn told Beatrice Patton that some 75,000 families had sent letters in favor of the program, with fewer than one hundred families asking for their loved ones to remain in Europe. Yet he hoped that others would follow her lead. "I do feel . . . that the burying of General Patton here in Europe is going to have a considerable influence upon the decisions of others," Littlejohn told her.

Others were even more outspoken.

Lt. Gen. Charles P. Hall told the Senate's appropriations subcommittee on military spending that returning the dead was a mistake ("at least, it would be in my own family") and he was discouraging it. He was backed by the committee's chairman, Oklahoma Senator Elmer Thomas, who praised the care and maintenance of overseas cemeteries. "I cannot understand why a family would want to bring a relative home from a place like that and put him in some isolated cemetery," Thomas said, "to be grown over with weeds and brush and briars in a few years, as I have seen in many places in this country."

It took another committee member, Senator Chan Gurney, to remind both men that 75 percent of families were requesting that their loved ones be brought home.

Col. Lyman R. Talbot, who oversaw field operations at all the military cemeteries in Europe, worried that families didn't truly grasp the fresh waves of anguish and grief they would encounter when bodies began arriving home. Better to honor them all in new, permanent cemeteries and instead use the money to support widows and their fatherless children. "After all," he said, "time is admitted to be the best cure for sorrow."

Even President Harry S. Truman, who had authorized the overall return program and its initial $92.5 million price tag, tried to appease opponents of returning the dead by suggesting the government pay families to visit overseas graves instead. During World War I, Truman had served as an artillery officer in France. Following that conflict, the American Gold Star Mothers successfully lobbied Congress to sponsor pilgrimages to France so mothers and widows could visit cemeteries. Nearly 6,700 women took advantage of the program and crossed the Atlantic.

Truman believed a similar offer should be made to families of World War II dead if they elected to choose burials in the new, permanent overseas cemeteries. He said,

> *I feel sure . . . that if they could see for themselves the care which is devoted to the graves of those who died in the First World War, and to the temporary cemeteries in which their own dead lie buried today, many of the next-to-kin would prefer that their loved ones should rest forever in the countries where they fell.*

His suggestions never gained traction with lawmakers.

* * *

The letters to Edwin Booth—preserved at Boston University's School of Theology, his academic home—are heartbreaking to read. I expected grief, sadness, and anger. What I didn't anticipate was finding one written by the parents of the co-pilot of my grandfather's doomed flight.

Lt. Marvin G. Niederjohn had been at the controls alongside pilot Leonard Mojica when their B-24 went down over Vienna in 1944. Survivors of the crash said Niederjohn was trapped in the cockpit as the burning bomber plummeted to earth. He had flown some thirty missions, but couldn't help save the plane from German flak. Before enlisting, Niederjohn had been an electrical engineer at General Electric, working on the superchargers of B-29 Superfortresses. A graduate of the University of Wyoming, he was mourned at home as "one of Laramie's best-known and most promising engineers" after his death was confirmed in 1945.

His parents, Russell and Gertrude Niederjohn, knew little else. All they had been told was that their son was likely buried as an unknown in Vienna. "If you can tell us anything about this cemetery, we'll be so pleased," Gertrude wrote to Booth.

It was April 1947, eight months after Graves Registration soldiers had exhumed the bodies of Marvin Niederjohn, my grandfather, and others from Vienna's Central Cemetery. But without a confirmed identification, Niederjohn's body was moved to France, marked only with an "X," and buried alongside fellow crewmates in the U.S. military cemetery at St. Avold. Because Niederjohn's remains had yet to be positively identified, his parents were left believing he was buried in Austria.

My grandmother, at least, had a bit more information than the Niederjohns. In January 1947, she received official notice that Delbert's body had been interred in France. It was the first detail she had received about the fate of his remains since being told, more than two years earlier, that her husband had perished in Vienna. There was no mention of him having been buried in Austria, or moving his remains between countries, or that Chaplain Howard Lee said a prayer for him at St. Avold.

The government had deliberately withheld such details. With hundreds of temporary cemeteries scattered across the globe, officials knew they couldn't afford to maintain all of them. Best to concentrate the bodies in larger cemeteries, narrow choices, and then inform families of the whereabouts of their loved ones. "It was one of the questions which makes the program difficult," a general told Congress.

The War Department told Virginia that Delbert was buried in St. Avold's plot JJJJ, row 10, grave 232. "You may be assured," the letter read, "that the identification and interment have been accomplished with fitting dignity and solemnity."

I don't know if my grandmother ever read Edwin Booth's essay urging Americans to leave the war dead undisturbed. When the War Department told her of Delbert's burial, she and her new husband, Russ Smalley, were living on the outskirts of South Bend, Indiana. He was teaching high school and coaching a struggling boys' basketball team; she was at home raising Judy. The local newspaper didn't carry the Booth article.

But my grandmother was a faithful subscriber to *Reader's Digest*. So perhaps she paused at the headline, "Let Them Rest in Peace," while thumbing through the May 1947 issue. Or she may have been focused on building a new life that would soon include another child.

* * *

Edwin Booth and his family remained in Europe for nine months, trying, as he later wrote, "to faith their way through their now broken life."

They visited Bray's grave at Margraten in sunshine and in rain, during the day and as the sun set. "By moonlight, too, we have stood by our son's cross and looked down the long glistening rows of his comrades' crosses bathed in mystic light."

When he wasn't at Margraten, Booth traveled to other temporary military cemeteries across Belgium and France. He took photographs of headstones for families who had written to him, leaving behind flowers. Visiting Margraten on Easter Sunday, he snapped pictures of the resting place of army Pfc. Hubert W. Chappel, killed in Germany, and mailed them to the soldier's grateful parents in Detroit. "Words cannot tell you how much you have done for us," the mother told Booth.

When the War Department eventually asked Booth where his son should be permanently buried, he checked the box for an overseas cemetery—specifically Margraten. He also requested that Bray rest alongside the bodies of two friends from the 513th Parachute Infantry Regiment, who had died in the same disastrous combat drop. But the parents of those two paratroopers requested their sons' remains to be shipped home, and the military honored their wishes.

Planners like Col. Robert Harbold, who had mapped out the scenario for managing the war dead, had always expected an overwhelming majority of families would choose U.S. burials. The first wave of responses arriving in the Office of the Quartermaster General in March 1947 reinforced their thinking: More than 77 percent opted for domestic burials, almost all saying they would inter their loved ones in private cemeteries.

As the months passed and more families were queried, there was a slight decrease in requests for hometown burials. Where analysts had first anticipated 80 percent of the war dead would be returned, family responses pushed the estimate downward to 70 percent. Still, most of America's dead would be coming home.

After learning in January 1947 that Delbert Trueman was buried in France, Virginia waited another nine months to hear from the War

Department again—this time about selecting a final, permanent resting place. It was November 1947, and he had been gone for three years. Month after month, she had wondered and worried about the fate of his remains. She wanted him brought home to Indiana—but would soon face more delays, shaped by factors both within and beyond her control.

Chapter 12
Delays

When Virginia Trueman married Russ Smalley, she started life over with a new husband and a new father for her daughter, Judy. But in doing so, she also ended any say she had in where her first husband was to be buried.

The army had firm rules about who could decide on the final resting places for the war dead. For soldiers who were single when they died, their fathers were considered next of kin. For married soldiers, spouses were given priority—unless they remarried. A new marriage for a widow or widower meant the burial choice reverted to a dead soldier's father or, if the father had passed away, the mother. The system created a cascading chain of next-of-kin designations that could spark confusion and conflict.

And it did. Fathers and mothers sometimes had no clue their son had married in the days before shipping out, leaving them with no say years later. Other times, parents had died since the end of the war, leaving a dead soldier's siblings to sort out matters. Divorce, estrangement, remarriage—all of it complicated the requests and approvals for final decisions.

Leonard Mojica, the pilot of Delbert's doomed bomber, had been a married man when he arrived in Europe with the 450th Bomb Group in 1944. His wife, Mary, was the first to be notified of his death. She received all his belongings left behind in Italy, including a pair of roller skates—the couple loved to skate together. But she never told Leonard's mother, Juanita Harding, when she learned he was buried in France. None of that sat well with Harding, who had to ask the War Department for details of her son's death. She at least wanted an American flag from the government to remember her only child.

But Mary Mojica would not respond to her mother-in-law. "I have not heard from or seen her since we got word of Leonard's death," Harding said.

Furious and frustrated, Harding told the War Department that her son had separated from his wife before flying to Europe, and he had intended to leave her after the war. He had a new girlfriend in Virginia and sent pictures of her to his mother.

She produced a letter Leonard wrote to her three months before his death: "As for Mary, no one realizes more than I how fine a girl she is. But that doesn't alter my decision. We're through irrespective of what she feels or wants, and as soon as I return to the States I want an immediate divorce. I don't want to hear any more on the matter. I guess men are pretty mean characters, aren't they, Mom?"

Harding spent two years writing to the War Department, particularly after learning that Mary Mojica had found a new husband in early 1947. "Being she has remarried gives my boy back to me, doesn't it?"

It didn't. Leonard's father was next in line as a survivor, unless Harding could prove she had legal custody of the boy as a child. She went to the San Francisco County Courthouse and got a copy of her divorce papers from twenty-three years earlier. She had raised Leonard on her own since he was in diapers. She also told the government she had no idea where the man was or if he was even alive.

All she wanted was her son. "I have the grave partly paid for and the hearse to meet the train and everything. Leonard's remains will be taken care of so we can be with him one night, and the priest will say prayers for him."

In January 1948, more than three years after Leonard Mojica's death, the government finally gave Harding the right to choose her son's burial spot. She wanted him to rest in Los Angeles. "I've been waiting for what seems like a thousand years," she said.

There were similar complications with the remains of Sgt. Kirk Mosher, who was first buried in the same grave with Delbert in the Vienna cemetery. Mosher had married Carmie Smallridge the day before he left Topeka, Kansas, for Europe; she had just turned eighteen. The two had been next-door neighbors as children growing up in Albuquerque, and reconnected when Kirk was in Air Corps training; he called her every time he was home on furlough. After the wedding, Carmie Mosher returned home to New Mexico to live with her mother. When she wrote letters to Kirk when he was away, she would number them—her last one was number eighty.

But it was Kirk Mosher's parents—not his wife—who were listed on his military records as the next of kin. It's unclear why: It could have been the last-minute wedding, with no time to update records, or that Mosher somehow wanted to appease the disappointment his parents voiced when he told them about the marriage. They received his belongings after his death and asked for his body to be returned to the United States. The army then paused the process: Mosher had a widow, and the decision was legally hers. She ultimately signed off—but only after Kirk's father submitted proof that Carmie had remarried. Carmie also burned the letters she and Kirk shared, which had become too painful to reread. She was certain they would have started a family after the war.

The government gave families thirty days to make a burial choice. Some couldn't bring themselves to decide and ignored the paperwork. Others had moved since the war ended, and the government needed new mailing addresses. By the spring of 1948, nearly a quarter-million letters had been mailed to families; one in five was either sent back because of a bad address or never came back. The army brought in the American Red Cross to help track down family members. Workers checked with postmasters, chiefs of police, and utility companies. They contacted ministers, rabbis, and priests, as well as neighbors, tradesmen, and local merchants.

Anyone trying to locate next of kin was cautioned to show understanding and patience once they finally found a parent, widow, or sibling. "It is often difficult to tell the next of kin what actually happened to their son, father, or brother," said one Memorial Division officer. "Many things cannot be related."

One of the most extraordinary efforts to reach a family member came in trying to find relatives of Pvt. Ernest E. Collier, a Missouri man killed in March 1945. The twenty-five-year-old infantryman was married with two children. He was buried in Belgium's Henri-Chapelle Military Cemetery, and the question in 1947 was where he should forever rest. His widow, Marie, told the government she wanted his remains left in Europe. She also shared that she had remarried, shifting the burial decision to Collier's father, Jesse.

The challenge was finding him.

Jesse Collier lived deep—very deep—in the Ozarks, some eight miles from the nearest speck of civilization. The only way to reach his home was on foot or by horse. That job fell to Edward P. Meisburger, a civilian employee with an American Graves Registration Depot in Kansas City. In September 1947, Meisburger left his office in Kansas City and drove more than 250 miles into the Ozarks, going as far as he could along rough mountain roads and then abandoning his army car. A local farmer carried him a short distance on horseback. Meisburger then walked four miles, following a trail that took him over two mountains. He stripped off his shoes, socks, and pants to cross a pair of streams. He got lost, backtracked, and walked several more miles.

Eddie Meisburger was not a young man. He was fifty-one, the father of four, and a veteran of World War I who had served with Harry Truman. Most of his career had been spent as a newspaper editor, and he'd only been with the American Graves Registration office for a few months as a publicity man when he trekked into the Ozarks. It's unclear why he was ordered to make personal contact with Collier. But, finally reaching the home of Jesse Collier, an exhausted Meisburger explained the government's burial program. Collier reviewed the papers and marked the box asking that his son be permanently interred in Belgium.

As the father signed the form, it dawned on Meisburger that the government required notarizing the request. The nearest notary was at least twenty-five miles, and a few mountains, away. He decided to skip the requirement and hope for the best.

In its driest language, the army concurred, saying "the possibility of bringing Mr. Collier and a notary together, for topographical reasons, is comparatively negative."

* * *

Along with securing a family's emotional decision about where to bury a loved one, the military required a far more benign—but no less essential—element for the return program to be a success: caskets. Graves Registration teams throughout the world would need new caskets for every dead soldier. And as loved ones began pondering their burial decisions in 1947, the military was facing a nationwide coffin shortage.

The army had precise standards for the caskets to be used to bring home the dead. Almost all of the human remains being returned home had never been embalmed. Many of the dead had been buried, exhumed, and reburied, and now would be exhumed a second time. That called for a seamless, leakproof casket to contain any liquid or odor. The design was, in effect, a deep bathtub created from a single sheet of steel. A one-piece steel lid fit snugly on top and, once bolted down, hermetically sealed the casket.

It was a 285-pound airtight container, lacquered with a bronze finish and a reverent appearance that designers felt Americans would appreciate. Every casket was then packed into a customized, 140-pound plywood crate to protect it during shipment across water and land.

Casket planning had already stalled in 1946 due to steel shortages and a steelworkers' strike. Families waited, and the army apologized. When a mother asked for her son's remains to come home, she received heartbreaking news from a lieutenant with the Quartermaster General: "The supply of steel for the manufacture of caskets is at present uncertain. Without this essential item, the projected movement of remains cannot be properly initiated."

Inside the Memorial Division, the issue became known as "C-Day"—the day casket supply would finally catch up with demand.

The army had contracted with five manufacturers to produce 250,000 caskets. The price tag was $35 million. Only one of the companies, Cincinnati Coffin Company, actually knew how to build caskets; the other firms had to retool existing plants. Caskets were scheduled to come off the assembly lines at the end of the year, but the first deliveries weren't made until February 1947.

"No further trouble is expected," an officer wrote, "and expediting is now being carried on to insure deliveries on time, and in certain vital cases, ahead of schedule."

It was false optimism. Workers at the casket factories had other plans. Welders, grinders, and toolmakers at two casket plants walked off their jobs in April, demanding higher pay and more vacation time. Most notably, more than three thousand employees at Goodyear Aircraft in Ohio manned picket lines for six weeks. The War Department lost two hundred coffins for every day the plants were closed. Goodyear Aircraft acquiesced eventually and gave workers a pay raise and additional time off.

While labor negotiations unfolded at Goodyear, other plants managed to produce some caskets, and enough were in stock for the first shipment to cemeteries in Europe. By early May, approximately 6,200 caskets were loaded onto the U.S. Army Transport *Joseph V. Connolly*, and the ship would sail from New York to Antwerp. Built as a Liberty ship, the *Connolly* had undergone a retrofit to equip it to carry thousands of coffins, both empty and full, across the Atlantic. The availability of caskets had a direct impact on when the first bodies could be exhumed, and with the *Connolly* on its way with coffins, Graves Registration teams began emptying Henri-Chapelle of more than 17,000 American bodies in July. It was the first military cemetery to offer up the dead for shipment home.

The army was feeling confident going into the fall of 1947. All remains recovered from far-off burials were now concentrated in the temporary cemeteries, and caskets were on their way by the thousands. Family requests for burials were arriving with consistency, with nearly 73,000 next of kin making their selections. New permanent cemeteries were in development.

More than three years after Col. Robert Harbold began sketching out a strategy for bringing home America's dead, the repatriation was in full motion.

"The plans which have been drawn and redrawn on paper have become reality," said Brig. Gen. George A. Horkan, who had followed Harbold as head of the Memorial Division. "Within a short time, flag-draped caskets will be moving into thousands of communities throughout the United States, bearing silent witness to the tremendous and tragic cost of international strife."

Horkan was addressing VFW members who had gathered for their annual conference in September 1947, and provided a detailed review of how bodies were being managed "because you fought with and died beside many who gave their lives."

The first of the war dead—carefully sealed, reverently handled, and long-awaited—would arrive on American shores in October.

* * *

Virginia Smalley received the government's long-anticipated paperwork in late October, almost three years to the day of Delbert's death. "The Quartermaster General of the Army has been entrusted with this sacred responsibility to the honored dead," wrote Quartermaster General Thomas B. Larkin.

Virginia and Russ had celebrated their first anniversary two months earlier, and they were expecting a baby the following January. When she was married to Delbert, the two had talked about having another child after the war. Now, at thirty-one and remarried, she was facing two of life's most emotional milestones: bringing a new life into the world and burying a spouse.

She reviewed all the government paperwork about disinterments and cemetery choices just as the nation began welcoming home those who had been buried overseas. The first to have died were also the first to come home when the U.S. Army Transport *Honda Knot* slid into San Francisco Bay on October 10, bearing the bodies of 3,027 men from Hawaiian military cemeteries, including those killed in the Pearl Harbor attack. Sixteen days later, the USAT *Joseph V. Connolly* arrived in New York with the first dead from Europe in its hold—6,248 bodies, most from Henri-Chapelle Cemetery in Belgium.

On both days, when the ships arrived, flags across the nation were lowered to half-staff. Six thousand people, including Gold Star mothers, gathered at a San Francisco park to watch the *Honda Knot* slide under the Golden Gate Bridge. New Yorkers turned out in more extraordinary numbers. Four hundred thousand people lined the streets of Manhattan in silence to witness a funeral cortege carrying a lone flag-draped coffin from the *Connolly* to Central Park. Six thousand servicemembers and veterans flanked the caisson, and one hundred military aircraft flew over the island.

At the park's Sheep Meadow, 150,000 people sat and stood for speeches by elected leaders and military officers, who were often drowned out by a helicopter buzzing over the scene. Women and men wiped their eyes at the sight of the solitary casket.

The *Washington Post*, which had repeatedly criticized the return program, offered a reluctant editorial welcome home, saying the war dead had made the ultimate sacrifice and deserved to be honored. But there was a dig. "As we have said before, to us it seems a desecration of the cemeteries abroad, and a sort of breach of final trust with the dead, to disinter their broken bodies and commence the whole sad process of burial again in this country," editors wrote. "Perhaps some families will derive consolation from the return that they could not have gotten otherwise."

Back in Indiana, Virginia studied the burial request forms—technically a disinterment directive, or what men in the field called "DDs"—and spoke with Delbert's parents. She waited more than a month before mailing the paperwork to Washington. She was forced to defer the decision: Paul Trueman, she wrote, was Delbert's next of kin. The final choice was his.

It would be another three months before Paul Trueman received the same packet of materials that had gone to Virginia and thousands of other next of kin. It was January 1948. By then, the army was well behind its original schedule, which called for nearly all the dead to have been returned by the end of 1947. Instead, the celebrated shipments to San

Francisco and New York were the only bodies returned that year. The new year would be very different, to the point of overwhelming workers tasked with helping caskets reach their final destinations.

Paul Trueman didn't hesitate. He filled out the forms and sent them back promptly. Bring my son home.

Chapter 13

Bodies

Karl Kasca was a newly licensed embalmer when he arrived in France in the fall of 1947. Just a year earlier, he had earned a bachelor's degree in mortuary science in San Francisco and passed his California state board exams to care for dead bodies. He worked at a funeral home in Napa, where people commended his skills in embalming, cosmetics, and creating a body that appeared lifelike.

None of it prepared him for what waited in Europe.

Kasca had answered the government's call for civilian embalmers to work with the return of the war dead, where the expectation was to deliver the same level of professionalism provided at a funeral home. But funeral homes didn't process dozens of bodies, many mangled and most reduced to bones, day after day.

His first assignment was at a small temporary military cemetery in Liege, Belgium, helping to identify unknown remains. He quickly learned how to search for clues. He discovered that after soldiers had returned from the front lines and had their uniforms laundered, they would grab fresh clothes, regardless of the name stenciled on the fabric. That made for confusion and false leads when confirming the identity of a dead man who was wearing another soldier's uniform.

From Liege, he moved to a military cemetery in Epinal, in France's Vosges Mountains, where Kasca set up a morgue for processing the remains of five thousand dead. The cemetery sat on a plateau, where workers could look out over a valley and see the Moselle River winding in the distance. Everyone agreed it was a beautiful location, but the work was grim.

Kasca's final and busiest assignment was the cemetery at St. Avold. He worked long days, overseeing other embalmers and their assistants as they prepared bodies for the final journey home. Each body was disinfected, sprinkled with a chalky white preservative, and then wrapped tightly—first in linens, then a blanket—and placed face up in a casket.

As his hands moved, Kasca's mind churned: *There but for the grace of God go I.*

In a makeshift warehouse that served as St. Avold's morgue, teams kept placing muddy remains in front of him at a processing table. Conveyor belts churned as they moved caskets and shipping cases along a morbid assembly line. More washing, more disinfecting, more shrouding. Here would come a body, twenty pounds of fractured bone and no more. Nothing that resembled a man. An army serial number, 35900811. My grandfather.

* * *

When Paul Trueman asked the U.S. government in January 1948 to return his son's body to Indiana, the military cemetery at St. Avold was on the verge of closing. As Graves Registration teams closed smaller cemeteries in eastern France and concentrated the remains in St. Avold, the graveyard had come to hold 26,000 bodies. It was closed to new burials in February, when crews began exhuming bodies to either return to the United States or be buried in permanent cemeteries in Europe. Delbert Trueman had been buried there for eighteen months.

As the military prepared to empty all its temporary military cemeteries, officials overseas worked with local authorities to comply with public health laws. Some European nations worried about the spread of disease when bodies were exhumed, particularly if a soldier died in some way other than killed in action; cholera, smallpox, typhus, and other diseases could potentially linger in remains and become virulent again. After World War I, townspeople in French villages had worried, to the point of hysteria, that clearing cemeteries of American dead would unleash epidemics.

The Quartermaster General was determined to avoid that as his troops began exhuming the dead of World War II. They needed two tools, one practical and the other perceptual: disinfectants and public relations.

Before laborers and morticians began pulling up bodies, army public relations officers reassured residents that embalmers would disinfect and hermetically seal all remains in caskets. Workers would treat the soil that held the dead to kill off insects and larvae. The army pledged that no local buses or trains would be used to transport remains, and convoys of military trucks would take alternate routes to avoid passing through populated areas.

In France, where Delbert and thousands more Americans were buried, American and French officials brokered an agreement in October 1947 that allowed Graves Registration teams to bypass local permits for exhuming and moving remains, with an understanding they would follow all sanitary practices.

While there was little chance of unleashing an epidemic, embalmers like Karl Kasca still used copious amounts of disinfecting and deodorizing sprays on remains. Once a body was exhumed and unwrapped, morticians and their assistants saturated it in fluid that both killed germs and preserved the remains. It was a brew of chloroform, formaldehyde, rosemary oil, methanol, camphor, and dichlorodiphenyltrichloroethane (DDT). Sheets for wrapping the remains were also saturated in the same chemical concoction.

No residents would have been near the cemetery as men lifted bodies from the earth. The army made it clear that visitors were not allowed once exhumations began. There was also a ban on photographs, unless they were for official War Department purposes, and these were stamped "restricted." The War Department would only release photos of the cemetery to the public—namely, the print media—if the images would not "cause next of kin unnecessary pain and anguish, or be detrimental to military morale." Whenever bodies were being removed, a cemetery's flag was lowered to half-staff.

All of the European cemeteries were busy. Since the USAT *Joseph V. Connolly* had made its first delivery to New York, 13,000 bodies had been prepared and shipped home in 1947. The number would soar to more than 55,000 in 1948. Where just two ships had made two deliveries in 1947, thirteen vessels would depart Europe with the dead the following year.

* * *

As deadlines neared for closing and clearing cemeteries like the one in St. Avold, the time also arrived for the War Department to hand off stewardship of the dead who would remain buried in Europe. Since 1923, the American Battle Monuments Commission had assumed responsibility for creating and maintaining permanent military cemeteries in Europe for the dead doughboys of World War I. That included the immense Meuse-Argonne American Cemetery in France, with more than 14,000 dead; the Aisne-Marne American Cemetery near Belleau Wood; the Flanders Field American Cemetery in Belgium; and the small but poignant Brookwood American Cemetery outside London.

The agency's mission would continue in 1947 with the dead of World War II. Since the war's end, the American Battle Monument Commission and War Department had worked to identify locations for permanent burial grounds in Europe and the Pacific Islands, knowing that some families would want their loved ones to rest permanently where they had died.

The War Department and American Battle Monument Commission settled on fourteen new cemeteries worldwide, with the majority located on the European continent, one in England, one in North Africa, and one in the Philippines. Five would be located in France alone, including the Lorraine American Cemetery to hold the remains of the dead being exhumed from the temporary cemetery at St. Avold. Constructed just a half mile from the temporary military cemetery, Lorraine featured a limestone memorial towering sixty-seven feet high that would come to dominate the 113 acres of graves. Of all the new, permanent cemeteries established in Europe after the war, Lorraine American Cemetery was the only one built entirely separate from its earlier temporary space. At least ten thousand soldiers could rest there.

Military leaders selected sites for the new cemeteries for their natural beauty, topography, and potential for expansion. Historic significance and sentiment also played a critical role. The lone burial ground in the United Kingdom, for example, was established in Cambridge as the final resting place for thousands of Eighth Air Force men who had called England home throughout the war. Normandy American Cemetery, overlooking the Atlantic Ocean, would hold the remains of men killed in the D-Day invasion. Luxembourg American Cemetery would be the final resting place for men who died during the Battle of the Bulge and the Allies' eastward push toward the Rhine River.

Gen. John J. "Black Jack" Pershing, commander of the American Expeditionary Forces in World War I and chairman of the American Battle Monument Commission from 1923 until he died in 1948, believed the overseas cemeteries were more than pristine burial grounds. They were shrines that would "outlast time itself."

* * *

By the end of 1947, after the *Joseph V. Connolly* and *Honda Knot* returned the first of the war dead, more than a hundred thousand families had told the U.S. government of their burial choices. Seventy-five percent requested that their loved ones be shipped home.

At the temporary cemeteries across Europe and the Pacific, workers were preparing and casketing remains at a rate of 2,100 bodies a week. In Washington, officials aimed for the weekly number to reach 3,275, to make sure at least 31,000 dead would be sent home by mid-1948.

"During the coming year, we will have to work under pressure and work hard, not only with our minds but with our hearts as well," said Gen. George A. Horkan, head of the Memorial Division. "It is the final burial which is the payoff."

The military hoped to have all the dead returned by mid-1949. There were small setbacks. The *Joseph V. Connolly*—the same Liberty ship that had carried the first wave of dead from Europe—was swept by fire in the North Atlantic. An oil leak sparked a blaze in the early morning hours as the ship made its way from New York to Antwerp with a hold filled with caskets. The vessel lost power, leaving the men in darkness and smoke.

As the blaze raged, the captain sent out a distress signal and ordered all forty-six men aboard to abandon ship. Even the rope ladders were catching fire as men lowered themselves into lifeboats and a cold, churning sea. Some men suffered burns, but no one died. Three ships raced to the burning transport and rescued the crew later that day.

But the ship was doomed. For two weeks, the *Connolly* drifted, listed, and smoldered, fueled by its cargo: 6,445 shiny new coffins, sheathed in plywood shipping cases, tightly stacked in the hold, and packed in with wooden dunnage. Overhead, six hundred five-gallon cans of embalming fluid sat on the buckling deck. It made for an inferno. The ship glowed red and then white. Despite efforts to tow it nine hundred miles back to New York, the *Connolly* and its caskets—still a commodity for the return program—sank into the Atlantic during a blinding snow squall.

Just two weeks after the *Connolly* loss, a second funeral ship foundered in the Atlantic. The USAT *Corporal Eric G. Gibson* lost its propeller six hundred miles east of New York as it plowed toward Cherbourg, France, with a shipment of coffins. It was returning to Europe after bringing a shipment of remains to the United States—1,753 soldiers, including many who died at Omaha Beach on D-Day. The *Gibson* had to be towed back to New York for repairs, holding up another delivery of caskets for six weeks.

However, the biggest concern for the army wasn't troubled ships. It was a shortage of licensed morticians—professionals like Karl Kasca.

The army did not assign enlisted men to embalm the dead. As one general said, "The policy of the Army is not to use enlisted men on that work. The enlisted man is a soldier." But the countries where America's soldiers were buried required licensed professionals "for this disagreeable but necessary task" of handling and preparing the dead. For each temporary cemetery being cleared, the military needed civilian morticians to supervise the preparation and casketing of bodies. Of all the specialists needed to launch the repatriation effort, General Horkan declared, "Embalmers are the most urgently needed."

The War Department appealed to state employment agencies nationwide, offering jobs for morticians in Europe, the Pacific, Japan, Korea, and the Philippines. Compensation was key, and the annual salary for morticians was nearly $4,200, one of the highest for civilians working in the return program. Karl Kasca was definitely interested.

* * *

When he first went to mortuary school after the war, Kasca believed he was embarking on a career that would bring comfort to others. He had known since high school that he wanted to be a mortician, even if other kids couldn't quite believe it. He liked the quiet, the methodical work, and the sense that he would bring some peace to grieving families.

It was a balm for the loss and devastation that marked his erratic upbringing in rural southwestern Pennsylvania. His father Andrej Kasca, a Slovakian immigrant, was a coal miner. He was sixteen years older than Karl's mother, Louise. She had lost her first husband to suicide six months before marrying Andrej, and came to the marriage with an eighteen-month-old daughter. The family lived in a mining town called Dunlo, where all the men—many from Eastern Europe—worked for a coal company that fed the steel mills in nearby Johnstown. It was dangerous work. Andy Kasca was injured at least once when he got tangled up in a coal car as it dumped its load.

When Karl was twelve years old, his father killed himself by using his toe to fire a 12-gauge shotgun into his chest. It was a horrible loss. His mother had never been a warm woman, and quickly abandoned Karl and his sister in hopes of being more appealing to a potential new husband. Karl's sister went into a convent, and he moved in with a foster family a hundred miles away on a farm. Two years after his mother left him, Karl's maternal grandfather died by suicide as well—turning on a gas oven and breathing in the toxic fumes.

On the farm, he rose every morning at five o'clock to begin his chores, including caring for fourteen cows. The animals always needed to be milked in time for a delivery truck to make a collection. But the new home felt stable. There was always a bowl of cookies on the kitchen table. He became active in high school plays and a church youth group.

At eighteen, Kasca joined the navy straight out of high school, enlisting in Pittsburgh in 1939. He joined the crew of the USS *Nashville* just as it ferried Gen. George C. Marshall to Rio de Janeiro on a goodwill tour. Like Kasca, Marshall was a Pennsylvania native, and the two struck up a conversation that led to long talks on the bridge after dinner. Kasca was a lowly seaman, fresh from the farm and away from home for the first time, talking every night with an army general. As Marshall went on to a distinguished career as army chief of staff, secretary of state, and architect of a postwar plan to rebuild Europe, Kasca never forgot their evening conversations at sea.

He spent four years on the *Nashville*, including an overhaul in San Francisco that allowed him time to explore nearby Napa. He met a local girl named Berenice Montellier at a dance party, and after dating for three years while he crisscrossed the world, the two married in 1943.

Life at sea soon became very dangerous for the groom.

As a chief machinist's mate on a new ship, the destroyer escort USS *England*, Kasca and his crewmates zigzagged the South Pacific in search of Japanese submarines. On an attack, the ship would lob sixty-five-pound anti-submarine mortars called Hedgehogs into the sea. A few minutes would pass, and then the ocean would erupt with a violence that knocked men off their feet. More minutes would go by, sailors would scan the sea, and then bubbles of oil would burst through the water, followed by pieces of cork, deck planks marked with Japanese characters, and fragments of clothing. One time, a giant sack of rice bobbed up. So, too, would blood and human limbs shredded by the underwater explosions.

In May 1944, the *England* crew tracked and destroyed six Japanese submarines in twelve days. There were never any survivors, and at least 378 Japanese sailors perished. "I regret that we had to kill those people in order to win. Unfortunately, war is killing," the ship's executive officer wrote later. The *England* was hailed as the mightiest sub killer in the navy, and no ship has ever matched its record.

The *England*'s crew would be tested in May 1945 when American soldiers and marines invaded and secured Okinawa. Sailors repeatedly repelled Japanese suicide planes that attacked the ship. But on May 9, just as the sun was setting, three enemy aircraft roared toward the *England*. Navy gunners hit one of the approaching planes—a fully loaded dive-bomber—which then slammed into the ship's bridge. One of its bombs tore through the ship and exploded, turning the ship into an inferno. Everywhere, men were burned, dying, and dead. Twenty-seven sailors lost their lives, forty were injured, and ten vanished forever, most likely blown overboard.

Called up to the deck from the engine room, where he worked in the noise and grease, Kasca received an order: Gather the remains and do your best to assemble them. Other sailors knew Kasca wanted to be a mortician, and this job was for him. He gathered limbs and torsos and tried to piece together the fragments of friends.

The war was over for the USS *England* and Kasca. But he would come to witness the same horrible damage in the cemeteries of Europe. When he read the advertisements seeking embalmers to work overseas, he and Berenice discussed it. They had been married for four years and saw Europe as both a mission and a vacation. American families wanted their husbands and sons brought home. Kasca would help make that happen. He and Berenice also would have time to be tourists, exploring France, Germany, and Belgium before settling down and starting a family back in California. They were twenty-seven years old.

Once overseas, they lived in different worlds. At St. Avold, Karl stayed in military barracks at the cemetery. Berenice lived in the village with a family that provided her with a bedroom and the use of a bathroom. She would eat at cafés and sometimes have dinner with her husband at the cemetery. She enjoyed visiting the village market, watching a farmer carry a piglet in a sack slung over his shoulder, and marveling at the fresh vegetables and fruit on display. Other commodities were hard to find, including sugar, and pastries were bland and heavy. Medical supplies were sparse; she once saw a doctor grab soiled, bloodied gauze from a wastebasket to wrap a deep cut on a young boy's leg. Despite the shortcomings, it was unlike anything in Napa.

Karl, meanwhile, confronted the unspeakable. He discovered the landscapes were gorgeous, but the sights at work were horrific. It was a harvest of death, with cemeteries being torn open and cleared of bodies. At St. Avold alone, some 16,000 graves awaited emptying, with local laborers using shovels and pickaxes to uncover the dead. Pulled from the earth, mud-caked remains consisted of shattered men, scraps

Mortician Karl Kasca alongside the grave of an unidentified soldier buried in a temporary American cemetery in Neuville-en-Condroz, Belgium, in 1947. *Karl Kasca II photo*

of uniforms, charred bones, and rotting boots. Some bodies, buried immediately after combat, were being exhumed for the first time, with soldiers still fully clothed and wrapped in tent pieces and mattress covers. For others, such as Delbert and the airmen first buried in Austria, this was a second uprooting of their remains. Almost all were in the final stages of decomposition. Crews placed everything pulled from a grave in a wooden box and moved it to the mortuary.

First Lt. Henry F. Alzmann oversaw the workers who unearthed Delbert's body. He had arrived at St. Avold just a month earlier, and was a bit overwhelmed by all the activity, from disinterring bodies to attempts to identify unknown remains. He was struck by how many dead men were still wearing their army uniforms and boots. His top priority: No body would leave St. Avold unless positively identified. He worked alongside embalmers in the morgue.

Inside, Kasca and other embalmers lifted remains to a processing table and worked gingerly; protocol called for reverence and dignity, but also a keen eye to spot any ammunition or grenades obscured in the remains. More disturbing was what was missing: limbs, dog tags, faces, names.

Men washed what was left of a body, which was then disinfected, sprinkled with a hardening compound that included plaster of Paris, swaddled in fresh blankets, and placed in coffins. Casket upon casket was processed and sealed, and marked for final burial. Most coffins were destined for ships heading to the United States; others would remain in St. Avold for burial in the new, permanent military cemetery being laid out down the road.

Kasca handled Delbert's remains in mid-May 1948. His dog tag, once buried with him, had vanished, but Kasca confirmed his identity through dental records and earlier documents. He assembled the remains neatly on a white blanket, wrapping the bones tightly and using a safety pin to hold everything together. An embossed metal ID plate that had been nailed to the wooden cross marking Delbert's grave was placed on top of the blanket. Men lifted the bundle into a casket, sprayed it again with disinfectant, and covered it with a white sheet. Kasca and other morticians then packed padding around the remains to secure them during the overseas journey.

A crew lowered a lid onto the casket's rim, which they coated with a type of asphalt paint for a permanent seal. Workers then secured the lid with bolts. A tight casket was essential. These caskets would travel by truck, rail, ship, and hearse—and were never to be reopened. Kasca checked each one for dirt or smudges. Lieutenant Alzmann signed off.

At the time, no one at St. Avold knew the wishes of the Trueman family. Delbert's casket and thousands of others were stacked and stored under tarps on the cemetery grounds until the paperwork came through, waiting for ships to carry them to the United States.

* * *

Three weeks after Karl Kasca sealed Delbert Trueman's remains inside a coffin at St. Avold, the village's mayor traveled to Paris for a solemn ceremony. The president of France was there, as was America's ambassador to France. In the Saint-Louis Cathedral of the Hôtel National des Invalides—the official church of the French army—the focus was a modest monument just four feet tall. Carved into its granite face were the words *VOIE DE LA LIBERTÉ 1944*, with a sculpted flaming torch beneath and forty-eight stars encircling its dome.

This was a Liberty Road marker like the ones installed throughout France to mark the route followed by Patton's Third Army as they liberated the country. But the Paris monument held deeper meaning. It bore the names of seventeen temporary military cemeteries that U.S. troops created in places like Blosville, Limey, Andilly, and St. Avold—the burial grounds now being cleared of bodies. The mayors of all the communities each came to Paris with a small amount of soil from their wartime cemeteries, which they poured into the hollow of the marker.

I never considered visiting St. Avold. The temporary cemetery there, once vacant and closed, became land for a housing development. Nothing remains to suggest that it once held thousands of American war dead, including my grandfather. But seventy years after Delbert's death, I found myself standing in the quiet, cool air of Saint-Louis Cathedral while touring Paris with my husband. We had come to the sprawling complex of Hôtel National des Invalides to see the massive tomb of Napoleon.

I did not expect to come across a memorial that held the soil that had once blanketed Delbert Trueman. But it provided the same sense of connection to my grandfather that I'd felt standing among the headstones at the Vienna Central Cemetery. It was distant, but real.

* * *

When the final casket holding the dead of St. Avold was sealed and the morgue shuttered, it marked a solemn moment for Kasca and his colleagues.

"There was no whooping, hollering, or frivolity," he wrote later in a letter to a family friend. "We walked together to our club, had a drink or two, shook hands, and dispersed, each with his own thoughts and memories."

Before the cemetery was dismantled, Berenice Kasca snapped several pictures of the pristine and orderly grounds. They were souvenirs of their time in Europe, mementos of what she remembered as the first big trip in their lives. For Karl, the images captured a place he was determined to forget.

Fifty-five years later, he slipped the photos between two thin pieces of cardboard, sealed them in a manila envelope, and carried them to the mailbox. He did not need to see them again. A few days later, I opened the envelope and held black-and-white images of the French cemetery where my grandfather was buried—his second resting place.

First there had been Margaret House, sharing her photographs of the cemetery in Vienna, where Delbert was initially buried and where she and her husband, James, worked in Graves Registration. Now came the Kascas, offering photographs of Delbert's second burial location: rows and rows of white crosses. Endless, repetitive, precise white lines stretching from one edge of the photo to the other, left to right, top to bottom, row upon row, sprouting from the earth.

But to Karl Kasca, all he saw was what lay beneath. "Bodies, bodies, bodies by the hundreds," he told me, "multiplied into many thousands, day after day after day."

He calculated that the remains of more than 10,500 men passed through his hands at St. Avold. Among them was Delbert Trueman—tail gunner, husband, and father.

* * *

After families told the government they wanted their loved ones returned from Europe and the Pacific, the War Department urged patience—and cautioned them against making any funeral plans. The exhumations of thousands of bodies would take time, and the military could not guarantee their arrival in the United States. Instead, families should wait for a government telegram confirming their loved one's return.

For many, the wait was an extension of the limbo they'd felt since the first terrible telegram from the War Department. In Los Angeles, Juanita Harding begged for details about her son, Leonard Mojica. Five months after asking that his body be returned, she still had no information.

"It would help me so much if only I could know within a month or so of the arrival of his remains. The strain of waiting is rather hard to put into words," she wrote. At the time, workers at St. Avold were exhuming her son's body. A Memorial Division officer assured Harding she would have "ample time" to make funeral arrangements.

The families of the other men who died with Delbert—all buried near him at St. Avold—had made their choices. Arthur and Nina Webb wanted their son George, the plane's bombardier, to be buried in Europe. The parents of gunner Elvin Killingsworth planned to inter him in California, where he had grown up.

As laborers exhumed Webb and Killingsworth, they also brought up the body of gunner Charles S. Kleinhenz. But as he had done since learning his son was reported missing and then dead, Kleinhenz's father refused to acknowledge the boy's death and ignored the government's repeated requests for burial instructions. The airman's casketed remains sat in storage. If a family never shared their burial wishes, the policy of the return program was to bury a soldier in an overseas cemetery. Still, the Memorial Division waited a little longer for a signal from the Kleinhenz family.

Paul Trueman had submitted his request in January 1948. Delbert's remains were disinterred and casketed that May, then placed in storage. In September, men removed the coffin from storage and lowered it into a shipping case, which they tagged and stenciled with Delbert's name and service number. They packed the crate with sawdust and loaded it onto a train bound for Antwerp, more than two hundred miles to the north, where army transport ships were regularly departing with thousands of war dead. The Belgian port served as the final European stop for bodies from northern France, the Netherlands, Belgium, and Luxembourg.

As the funeral ships were scheduled to arrive, with each destined to carry upward of seven thousand caskets, the army rented a giant two-story warehouse for storing the dead at the Belgian port. It sat close to rail lines, roads, and inland waterways; some caskets were even floated to the port by barge along French and Belgian canals.

Delbert's casket arrived in November on a train, watched over by a twenty-six-year-old army private named John A. Mountford, who traveled with the remains from St. Avold. It was Mountford's job to guard the shipping cases and check for any damage. He also made sure that paperwork from the cemetery, with details about the dead and their final destinations in the United States, reached the hands of the sea captain and the ship's crew. In a mission built on reverence and precision, accuracy mattered deeply.

Delbert's body sat stacked in the warehouse among other caskets, and 1948 drew to a close. The army had returned more than 114,000 bodies from all areas of the world—60,000 from Europe alone. Where early plans drawn up by Col. Robert Harbold had projected that upward of 90 percent of families would request the return of their loved ones, the reality was that numbers were shifting downward to 60 percent. This helped with officials' desire to shut down the program sooner than its 1951 deadline.

Almost all temporary cemeteries in Europe were now empty. Ships that had once carried two thousand or four thousand casketed remains were now taking on more than seven thousand bodies on trips from Antwerp or Cherbourg.

The acceleration, said Brig. Gen. Kester L. Hastings, was not a sign of impatience but of compassion. "The bodies must get back to the next of kin," he said, "in order to settle their fears and anxieties."

In early December, an army transport ship named the *Barney Kirschbaum* pulled into the Port of Antwerp. Workers began transferring coffins from the nearby warehouse, draping each one with an American flag before moving it aboard the ship. One of the cases contained the remains of Cpl. Delbert Trueman.

On December 7, 1948—seven years to the day after Pearl Harbor—Delbert began his journey home.

Chapter 14

Homeward Bound

Delbert Trueman left the United States in 1944 aboard a heavy bomber, flying toward war alongside nine fellow airmen he had come to trust with his life. They shared stories about each other's wives and children, forming bonds of trust and friendship as they prepared for the challenges of combat.

When he returned to the States in 1948, he came back as a body sealed in a casket, placed in the hold of a Liberty ship with nearly 4,400 others who had lost their lives in the war. The journey—from Europe to the United States and then to his Indiana home—would require a choreography of trucks, cranes, forklifts, car floats, trains, and a hearse.

Shipping America's war dead from all over the world to the United States was not unlike the logistical handling of oceangoing cargo carried out every day in port cities. But the atmosphere of reverence was extraordinary. The dead were never referred to as bodies or remains—they were passengers. They were not unloaded from ships, but disembarked. Each shipping case was wrapped in red, white, and blue; the American flag's field of white stars was positioned at the head of the case, over the heart of the deceased. And their final recipients—mothers, fathers, wives, and children—were among the most grateful ever to accept a delivery.

The army compared the shipment of the dead to the movement of troops—an unseen army heading to a new destination. *Atlantic Monthly* writer David L. Cohn called it "the strangest and most melancholy immigration movement in the history of man."

* * *

When Delbert's body arrived at the Port of Antwerp, two men stood waiting. One was 1st Lt. Robert B. Howard, a Graves Registration officer. The other was Adam Brown, the civilian captain of the USAT *Barney Kirschbaum*.

Howard had been selected for the ship's seven-man honor guard to escort the war dead home due to his composure, his respect, and the sharpness of his uniform. He was a lanky kid from Sarasota, Florida, who'd joined the Reserve Officer Training Corps in high school and enlisted just as the fighting ended. For three years, he'd served quietly in the shadows of war—documenting the dead, overseeing disinterments, and watching morticians prepare bodies ravaged by time and battle. Howard was scheduled for reassignment at the end of 1948. The *Barney Kirschbaum* would be his final assignment before returning stateside.

While dockworkers loaded the ship—two caskets at a time, each draped in the Stars and Stripes and carefully lowered into the ship's hold—Howard marked his twenty-second birthday. His role was solemn but clear: to ensure a dignified, respectful loading and unloading of the caskets. An honor guard member always stood duty as bodies were loaded, and the shipping cases remained shrouded in American flags until they were in the hold. The three officers and four enlisted men of the honor guard were the only living servicemen aboard the ship. They joined forty-four civilian officers and seamen who made up the ship's crew.

Like Howard, the *Barney Kirschbaum* had Florida roots. As the young soldier was leaving the sunshine of Sarasota for Europe in 1945, shipbuilders to the north in Panama City were launching the new Liberty ship. The J. A. Jones Construction Company shipyard was one of eighteen shipyards across the country churning out thousands of Liberty ships, which were used to carry cargo and troops. Costing $1.7 million and built at government expense for the War Shipping Administration, the *Barney Kirschbaum* stretched more than 441 feet long and was

The U.S. Army Transport *Barney Kirschbaum* ferried the dead from Europe to Brooklyn, New York. *Wikimedia photo*

designed to carry aircraft. Its actual cargo would vary wildly over its first several years.

The *Barney Kirschbaum* was one of nine converted Liberty ships, which carried thousands of coffins homeward as part of the return program; five sailed in the Atlantic and four in the Pacific. Managed by the Army Transportation Corps, the vessels were retrofitted with a 'tween deck to accommodate up to 6,200 caskets in shipping cases. After her sister ship, the USAT *Joseph V. Connolly*, sank with six thousand coffins aboard, the *Kirschbaum* became the next in line.

When a funeral ship was underway with remains, the crew always flew the American flag at half-mast from the gaff. The army also made certain the vessels were specially outfitted with radar. Avoiding collisions and navigating rough seas was essential—this cargo could never be replaced.

Caskets in the hold of the *Barney Kirschbaum* weren't the only evidence of the war's wrath. The ship itself was named for an American merchant mariner who went down with his ship when a German U-boat torpedoed it in 1943. Barney Kirschbaum was the son of Russian immigrants who went to sea at the age of seventeen with a permission slip from his father. As the forty-year-old master of the cargo ship *Collingsworth*, Kirschbaum was among thirty-seven seamen killed when the enemy submarine sank four vessels in the Atlantic within ninety minutes. He was the first Merchant Marine captain killed in the war. His body was never recovered. His name remained alive, painted on the bow of a gray-and-red vessel that would carry others home.

If Captain Kirschbaum spent his life at sea, Adam Brown had an on-again, off-again relationship with ships. The *Barney Kirschbaum* was the first vessel he commanded, but he had spent years on the water. Raised in Texas, he enlisted in the navy just eleven days after the United States declared war on Germany in 1917. He spent most of his war service as an armed guard aboard an oil tanker. In 1918 he found himself battling influenza along with dozens of sailors in a navy hospital in Key West, Florida, but managed to survive the pandemic. He continued working on ships after the war before settling into civilian life in Brooklyn, New York. Marriage, fatherhood, and tragedy followed—he lost his wife in childbirth during the Depression, then lost his home. Working sporadically as a house painter, he missed too many mortgage payments and was forced to move into a rented cold-water flat with his two young daughters.

The start of World War II gave Brown the opportunity for a steady paycheck and the chance to return to the sea—this time with the Merchant Marines. He served as an officer on several army transports, including a hospital ship carrying wounded soldiers from North Africa. For three years he was the first officer—or second-in-command—on the USAT *Thomas H. Barry*, a former passenger ship. He was aboard the ship with 3,320 army personnel and Red Cross workers headed to France in 1945 when it accidentally rammed a fishing boat off the coast of Nantucket, killing seven aboard and sinking the trawler.

He was also aboard the *Thomas H. Barry* when Chaplain Howard Lee crossed to France in 1946 to help bury Delbert Trueman. Now, Brown would carry Trueman home.

Most of Brown's voyages on the *Thomas H. Barry* were happy ones: ferrying U.S. troops, their war brides, and babies from Europe and North Africa to the United States. The ship also carried hundreds of American women to their army officer husbands stationed in Germany and Austria, with dozens of children along for the ride. By the time Brown took command of the *Barney Kirschbaum* in mid-1948, the transport ship had carried everything from potatoes and sugar to Lockheed P-80 Shooting Star fighter jets.

Now, it bore a quieter, more solemn purpose—one of sacrifice and remembrance.

The December journey from Antwerp marked Brown's first time carrying the dead. The honor guard rode with its silent cargo while Brown kept an eye on his civilian crew. At forty-eight, thick-necked and blue-eyed, he ran a tight ship. Everyone on board was expected to behave with dignity because of what they carried.

* * *

While Captain Adam Brown and the *Barney Kirschbaum* steamed westward toward New York, the families of the dead men in the hold began receiving long-anticipated government telegrams: Their loved ones were finally on their way.

The telegram offered no mention of a ship, where it would dock in the United States, or when to anticipate the arrival of a body. Instead, families were asked to confirm where to deliver a body and prepare to wait several more weeks before the actual delivery. Use this time, families were advised, to finalize funeral arrangements.

One week before Christmas, Paul Trueman received his telegram from Western Union. Nearly a year had passed since he asked the War Department for a hometown burial. Now, Delbert's remains were weeks—maybe days—from appearing in Marion. The government assured him that a military escort would deliver the body "as soon as practical."

Paul Trueman quickly confirmed his family's wishes: They would use the same funeral home that handled the service and burial for Delbert's brother, Dale, in 1943. Delbert's parents spent the holidays preparing, finally, for a funeral.

For Virginia, it was a holiday season of mixed emotions. It had never felt right to her to have a funeral without Delbert's body, and the reality of that day was fast approaching. The sadness was tinged with the sparkle of the season. Eleven-year-old Judy was doting on her baby brother, Joe Eddie, who was celebrating his first Christmas. The family had recently moved into a new house in Gas City, a small town near Marion, after Russ secured a teaching job there. They were back where they had grown up, and were closer to both the Smalley and Trueman families.

* * *

The *Barney Kirschbaum* was late.

Scheduled to arrive in New York on December 28 after seventeen days at sea, the ship was slowed by heavy storms and churning seas. At last, on the morning of New Year's Eve, Capt. Adam Brown and his crew maneuvered the freighter into Pier 3 at the massive Brooklyn Army Terminal.

Anticipating the ship's arrival, a *New York Daily News* columnist by the name of Ed Sullivan penned a tribute, giving voice to the silent passengers:

> *We didn't expect to celebrate New Year's Eve, 1948, this way, we the dead. Now we are coming home, recruits from cemeteries. . . . We died for the flag that covers our coffins—we died for an ideal—we died groping for a better world, greater understanding, greater gentleness.*

As each funeral ship arrived in either New York or San Francisco, the army's level of ceremony and personal engagement intensified. When the *Barney Kirschbaum* docked, officials conducted a memorial service on the pier. An honor guard stood in formation alongside the freighter, joined by a military band. The weather danced between rain and snow, and the *Barney Kirschbaum*'s forty-four crew members pulled tarps over the ship's open hatches to shield the shipping cases and their flags.

The chaplain of the New York Port of Embarkation led the ceremony for the two hundred people—Gold Star mothers and other next of kin from the area—standing at the pier. It was the fifth and final time that year he led funeral rites at the dock, having blessed nearly 25,000 dead upon their arrival. A bugler played "Taps" and, as the honor guard marched away, the band broke into "Onward Christian Soldiers."

The *Barney Kirschbaum* carried the final delivery of war dead for 1948. Ships and men had already brought home more than 114,700 bodies to New York and San Francisco ports in the first fifteen months of the return program. That included nearly sixty thousand from St. Avold and other temporary cemeteries in Europe.

* * *

Starting with the arrival of USAT *Joseph Connolly*, the body of every soldier who died in the European Theater and was returned to the United States passed through the Brooklyn Army Terminal. It was a solemn bookend to the hundreds of thousands of anxious, eager soldiers who streamed out of the port years earlier, bound for overseas battlefields.

It was bitterly cold the day I wandered the grounds of the terminal, with biting winds whipping across the gray water of New York Harbor. Three of the base's four original piers were gone. Pier 3—where my grandfather arrived on the army transport—was a memory. The lone remaining pier had become a very long parking lot.

Two massive warehouses, threaded by now-abandoned railroad tracks, form the heart of the terminal. When it opened in 1919 as an army facility, the larger of the two warehouses was the world's biggest building—stretching farther than three football fields and rising eight stories high. Two lines of rail tracks ran directly through the building's center, creating a canyon where cargo from overseas ships could be hoisted directly into idling freight trains.

This is where my grandfather's body first returned to American soil. In the first days of 1949, workers moved his casketed remains off the

Barney Kirschbaum and across a skybridge connecting the warehouses. Both buildings had mortuaries for inspecting any damaged or leaking caskets, but Delbert's coffin looked as pristine as when it left St. Avold. From the warehouse, men loaded his casket and others into idling railcars that the army had customized for moving the dead to towns and cities across the country.

The train cars had been transformed from Pullman sleeping cars for civilian passengers to army hospital cars for wounded and sick soldiers and now hushed shuttles for the war's dead. Each mortuary car was gutted, with tiers of hospital beds, bathrooms, and kitchens ripped away to make way for racks that could hold up to sixty-six coffins. The bodies, still referred to as passengers, traveled at reduced rates charged by railroads to the army. Steel plates covered the car windows. No one could peek inside. But the olive-green cars—with "United States Army Transportation Corps" stenciled in white on their sides—were a clear signal for most Americans that the dead were coming home.

Lifting thousands of caskets from the hold of a ship into specially fitted railroad cars was elaborately choreographed to guarantee that mortuary trains could efficiently deliver bodies to army distribution centers throughout the country. It was, in effect, an assembly line of the dead.

Eighty years later, sunlight streams through the central atrium and brightens the warehouse's drab concrete walls and vintage railcars that straddle abandoned tracks in the well of the building. Moss creeps over the rail ties. The vast space under the atrium is eerie and quiet.

The terminal is no longer a military hub. Instead, it is alive with tech start-ups, small businesses, and artisans. Workers and tourists sip espressos at café tables, just feet from where thousands of soldiers' bodies once passed.

When my grandfather's coffin left here in 1949, it returned to the water. Moving the dead from the western tip of Long Island to points west and south of Brooklyn meant crossing New York Harbor. Loaded railcars rolled out of the warehouse and onto car floats—barges fitted with train tracks. A float carrying Delbert's casket made the four-mile crossing to Jersey City, gliding past the Statue of Liberty as it moved inland.

For my grandfather, four states and seven hundred miles of train tracks lay ahead. It would take more than three weeks to reach Indiana, including a very important stop in Columbus, Ohio.

* * *

More than 8,100 Hoosiers died in World War II, and their bodies had been arriving in Indiana since the *Honda Knot* delivered the first remains from the Pacific Theater in October 1947. That month, five thousand people gathered in downtown Indianapolis to welcome home the body of Seaman Second Class Ira Lincoln Lee. He and his father had been the first men in the city to volunteer for duty after the Pearl Harbor attack. His dad failed a physical, but the navy accepted Ira. Seven months after enlisting, the eighteen-year-old was killed in a loading accident aboard his ship. Now he became the first of Indianapolis' war dead to be returned home.

When the *Barney Kirschbaum* docked in New York at the end of 1948, the remains of 152 Hoosiers were in the ship's hold—including Delbert and three other men from Marion and Grant County. One of them was a fellow airman named Charles M. Garrison, a waist gunner with the 92nd Bomb Group based in England. On Christmas Eve 1944, Garrison died when his B-17 was hit by German flak and exploded over Belgium during the largest aerial attack of the war. Nearly three thousand bombers and fighters flew that day. Garrison was twenty-three years old. A year passed before a local Belgian stumbled upon Garrison's remains in a wooded area and buried him, marking the grave with a cross made from birchwood.

Garrison's widowed mother wanted him home and buried next to his father in Indiana. His body left Brooklyn aboard the same train carrying Delbert Trueman.

As funeral ships plowed toward the United States from Europe and the Pacific, the army typically released the names of the returning servicemen to local newspapers. Ideally, families had already been informed of loved ones' arrivals at least twenty-four hours before their names appeared in print. Officials viewed the coverage as a public demonstration of the government's commitment to bringing the dead home. But some in the return program cautioned that it was essential to respect the privacy of loved ones. Not all families appreciated the publicity.

"My mother is the next of kin and the body is coming home," one man told the army's Public Information Division. "She is very sick and the shock will probably kill her." At his request, the army dropped the dead soldier's name from its press release.

Maintaining good relations with families became increasingly critical as the dead were unloaded from ships and moved to fifteen distribution centers around the country. Each center was responsible for receiving and storing remains for its multistate region, and then transferring them to communities under the watchful eye of a military escort.

It made some families anxious, having learned that a son or husband had arrived in New York or San Francisco, but with no definite delivery date. Weeks could pass between a casket's arrival at a distribution center and its final departure aboard another train to head toward its final stop in places like Pittsburgh, Iowa City, or Boise. The delay heightened the emotional strain between the military and families, who knew their loved one's remains were so close to home after so many years apart.

Military diplomacy became more important than ever.

"If we wish to have the next of kin and the public in general to think well of us and magnify our good points in this program and minimize our mistakes, we need to make friends with the next of kin and with people with whom we come in contact," Gen. George A. Horkan told leaders from the American Graves Registration divisions. "We will be judged by the next of kin, and your relationship with them will measure the success of your operation in the field."

Maj. Gen. Thomas B. Larkin, the Quartermaster General, was more direct: "You are dealing not with reason and logic," he said, "but with sentiment."

* * *

No one bore the weight of human compassion more heavily than the military escorts who accompanied the bodies home. After years of bureaucratic letters and impersonal telegrams from the government, an escort in uniform was the first flesh-and-blood connection a family had to the military that had claimed their son, brother, or husband. Escorts were met with tears of anger, gratitude, frustration, and grief.

Of all the responsibilities of the return program, from locating wartime graves to delivering caskets to hometowns, the escort's duties were "the most sensitive and significant part of the mission," Horkan said. "His appearance and the manner in which he conducts himself have a profound effect on the family's impression of the quality of this last honored service rendered by the government."

CMM Piersel R. Penning understood the burden. He had joined the navy at age seventeen in 1930 and volunteered after the war to escort the bodies of deceased sailors. It demanded every ounce of his stamina. "To be met at the railroad station by a bereaved family and the friends of the deceased is one of the hardest parts of my duty," he said in 1948. Penning considered it a privilege, not an obligation, to be an escort, but he would never become fully comfortable with the cascade of emotions.

Escorts were trained to navigate the emotional demands of their work. "They had the best psychiatrists available, telling us what to expect when we delivered these bodies back home," recalled one Army Air Forces escort. "They taught us answers to every conceivable question—how to conduct ourselves." Another, a survivor of combat in the Philippines, called escort duty "the roughest assignment" he ever had.

Soldiers, sailors, marines, coast guard members—many of them reservists—stepped forward to accompany their comrades home. No one was ever ordered to be an escort. They were always of the same gender and race as the person in their care, belonged to the same branch of service, and at least held the same rank, if not a higher one.

Only the very best were selected.

They had to be beyond reproach. Fingernails clean and trimmed. Hair neat. Faces shaven. Shoes polished to a shine. White gloves on their hands. A black mourning band wrapped around the left arm. No body odor. No bad breath. No nicotine-stained fingers. Alcohol was strictly forbidden. Escorts were trained not only for solemnity, but for perfection.

They had one all-encompassing responsibility: Do not lose the body. That meant always watching as a casket was loaded onto a train and stored in the baggage compartment, and checking it every time the train made a stop. It meant repeatedly leaving their first-class coach seats to check on the remains. The worst possible scenario would be for a baggage handler to drop off a coffin at the wrong destination. Escorts always held a round-trip train ticket—and a one-way fare for their charge.

Early in the return program, some escorts delivered remains to funeral homes but never met with families. That changed when families complained. One funeral director accepted a soldier's remains and told the escort there was no need for him to stay. The mortician then turned around and told grieving relatives that their loved one had arrived in a shoddy military casket, and convinced them to buy an expensive new one. From then on, escorts were expected to stay for the funeral and meet the family personally.

When meeting an escort, parents often saw their sons, alive and in dress uniforms. Mauretta Pace was reluctant to say goodbye to the Air Corps lieutenant who brought the body of her son, Flight Officer William K. Pace, home to Arizona.

"Perhaps I was selfish to hold him so long," she said, "but he was so similar to my son, I felt his presence at the final rites would help to ease the sorrow and grief of our loss." Pace hoped every mother met such a courteous and kind escort. In almost all cases, they did.

The body of marine Pvt. Chester J. Rej was among the first returned by the *Honda Knot* in the fall of 1947. The twenty-one-year-old had served only eight months before being killed in the Pacific in 1943. When Rej's body was delivered to his family in Ohio, M.Sgt. Francis P. McGrath was by his side. Rej's parents, John and Julia, thought he was wonderful.

"We have grown so fond of him in his short time that we really miss him a lot," the Rejs wrote to the Quartermaster General. "He has certainly done wonders in comforting us and seemed like one of the family."

William J. Burnett felt the same about the sailor who traveled with the remains of his son, William R. Burnett. The younger Burnett had died of tuberculosis meningitis while serving with the navy in the

Pacific. His body was in the care of CMM Ernest Werner, a sailor whose empathy and tact moved the family. "His very presence in our household made us a lot braver," Burnett said, "and our burden a lot lighter."

Said another parent: "I suppose the boys receive some sort of special training for that unhappy task, but I can only say that nothing he did seemed like training. Every gesture he made seemed to be completely heartfelt."

Grateful parents and widows often wanted to thank escorts—with money, baked goods, or overnight stays in their homes. The army told escorts that accepting gifts was against regulations and, more importantly, degrading to the dignity of returning the dead. But some gestures were too meaningful to refuse.

Edna H. Keighley, a member of the Osage tribe, had a present for her son's escort: a horse. Her son, Pfc. Charles G. Keighley Jr., had died in Europe in 1945. His mother's gift of the animal was a traditional gesture of gratitude. The escort, T.Sgt. Walter F. McFarland, politely declined. Edna Keighley next offered him a colorful blanket. A local funeral director quietly told McFarland that refusing would be an insult. The sergeant thanked her for the blanket, and the Quartermaster General lifted its ban on accepting gifts.

Congress also showed its appreciation for escorts' sensitive and demanding duties. When lawmakers learned that many men were dipping into their own pockets to pay for meals, motels, and laundry because the government's daily allowance only went so far, they hurried to raise the stipend. An escort's daily allowance soon became the highest in the army.

Now and then, loved ones would confront escorts, suspecting that the government had sent home the wrong body. They insisted on opening the casket. Escorts were trained for this, too. They always carried a small pocket photo of an empty coffin's interior and would show it to relatives, hoping it somehow would ease their concerns to see what surrounded the remains of their son or husband. Escorts were not allowed to open a casket while on duty. Instead, they would gently explain that viewing the contents would be horrifying. Still, once relatives received a body, they could pry open the lid in hopes of putting their minds at ease.

In Ohio, Ernest and Selma Peterson had their doubts about the casket delivered to their suburban Cleveland home, unsure if it truly contained their son. Lt. Garrett E. Peterson was just twenty when the C-46 cargo plane he was co-piloting crashed in Burma in 1945. The China-India-Burma Theater, with its dense jungles and towering Himalayas, was a challenging place to locate missing airmen. Despite this, a Graves Registration team found Peterson's body two years later. Even after the army verified his identity through dental records, his parents remained skeptical. But opening a sealed war casket was illegal under Ohio law.

The parents went to court, won, and stood by as the casket was opened in 1948. One can only imagine what they saw, but they were satisfied their son was truly home. They buried him the following day.

* * *

S.Sgt. George W. Goff witnessed the first American deaths in World War II. He also stood in uniform to see that the last of the bodies to come home were treated with dignity.

Goff had been with the Air Corps for less than five months when he was wounded in Japan's attack on Hawaii. A technician at Hickam Field, just four miles from Pearl Harbor, his job was to keep the air base's bombers and fighters in top condition. Japanese planes destroyed many of those planes, both on the flight line and in hangars, as well as Hickam's massive barracks where Goff, then twenty-three, and 3,200 other men lived. Amid explosions, flames, and thick smoke, men fired rifles and pistols at the enemy planes screaming overhead and strafing anything below. Dying and wounded men like Goff overwhelmed doctors and nurses at the airfield's forty-bed hospital.

It was as if Goff couldn't outrun loss and death. Growing up in West Virginia, he faced the heartbreak of losing his mother to an infected gallbladder when he was only four years old. Three years later, his cancer-ridden father died at the hands of a quack doctor. Orphaned, Goff was raised by a widowed aunt in Charleston. Not long after enlisting and arriving in Hawaii, he faced another tragedy when his older brother was electrocuted on a job site.

For his wounds at Hickam Field, Goff was awarded the Purple Heart. That medal likely adorned his uniform when he reported to the Columbus Distribution Center in January 1949. For ten months, he had been riding trains as a military escort, accompanying the remains of airmen to their hometowns in Ohio, Michigan, Pennsylvania, West Virginia, Kentucky, and Indiana. He spent seventy-two hours on duty, followed by seventy-two hours off. His final trip of the month would be to Marion, Indiana.

As with every journey, a mortuary supervisor at the depot handed Goff an envelope containing the documents he needed for his mission. Inside, paperwork told Goff he would be escorting the remains of Cpl. Delbert W. Trueman. Goff only knew Delbert's name and rank, and that a funeral director would meet him in Indiana. There were no details about Delbert's death or who he left behind.

Delbert's casket had sat at the Ohio depot for twenty days since it arrived from Brooklyn. Neat rows of shipping cases containing coffins filled a depot warehouse, awaiting delivery orders and outbound trains. The Columbus center was one of the army's busiest, and some 1,700 sets of remains had arrived that month alone. Shipping cases were never stacked, and a guard always watched over the silent inventory.

With a final careful check for any damage or odor, men lowered an American flag over Delbert's shipping case. Goff carried a second flag to lay across the coffin at the funeral that the Trueman family had long anticipated.

On the morning of January 27, Goff—joined by the remains of an airman cloaked in stars and stripes—boarded a Pennsylvania Railroad passenger train bound for Indiana.

Chapter 15

At Rest

For the fourth straight day, rain soaked Marion.

It was warm for late January in northeast Indiana, and the weather shifted between rain, a stinging sleet, and bursts of snow flurries. Anyone walking outside did so quickly, head tucked into chest.

Freezing rain greeted George Goff and the Pennsylvania Railroad's *Fort Hayes* as they pulled into the city's train station just before lunch-time. Two-and-a-half hours out of Columbus, Ohio, the passenger train was halfway through its daily run between Pittsburgh and Chicago. Marion was one of a dozen small-town stops the *Fort Hayes* made as it bisected Indiana. At each, Goff had left his seat to check on the casket riding in the baggage car—ten times in total since departing Ohio.

Passengers stepping off the train in Marion might not have noticed the hearse idling next to the brick-and-limestone station. The Raven Funeral Home was just a block away. As travelers moved from the coaches into the rainy day, Goff left his coach seat. It was time for one final check of the shipping case containing Delbert's coffin. The flag had to be perfect. He also slipped on his white gloves and gave himself a final look-over. No one would mistake him for anything less than a military escort.

The funeral home staff lifted the shipping case from the train and carried it to the funeral car.

The trip had been a smooth one for Goff, but now came the tough part: Meeting the Trueman family, working with the mortician and minister, and making certain that volunteers from the local American

Legion post carried out a perfect military ceremony. He knew his job was to stay in the background, offer to help when needed, and never burden the family.

The next twenty-eight hours presented Goff with what George Horkan, chief of the army's Memorial Division, called "the payoff"—the culmination of years of work to bring the dead home with dignity.

"We can do a perfect job from overseas to the cemetery at home," Horkan said, "but if we muff the funeral, the whole process can be ruined."

* * *

An hour after George Goff's train arrived in Marion, a second Pennsylvania Railroad train pulled into the passenger station. It had departed Chicago that morning, carrying another military escort and another flag-covered coffin.

Marine Pfc. Robert E. Beard was nineteen when he was killed in action during the Battle of Saipan five years earlier. His fellow marines wrapped him in a poncho and buried him in a temporary trench grave. Beard was posthumously awarded the Silver Star for trying to save the lives of comrades under fire.

After recovering his skeletal remains in 1948, the marines and the army shipped Beard from Saipan to San Francisco, and then on to Indiana.

Beard had lived in Marion when he was a young boy. But after his father was fatally crushed in a car crash, his mother was left unable to care for her children. She placed Robert and his siblings in an orphanage seventy miles away. But she stayed in town, and after the war, she requested that her son be brought home. Anna Beard wanted to be buried alongside her son when the time came.

Robert Beard and Delbert Trueman shared more than a solemn homecoming on that drizzly day. Years later, the families of the two men would be bound in another way: Delbert's niece and Robert's nephew would meet, fall in love, and marry, linked by fallen uncles they never knew.

* * *

The soldiers' returns received quiet mentions in the paper. Marion's headlines focused on cars and basketball. Crosley Motors announced plans to double vehicle production in 1949, with five new models rolling off Marion's assembly line. At Memorial Coliseum, the Marion Giants were struggling to win, stuck at the bottom of their conference standings. Orville Hooker, who had once coached Delbert Trueman and the boys' team to championships in the early 1930s, was now the superintendent of Marion schools.

Talk of World War II had faded. A new enemy was emerging. The editors of the *Marion Leader-Tribune* warned of a growing U.S. confrontation with the Soviet Union. "Five years ago it was said that Russia would not have an atomic bomb 'until 1950.' Since then it has been said that if war comes, it will not come until 1950 or 1952 or 1955. Five years ago those dates seemed safely remote. Now they are almost upon us."

But there were still the dead from World War II to bury.

The Trueman family had known for three days that Delbert's body was on its way. They never doubted whether the army had shipped home the right body. They told friends and relatives about the funeral, ordered flowers, and asked the Rev. Paul Benedict to lead the memorial service.

Benedict had been comforting people since his days as an army chaplain in World War I. He stayed in the reserves while serving Methodist Episcopalian congregations across Indiana for the next two decades. By the time World War II arrived, the idea of returning to full-time work as an Army chaplain was discouraging. Benedict was forty-eight years old, with a wife and two children at home and 1,200 parishioners in the pews of his Fort Wayne church. He asked the army's Chief of Chaplains for a deferment, suggesting, "The first call just now should come to the younger pastors." The army responded by calling him to extended active duty.

For more than two years, Benedict served at stateside army bases, leading services, visiting sick soldiers in the hospital, and performing a marriage every now and then. He put religious tracts and Bibles into the hands of thousands of soldiers. After men repeatedly asked to sing the tune, "Praise the Lord and Pass the Ammunition," Benedict wrote to the chief of chaplains in Washington: Was this tune a gesture of gratitude or outright blasphemy? The head army chaplain declined to weigh in on a song written by a navy chaplain.

New soldiers praised Benedict for helping them feel at ease as they moved through reception centers. Episcopalians, Baptists, Methodists—they all appreciated a style that combined scripture with compassion, concern, and the realities of war.

"I have never forgotten your sermon," one private told him. "I hope our men will live as near right as possible, for we are trying to save the world for living right and free." Added another private, who was becoming a new soldier at age eighteen: "I am sure I'm not speaking for myself alone when I say we need your prayers. We want you to pray for us, for I know that all of us want to be ready if and when the time comes."

In 1944, Benedict left his wife and teenage children to help set up a thousand-bed military hospital in France. After seeing thousands of young men in the United States prepare for combat, Benedict now watched over soldiers whose war was over. Working out of the 191st General Hospital on the outskirts of Paris, Benedict offered solace to men evacuated from combat zones with physical injuries and, more often, psychological wounds. The hospital building had previously been a French mental institution, and the army continued that mission—caring for soldiers torn apart by combat. Doctors gave high doses of insulin and administered electric shocks, hoping to ease soldiers' combat fatigue.

The hospital was always overcrowded and understaffed, with many workers having little training to care for psychiatric patients. Despite the chaos, Benedict—one of only two chaplains—was known for his calming presence. He offered not only prayers, but also patience, insight, and a deep well of compassion.

He would draw on that compassion for Delbert Trueman's memorial service.

Benedict had been serving at Marion's First United Methodist Church for less than two years. One of the first weddings he officiated after arriving in the summer of 1946 united Virginia Trueman and Russell Smalley as they started their life together. Now, walking the short block from the parsonage to the funeral home, he joined Virginia, her daughter, and the Trueman family for Delbert's farewell.

The funeral parlor was filled with more than a dozen vases of flowers bearing sympathy notes. The American War Mothers sent a wreath. Delbert's casket, now removed from its shipping case, was draped with the second American flag that Goff had carried from Columbus.

Dozens of family members and friends gathered: Delbert's parents and two sisters, cousins, classmates from his high school basketball team, friends from work, his old boss, neighbors, and veterans from the local American Legion post. Dale Trueman's widow, Leah, was there, too. Six years earlier, she had sat in the same parlor with a grief-stricken Trueman family. She and Virginia had long shared a quiet bond—sisters-in-law and widows of fallen brothers. Dale had been gone since 1943, and Leah was now engaged to be married later in the spring. Virginia would be her matron of honor.

Guests signed their names in a memorial book filled with Bible verses and poetry; Delbert Trueman, Tennyson assured, was crossing the bar. Each mourner held a small red, white, and blue memorial booklet bearing a gold star and a passage of scripture. "The Lord shall preserve thee from all evil: He shall preserve thy soul. The Lord shall preserve thy going out, and thy coming in, from this time forth, and even for evermore."

* * *

When I asked my mom about her father's homecoming, she became very still.

The day his body arrived in Marion, she and her sixth-grade classmates were away on a field trip. That evening, she and her mother walked quietly into the funeral home. She remembered speaking with George Goff and was touched by his kindness. Escorts were trained to greet all family members with the same words: "On behalf of the Army, I wish to extend my deepest sympathy. Please be assured that I would consider it an honor to be of assistance in any way possible."

As with her father in uniform, my mom recalled that Goff was tall. Until then, her father's death had lived in telegrams and quiet conversations—news delivered when she was just six years old, back in 1944. But now, standing beside the casket, the loss became unmistakably real. Her father wasn't away, he was right there in the room, and so was the weight of everything she hadn't fully understood years earlier.

She and her mother returned to the funeral home the next afternoon; Russ Smalley stayed home with the baby. Inside the parlor, she saw her grandparents, Paul and Nellie, seated in the front row. She had always loved being with them, spending time at their house, poking through closets and storage rooms for hidden treasures. Her aunts, Virginia and Babe, were there, too. Just like with Dale, they were bracing for saying goodbye to another brother.

Sitting a few rows back with her mother, she noticed her grandmother motioning to her: *Come sit with us.* She was Delbert's only child, the Truemans' first grandchild. She slipped away from her mother and joined them in the front row for the minister's words.

Decades later, telling me this story, my mom begins to cry. Not for her deceased father or her grieving grandparents, but for her steadfast mother, sitting alone. "I should have stayed with her," she says, voice breaking with regret.

* * *

The ceremony was brief. Afterward, a six-man color guard from Byron Thornburg American Legion Post 10 carried the coffin to a hearse, with Reverend Benedict leading the procession. The army usually didn't provide pallbearers for civilian cemetery burials and relied on the Legion and Veterans of Foreign Wars instead. With the bodies of Delbert Trueman, Robert Beard, and Charles Garrison arriving in Marion within twenty-four hours, the men of Post 10 stayed busy providing military honors.

The post's namesake was a soldier killed in World War I while driving an ambulance. Like Delbert and others, his body had arrived at the Marion train station for a final burial.

Everyone gathered at Grant Memorial Park at the edge of Marion. As he always did, George Goff carried rounds of blank ammunition in his pocket. He handed them to seven Legionnaires, who fired twenty-one volleys that would echo across the cemetery. A bugler blew "Taps," marking a long, final rest. The veterans solemnly removed the flag from Delbert's casket, folded it into a crisp triangle, and placed it in the hands of Paul and Nellie Trueman.

For the third and final time, Delbert Trueman was lowered into the ground—this time beside his brother, Dale, and surrounded by the people who had raised and loved them both.

For the Truemans, the war was finally over.

* * *

There was no grave marker when my grandfather was laid to rest, for the last time, on that gray January day in 1949. Several months went by before an engraved slab of polished white rock arrived in Indiana, courtesy of the federal government. Once set in place, it flanked the pink granite headstone of Delbert's younger brother. Both had died aboard B-24 bombers, each falling from the sky, trapped in metal and flame. Their deaths, fifteen months apart, left my great-grandparents with no sons and shattered hearts. The brothers' graves are just inches apart.

My grandfather perished at twenty-seven, and his brother at twenty-four. In our family, they are forever "the boys."

The Trueman brothers rest side by side in Marion, Indiana. *Kim Clarke photo*

Delbert Trueman was first laid to rest in one of Europe's most beautiful cemeteries. His second burial took place in a temporary but tidy American military cemetery, where an honor guard was always on duty over the silent troops. His final burial was in the shadow of the Indiana city where he grew up, started a family, and volunteered to avenge the death of his brother.

This is the cemetery that speaks to me: eighty flat acres bordered by soybean fields, a string of greasy fast-food restaurants, and a noisy highway bypass. No gleaming statues or soaring monuments. No uniformed soldiers or stiff military protocol. I've never needed a map to find my grandfather's grave, thanks to visits here with my mother and grandmother, as well as other trips I've taken on my own. It is a place rich with stories, family, and love.

Staring at his headstone, and a tiny American flag that pokes from the soil, I blink away tears at every visit.

My grandfather's first grave, in a remote section of a grand Viennese cemetery, held only a body. The last, where Delbert lies with his brother and parents, holds a life.

Epilogue

Delbert Trueman was the first of the six airmen from his doomed flight to be permanently laid to rest. It would take three more years for the others who died with him in Vienna to be finally buried. Their ultimate fate reflected the options available to next of kin.

Pilot Leonard Thomas Mojica was buried in Holy Cross Cemetery in Los Angeles in 1949, just six days after Delbert's funeral. For years, Mojica's mother had pleaded for his return. "I thank God that he is here where I can visit his grave as often as I wish," she wrote to the army's Memorial Division.

Still, she was haunted by questions for months afterward. Where, exactly, had Leonard's body first been found? Was it possible that somewhere, anywhere, the army still had some of his belongings, like letters and birthday presents she had mailed to him? Her former daughter-in-law had broken all promises to share Leonard's personal belongings. And was her son's body really in the casket that arrived in California?

"I've heard so many stories that I just can't believe, about sending the wrong body home to a family," she wrote. "I've just got to know all the details about recovering my son's body."

The Memorial Division assured her that Leonard's remains were first discovered with his crew in Austria and positively identified at an army laboratory in France. "May you bear your grief bravely and proudly because of the courage and ideals that your son's life and service exemplified," a lieutenant colonel told her.

Marvin Niederjohn, Mojica's co-pilot, had no marked grave of his own. His remains were mixed with twenty-six other airmen recovered in 1946 from the chaotic wartime burials in Vienna's Central Cemetery.

They represented thirteen different bomb groups that had targeted the Austrian capital in 1944 and 1945. While the army knew the names of the men, they could not identify them individually. Still, each man was honored with a flag-draped casket at a mass burial service at Jefferson Barracks National Cemetery in St. Louis, Missouri, in September 1952. Servicemen in uniform and family members from twenty-six states surrounded the coffins, joined by Catholic, Jewish, and Protestant chaplains.

Bombardier George E. Webb's body traveled the shortest distance from St. Avold Military Cemetery for final burial. His parents asked that their son remain in France, and his body was reinterred in March 1949 at the new Lorraine American Cemetery, just a half-mile from the St. Avold burial ground.

Elvin R. Killingsworth, the young gunner nicknamed "Killer" by his crewmates, came home to the United States in March 1950—fourteen months after Delbert's burial. For years, Killingsworth's remains were unidentifiable and labeled X-7122. His identity had been a mystery because German troops, when burying him in Vienna, placed the dog tags of another airman in Killingsworth's coffin. Finally, in the fall of 1949, technicians matched his teeth and clothing with earlier records. His obituary appeared on an inside page of the local newspaper he once delivered as a boy. He was buried in Golden Gate National Cemetery in San Bruno, California.

Charles Kleinhenz Jr., another gunner, was among the last of the Mojica crew to be buried permanently. His father had for years refused to sign the paperwork indicating where his son should be laid to rest. He still denied that his only child was gone.

"Mrs. Kleinhenz is rational and accepts the facts of her son's death," a Red Cross worker reported, "but is afraid to say so because she does not feel able to act contrary to her husband's wishes."

The elder Kleinhenz, though active in his local American Legion post and serving with honor and firing guards for military funerals, would not acknowledge his son's death. When the army sent a final letter to Charles Sr. stating the remains of his namesake would stay overseas if he did not respond, the father relented and asked for a burial in Europe.

After two years in storage after being exhumed from St. Avold, Charles Jr. was finally interred in Ardennes American Cemetery in Belgium in July 1950.

The two airmen buried in the same grave as Delbert in Vienna were laid to rest permanently in 1948.

Sam Holquin, the young man who had served time in prison before the war and whom the army had once rejected, was buried three days after Christmas in Lorraine American Cemetery on the outskirts of St. Avold.

Kirk Mosher's body was loaded onto the USAT *Oglethorpe Victory* and then wound its way from New York to New Mexico, where he had grown up playing in swing bands with his father. His parents requested that he be buried in Santa Fe National Cemetery. In Albuquerque, a street developed by his family bears his name: Kirk's Court.

* * *

Four airmen on Delbert's doomed mission survived the deadly attack over Vienna and parachuted to a brief moment of safety before being captured by German soldiers. They spent the rest of the war in prison camps.

Gunner Richard L. Conkle returned to his home along Virginia's Rappahannock River after being liberated. He had flown thirty-seven missions before falling from the sky in 1944. During a brutal forced march across Europe, as POWs moved from northeast Poland to western Germany, Conkle drifted out of line, hoping to sneak a moment of rest in some woods. A German soldier caught him and drove a bayonet into Conkle's calf, adding, "I bet you will keep up now." After the war, Conkle later had a tattoo inked on his lower leg, a dagger plunging into one side and exiting the other.

Filling out a military questionnaire after his release, Conkle described the situation in the B-24 as it went into a flat spin. "Everyone was frightened," he scrawled. Back home, he had occasional nightmares, once climbing out a window, grabbing at his shirt, and screaming, "She's going down!" Still, he reenlisted and made a career with the air force. He died in 1980 at age fifty-four.

Photographer Richard J. Pinardi also reenlisted after being liberated in Germany in 1945 and served with the air force during the Korean War. He returned home to Massachusetts and dedicated a room in his house to all things World War II. He died in 2017 at the age of ninety-three.

Engineer Joseph J. Marallo survived prison camp, barely. In early 1945, as Red Army troops closed in on Germany, he and fellow prisoners were herded into train cars and moved to Nuremberg. "Fifty guys in a boxcar. It was brutal. Narrow-gauge cars. We were ten days in that boxcar. It was bad, really bad," he told me. They were forced to march again, this time walking one hundred miles from Nuremberg to Munich. Along the way, their captors told the Americans that President Roosevelt had died. "The Germans let one of the guys blow 'Taps,'" he said.

Once back home, Marallo traveled to Los Angeles for the funeral of his former pilot, Leonard Mojica. He married, became a father and grandfather, and retired after working as an engineer. He died in 1995 at age seventy-two.

Radio operator and gunner Robert A. Davis—the last man to speak with Delbert Trueman before their B-24 left Italy for Vienna—returned home to upstate New York to recover from his injuries. Life as a prisoner of war had drained sixty pounds from his already thin frame. He later worked as a radar controller at Griffiss Air Force Base near his upstate New York home. Years would pass before he and Joe Marallo reconnected and realized they lived just fifteen miles apart. When Davis and his wife, Kathleen—the young woman he had married just before leaving for the war in Europe—celebrated their fiftieth wedding anniversary, Marallo made a point of attending. Davis became the historian for the 450th Bomb Group Association, collecting and recording men's stories. After he died in 2012 at eighty-seven years old, Davis was buried in Arlington National Cemetery, with Kathleen at rest next to him.

While the four survivors languished in POW camps, the crews of the 450th Bomb Group continued attacking targets in Austria and Germany. Delbert's best friend in the service, Charlie Ward, survived thirty-four combat missions as a ball turret gunner. He returned home to his wife, Myrta, and their daughter, Carol—the Wards had been neighbors and friends with Delbert and Virginia when the men were stationed in Savannah for a steamy summer in 1944.

A year after the war ended, Charlie and Myrta welcomed a son. They named him Delbert.

* * *

The men who worked to recover Delbert Trueman's body and thousands of others from Europe moved forward with life after dealing with so much death. Some made careers in the military. Others walked away, haunted by their experiences of returning the dead.

After the army discharged him, Michihiko Hayashida returned to Boston University to finish the studies interrupted when he was drafted. He earned a bachelor's degree in 1949 and a medical degree in 1953. His interest in medicine had little to do with the countless bodies he saw during his service in Graves Registration. Instead, he had been drawn to the field as a teenager at the Topaz internment camp, and he had a part-time job working the night shift at a hospital in Salt Lake City. Assisting nurses and helping patients in the emergency department inspired him. He went on to become an ophthalmologist practicing in Hawaii.

When the St. Avold temporary cemetery closed in 1949, embalmer Karl Kasca and his wife, Berenice, made their way to Paris for a flight home to California. A phone call from the army convinced them to stay. They moved to Frankfurt, Germany, where Karl continued preparing the remains of Americans who had recently died while on duty as soldiers or civilian employees, often in car crashes, or by drowning, or sometimes in a fight. Kasca and two colleagues traveled constantly, flying across Europe, Africa, the Middle East, and the Azores to handle remains. Bodies needed to be embalmed and readied for funerals in the United States.

"Sometimes it took as much as three months for a body to reach home," Kasca said. "And they had to be presentable when they got there. Restorative art got to be one of my big things."

But it became too much. Between the desiccated remains of war dead and the fresh bodies of servicemen younger than he was, Kasca calculated he had worked with thirty thousand corpses. When he finally left Europe, he made a vow: No more coffins, no more death. He never returned to being a mortician. He worked as a machinist and then supervisor at a steel plant, dabbled in selling real estate, and closed out his working career by returning to the navy to refuel nuclear submarines. He would live to be eighty-four years old, but never again attended a funeral.

Robert Howard, who watched over Delbert as his coffin was moved from Europe to New York aboard the *Barney Kirschbaum*, made a career with the army. He served in three wars, was wounded twice in Korea, and earned two Bronze Stars. His experience with Graves Registration units and ferrying the dead of World War II across the sea was something he never shared with his family.

* * *

In the earliest days of planning how the nation would respond to a return of those lost in World War II, Col. Robert Harbold predicted that 95 percent of families would expect homecomings. The figure then dropped to 80 percent, and later to 70 percent, as parents and widows officially shared their wishes with the government.

Graves Registration teams recovered more than 281,000 bodies from across the globe after the war. During the busiest months of the return program, upward of 13,000 men and women, soldiers and civilians alike, devoted themselves to honoring the dead and ensuring they received proper burials in locations selected by families.

In the end, 61 percent of those who died overseas—about 171,000 bodies—were brought home. Fourteen military cemeteries were set up worldwide for nearly 110,000 war dead whose families requested they remain overseas. The Lorraine American Cemetery, which grew out of the temporary St. Avold Military Cemetery, holds more World War II dead than any other U.S. cemetery in Europe.

For American taxpayers, the six-year worldwide operation came in under budget at nearly $158 million, well below the projected $210 million.

Cost was never Col. Robert Harbold's concern. What mattered most was that families be heard. "Final disposition of our soldiers' remains, in accordance with the wishes of their loved ones, is an inherent obligation of the government as the final gesture of a grateful country to those who paid the supreme sacrifice." Those were the words of the original plan he submitted to the army in 1943.

The program to return the dead officially ended on the last day of 1951. Eleven months later, Harbold died in his sleep when his heart gave out. He was seventy-one, and it was Veterans Day.

Three days later, he was laid to rest with honors at Arlington National Cemetery. Soldiers fired a twenty-one-gun salute, and—as had happened countless times at countless cemeteries since 1945—a bugler blew the melancholy notes of "Taps." Harbold was buried among thousands of war dead he had worked to bring home, on a hillside below the Tomb of the Unknown Soldier.

* * *

When he was stationed in Texas in early 1944, Delbert Trueman wrote to his daughter, Judy, to say he was sending her a carton. It was a few days after Easter, and he was feeling hopeful. He imagined Judy was the "cat's ankle on Easter . . . all dressed up in your new clothes and all." He missed celebrating the holiday with her and Virginia. "Maybe next Easter, huh?" he told his daughter.

The box he mailed home was filled with letters and postcards. He told Judy to give it to her mother for safekeeping. "She can keep them somewhere so that you, she and I can sit down and read them sometime when this old war is over. We will probably get lots of laughs out of them, too."

There were, of course, no laughs to come. Delbert's death crushed those who loved him. Yet Virginia, my grandmother, always kept his memory alive for their daughter. She saved every letter he wrote to my mother, every photograph, every mundane military form, and every devastating telegram. Without her love and foresight, there would be far less to tell about Delbert Wayne Trueman.

Delbert's small collection of possessions was placed into the wooden crate that my mother unpacked for my sisters and me decades later, when we were young and she first explained the loss of her airman father. She eventually passed on the crate to me, handing me a touchstone to a man and grandfather I never knew but would come to know in a small way.

Just as meaningful as my grandmother's desire to honor Delbert's sacrifice was the generosity of my grandfather, Joseph Russell Smalley. I think of how fortunate my grandmother and mother were to have him in their lives after Delbert's death. He made them a family again. He graced my mom with unconditional love. He brought her into his large and welcoming Smalley clan; she loved visiting the family farm and playing with more than a dozen cousins. And he always respected my mother's unbreakable bonds with the Trueman family.

Major holidays like Easter, Thanksgiving, and Christmas often found our family traveling from Michigan to Indiana to stay with my Smalley grandparents. Those visits always included an evening with the Truemans—Delbert's sisters, their families, and his mother, Nellie. The adults sat around the dining room table, playing cards, smoking cigarettes, and drinking beer, while we kids played in the basement.

By then, my great-grandfather, Paul Trueman, was gone; he died in 1957, before I was born. But Nellie Trueman was present. As a child, I never quite understood my connections to these people, only that I had aunts and uncles, cousins, and a great-grandmother with snowy white hair. With the softest hands, she would cup my face and kiss my cheek. I was her first great-grandchild, born to the daughter of her lost son.

As I began to seriously explore Delbert's death and his long journey home, I sat down with my grandmother. I wanted her to know that my interest in telling Delbert's story didn't diminish the love I had for my grandpa, who had died years earlier and meant everything to our family. She said she understood and assured me he would understand as well.

Once, as we thumbed through a scrapbook filled with photos and clippings about Delbert, she admired his thick head of hair. "I've always wondered what he'd look like now."

She lived to be ninety-eight years old, with three children, six grandchildren, eleven great-grandchildren, and one great-great-granddaughter. She survived both of her husbands. When I asked if she ever thought about Delbert, she answered in a quiet voice: "I miss them both."

* * *

In her final years, my mother fought the cruelty of Alzheimer's disease. As she became weaker and more confused, she desperately tried to hold on to her sense of self. My siblings and I, terrified she might forget us, hung large black-and-white baby pictures in her room at the memory care facility. Beneath each frame, we added a name: Kim, Cory, Kelly, Curtis. Her most treasured memories remained with her. She always remembered us.

And she never forgot Delbert.

Entering her final weeks, she reached up from her bed and grasped my wrist. Her hand was bony and nearly as weak as her voice. But I did not pull away.

"Please. Promise me."

Are we in the present or the past? It was hard to tell anymore. Alzheimer's was strangling her brain. Whatever the subject, whatever the promise she wanted, I tried to deflect it.

Promise me.

I tried changing the subject. She looked hard at me, locking her eyes with mine. She wouldn't relax her grip or release her stare. She didn't budge.

Promise me.

And then I understood. She knew I had been gathering Delbert's story, and now she wanted a commitment. Honor him.

Promise me. Please.

I relented. I said I would share the story of absent fathers and grieving mothers, of Marion and Vienna and St. Avold, of uniforms and duty, of dirt and sky and death.

I have reflected on this wartime saga while sitting beside a bookshelf that holds the folded American flag from Delbert Trueman's casket, pressed into a tight triangle and encased in glass and wood. Nearby is his official black-and-white military portrait, his service cap slightly cocked on his head, the silver wings of an aerial gunner pinned over his heart. He is forever twenty-seven.

Promise kept, Mom.

Cpl. Delbert Wayne Trueman, 1917–1944. *Photo courtesy Kim Clarke*

Acknowledgments

Many people have made it possible for me to share a story I've always wanted to tell.

I am indebted to Stackpole Books and Globe Pequot for their faith and support in sharing this story. The collective contributions of editor Dave Reisch from Stackpole, production editor Nicole Myers from Globe Pequot, project manager Gomathy Ilammathe, and copyeditor Veronica Jurgena have been invaluable.

I have had the good fortune to learn from exceptional writers and editors at Boston University's annual Power of Narrative conference and the Iowa Summer Writing Festival at the University of Iowa. I would be remiss if I didn't single out Christine Hemp, an author and writing coach who always provided thoughtful feedback.

I have spent far too long researching this mostly unknown chapter of the war, and the veterans who shared their stories with me are no longer with us. The passing of these men does not lessen my appreciation or gratitude for their cooperation and insights.

I feel especially fortunate to have interviewed three of the airmen who survived the October 1944 bomber crash that took my grandfather's life. Robert Davis, Joseph Marallo, and Richard J. Pinardi were incredibly gracious with their time, and I am honored to have had the chance to connect with them.

Robert Karstensen, president and historian of the 451st Bomb Group, and Duane L. "Sparky" Bohnstedt, 460th Bomb Group historian, always responded to my questions and shared documents about airmen's lives in a combat zone.

Michihiko Hayashida was especially kind in explaining his duties in Vienna after the war and the dishonorable treatment his family and other Japanese Americans faced as World War II progressed for the United States. Karl and Berenice Kasca shared their experiences—some of them painful—of war-ravaged Europe and their time spent in American cemeteries, as did Henry Alzmann and Margaret House.

I am equally grateful to the family members of the men whose wartime lives I explored. They have been kind and patient in sharing letters, photographs, and memories of their loved ones. Carmie Campbell, Richard I. Conkle, Frances Hayashida, Kathryn L. Howard, Timothy B. Howard, Karl Kasca II, Daniel Mosher, Winona Speed, and Delbert "Chuck" Ward—all were generous with their time.

The duties and experiences of Graves Registration officers and enlisted men can be explored through the collections at the U.S. Army Heritage and Education Center in Carlisle, Pennsylvania. This is the army's top historical research facility, and I was honored to receive a General and Mrs. Matthew B. Ridgway Research Grant to conduct research there. Kate C. Lemay, director of USAHEC, was very supportive and encouraging about a topic that interests us both. Library technician Tom Buffenbarger provided all the materials I requested, and then brought out more holdings he thought might be helpful. They were.

At Boston University, Archivist and Preservation Librarian Kara Jackman went out of her way to share and explain the Edwin Prince Booth Papers kept in the School of Theology Library. At Butler University in Indianapolis, librarian Sally Childs-Helton at the Irwin Library's Special Collections, Rare Books, and University Archives, and Libby Holmes in the Registrar's Office helped locate what scant records existed from Delbert Trueman's short tenure as a student in the 1930s. Records related to Chaplain Howard Lee's academic journeys were provided by archivist Barbara Kievit-Mason at Sam Houston State University and archivist Jill Botticelli at the Southwestern Baptist Theological Seminary Libraries.

Renee Bissell-Cole of the Marion Public Library History Center in Indiana produced archival files and folders that helped illuminate the city's people and places during the war.

I am also grateful for the assistance of Samuel C. Shearin, Air Force Historical Research Agency; Laëtitia Desserrieres, Musée de l'Armée, Hotel des Invalides; Luther Hanson, U.S. Quartermaster Museum; Cindy Lindsay, Columbus (Ohio) Metropolitan Library; and archivists and technicians at National Archives and Records Administration locations in Washington, D.C.; College Park, Maryland; St. Louis; New York City; and Atlanta.

In New York, Andrew Gustafson of Turnstile Tours provided a fascinating exploration and history of the Brooklyn Army Terminal.

More than anything, I am indebted to friends and family who never wavered in their support or grew weary of my exploration of this story.

My friend John Stephenson is a longtime newspaper editor who has always made me a better writer. Add to that his deep knowledge of World War II, and his feedback made for a stronger manuscript.

I have been fortunate to work as a writer at the University of Michigan for thirty years. No one there has championed my work more than President Emerita Mary Sue Coleman. She is a mentor, role model, and, most importantly, a friend. She and her husband, Ken Coleman, have been relentless with their encouragement (and lovely dinners).

James Tobin is an accomplished author and historian, and I am incredibly lucky to call him a dear friend. No one has provided greater guidance and encouragement as I embarked on the journey of writing a full-length manuscript. His advice has been simply immeasurable.

This book is a story about family, and my siblings have been steadfast and supportive as I've worked through ideas, drafts, and memories. Cory Taylor, Kelly Rost, and Curtis Clarke—thank you. Our parents, Jack and Judy, are gone, but their love and lessons continually buoy me.

My husband Barry LaRue has truly been my rock. "For better or for worse" may not specifically describe enduring the ups and downs of authorship, but he has always stood by my side. He has kept me grounded while also constantly pushing me to never give up on a dream project I've subjected him to for, well, decades. He is the best partner. Period.

Select Bibliography

A Note on Sources

U.S. Army and War Department training manuals, guidebooks, memos, and film footage related to the work of the American Graves Registration Service have been invaluable in understanding and re-creating the duties carried out by soldiers and civilians who managed the dead of World War II.

Any exploration of the war dead and how the American government cared for them must begin with the epic work of historian Edward Steere. His study, *Final Disposition of World War II Dead, 1945–51,* written with Thayer Boardman, provides all manner of details and insight—from fascinating to bureaucratically dull—about the massive five-year program. An earlier Steere work, *The Graves Registration Service in World War II,* is an equally important examination of one of the least glamorous duties that come with combat. This includes the work of Graves Registration soldiers and officers in the Pacific Theater. Procedures were often the same, although burial and disinterment conditions—heat, humidity, water, countless islands—were more challenging.

The Office of the Quartermaster General commissioned both studies. Steere wrote them to document the history of what went right and wrong in handling the dead of World War II, and to provide a blueprint for future wars. "If these suggestions and activities should be carried out in any future hostilities," he wrote, "the American public has every right to expect that the lessons learned from mistakes and omissions of the past will result in a more efficient program for care and return of those who lose their lives in the cause of freedom."

BOOKS AND ARTICLES

34th Bombardment Group (H) 1941–1945. Turner Publishing Company, 1988.

450th Bomb Group (H): The "Cottontails" of WWII. Turner Publishing Company, 1996.

Anders, Steven. "With All Due Honors . . ." *Quartermaster Professional Bulletin*, Autumn/Winter 1994.

Arakaki, Leatrice R., and John R. Kuborn. *7 December 1941: The Air Force Story.* Pacific Air Forces Office of History, 1991.

Banny, Leopold. *Dröhnender Himmel, Brennendes Land: Der Einsatz Der Luftwaffenhelfer in Österreich 1943–45.* Österreichischer Bundesverlag Gesellschaft, 1988.

Birdsall, Steve. *The B-24 Liberator.* Arco Publishing Company, 1968.

———. *Log of the Liberators: An Illustrated History of the B-24.* Doubleday & Company, Inc., 1973.

Booth, Edwin Prince. "Let Them Rest in Peace." *Reader's Digest,* May 1947.

———. *From Experience to Faith.* Association Press, 1951.

Bowman, Martin W. *The B-24 Liberator 1939–45.* Rand McNally & Company, 1979.

———. *USAAF Handbook 1939–1945.* Stackpole Books, 1997.

Brown, David. "If I Don't Get Back." *American Legion Magazine*, June 1945.

Browning, Robert M. Jr. *United States Merchant Marine War Casualties of World War II.* McFarland & Co. Publishers, 2011.

Budreau, Lisa M. *Bodies of War: World War I and the Politics of Commemoration in America, 1919–1933.* New York University Press, 2011.

Buecker, Thomas R. "Prelude to Brownsville: The Twenty-Fifth Infantry at Fort Niobrara, Nebraska, 1902–06." *Great Plains Quarterly*, Spring 1996.

Carter, Kit C., and Robert Mueller. *The Army Air Forces in World War II: Combat Chronology, 1941–1945.* Office of Air Force History, 1973.

Central Identification Point, European Theater Area. American Graves Registration Command, 1947.

C'est La Guerre!: 612th Graves Registration Company, 1943–1945. Publisher not identified.

The Chaplain Serves. Chief of Chaplains, Army Service Forces, Department of the Army, 1944.

Cohn, David. "The Soldier Dead Come Home." *Atlantic Monthly*, May 1, 1947.

Conduct of a Military Funeral. United States War Department, 1947.

Conner, Thomas H. *War and Remembrance: The Story of the American Battle Monuments Commission.* University Press of Kentucky, 2018.

Cubbins, William R. *The War of the Cottontails: Memoirs of a WWII Bomber Pilot.* Algonquin Books, 1989.

Davis, Larry. *B-24 Liberator in Action.* Squadron/Signal Publications, 1987.

Dickon, Chris. *The Foreign Burial of American War Dead: A History.* McFarland & Company, 2011.

Dowling, Tom. "The Graves We Dug." *Army*, January 1989.

Effects Warehousing: A Study. Army Effects Bureau, 1945.

Escorting American War Dead. War and Navy Departments, 1947.

Final Report of the 191st (US) General Hospital. 191st General Hospital, 1945.

Fletcher, Marvin. *The Black Soldier and Officer in the United States Army, 1891–1917.* University of Missouri Press, 1974.

Flight Manual for B-24 Liberator. Aviation Publications, 1942.

Gage, John N. "Distribution Center." *Quartermaster Review*, May–June 1948.

Get That Fighter. Army Air Forces, 1943.

Graves Registration. *Technical Manual No. 10-630.* United States War Department, 1941.

Graves Registration. *Technical Manual No. 10-63.* United States War Department, 1945.

Gushwa, Robert L. *The Best and Worst of Times: The United States Army Chaplaincy, 1920–1945.* Office of the Chief of Chaplains, Department of the Army, 1977.

Handbook for Military Escorts. Headquarters Fifth Army, 1948.

Hasdorff, James C. *Interview of Major General Norris B. Harbold.* United States Air Force Oral History Program, 1987.

History of the American Graves Registration Service, Q.M.C. in Europe. United States Army, 1976.

Horkan, George A. "Postwar Mission Up To Now." *Quartermaster Review*, May–June 1948.

Hunton, Addie W., and Kathryn M. Johnson. *Two Colored Women with the American Expeditionary Forces.* Brooklyn Eagle Press, 1920.

An Interview with George W. Ciampa. Nimitz Education and Research Center, National Museum of the Pacific War, 2016.

Iritani, Joanne. *Oral History Interview with Beverlee Howe Filloy.* Florin Japanese American Citizens League, 2000.

Kidder, Warren Benjamin. *Willow Run: Colossus of American Industry.* KFT, 1995.

La Speranza, Marcello. *Bomben auf Wien: Zeitzeugen Breichten.* Ibera Verlag, 2003.

Lemay, Kate Clarke. *Triumph of the Dead: American World War II Cemeteries, Monuments, and Diplomacy in France.* University of Alabama Press, 2018.

Littlejohn, Robert M. *Passing in Review.* Publisher not identified, 1955.

Maguire, Jon A. *Gear Up! Flight Clothing and Equipment of USAAF Airmen in World War II.* Schiffer Publishing Ltd., 1995.

McGuire, Melvin W., and Robert Hadley. *Bloody Skies: A 15th AAF B-17 Combat Crew: How They Lived and Died.* Yucca Tree Press, 1993.

McKay, Neal H. "Port Operations." *Quartermaster Review*, May–June 1948.

Memoir of Ronald Croft (531st & 551st Quartermaster Groups—Graves Registration), 1944–1947. U.S. 7th Armored Division Association website, May 2009.

Military Escorts: Return of World War II Dead. United States Department of the Army, 1948.

Military Government of Austria. Report of the United States Commissioner, November 1945.

Mossman, Billy C. *The Last Salute: Civil and Military Funerals, 1921–1969.* Department of the Army, 1971.

Murrie, James I., and Naomi Jeffery Petersen. "The Last Train Ride: Return of the World War II Dead," *Railroad History*, Spring–Summer 2015.

North, Thomas. "Permanent Overseas Cemeteries." *The Quartermaster Review*, May–June 1948.

Operations of the Quartermaster Corps, U.S. Army, During the World War. Historical Report of the Chief Quartermaster, A.E.F., France, 1929.

Perkins, Paul, and Michelle Crean. *The Soldier: Consolidated B-24 Liberator.* Howell Press, 1994.

Perret, Geoffrey. *Winged Victory: The Army Air Forces in World War II.* Random House, 1993.

Phelan, Lawrence J. ". . . But for the Grace of God." *Army Information Digest*, January 1948.

Pilots' Information File: The Authentic World War II Guidebook for Pilots and Flight Engineers. Schiffer Publishing Ltd., 1995.

Plan for Repatriation of the Dead of World War II and Establishment of Permanent United States Military Cemeteries at Home and Abroad. United States War Department, 1945.

Plank, Ewart G., and E. H. Lastayo. "New York Port of Embarkation." *Army Transportation Journal*, March–April 1948.

Postwar Graves Registration Activities in an Overseas Theater. Office of the Quartermaster General, United States War Department, August 1947.

"Railroad Movement of World War II Dead." *Railway Age*, February 1948.

Ramsey, A. C. "Effects Depot." *Quartermaster Review*, September–October 1945.

Report of the Commission Appointed by the President to Investigate the Conduct of the War Department in the War with Spain. U.S. Government Printing Office, 1899.

Report on the Army Chaplain in the European Theater. The General Board, United States Forces, European Theater, 1946.

Report to the Secretary of War on American Military Dead Overseas. United States War Department, 1920.

Risch, Erna. *Quartermaster Support of the Army: A History of the Corps, 1775–1939.* Office of the Quartermaster General, 1962.

Risch, Erna, and Chester L. Kieffer. *The Quartermaster Corps: Organization, Supply, and Services, Vol. 2.* Department of the Army, 1955.

Ross, William F., and Charles F. Romanus. *The Quartermaster Corps: Operations in the War Against Germany.* Department of the Army, 1965.

Schuyler, Keith C. *Elusive Horizons.* A. S. Barnes and Company, 1969.

Shomon, Joseph James. *Crosses in the Wind.* Stratford House, Inc. 1947.

Sinclair, Francis and Lawrence J. Weidmann. *The Battle of Bourges: American Expeditionary Forces. Bourges.* Impr. L. Renaud, 1919.

Steere, Edward. *The Graves Registration Service in World War II.* Q. M. C. Historical Studies, 1951.

Steere, Edward, and Thayer M. Boardman. *Final Disposition of World War II Dead, 1945–51.* Historical Branch, Office of the Quartermaster General, 1957.

Steinbeck, John. *Bombs Away: The Story of a Bomber Team.* Viking Press, 1942.

Venzke, Rodger R. *Confidence in Battle, Inspiration in Peace: The United States Army Chaplaincy, 1945–1975.* Office of the Chief of Chaplains, Department of the Army, 1977.

Vezzano to Desert Storm: History of the Fifteenth Air Force: 1943–1991. U.S. Department of the Air Force, 1991.

Werrell, Kenneth P. "Friendly Rivals: The Eighth and Fifteenth Air Forces in World War II." *Air Power History*, 1991.

Whitlock, L. J. "Escorts and Honors." *Quartermaster Review*, May–June 1948.

Williams, Marc. *Flowers-by-Wire: The Story of the Florists' Telegraph Delivery Association*. Mercury House, 1960.

Williamson, John A. *Antisubmarine Warfare in the Pacific: Six Subs Sunk in Twelve Days*. University of Alabama Press, 2020.

Winkler, Allan M. *Home Front U.S.A.: America During World War II*. Harlan Davidson, 1986.

Wooley, Richard W. "A Short History of Identification Tags." *Quartermaster Professional Bulletin*, December 1988.

Wuest, Karl A. *They Told It to the Chaplain*. Vantage Press, 1953.

Your Body in Flight: An Illustrated "Book of Knowledge" for the Flyer. U.S. Army Air Forces, 1943.

Archival Collections

Boston University School of Theology Library
- Edwin Prince Booth Papers

Library of Congress
- Japanese American Internment Camp Newspapers, 1942 to 1946
- Veterans History Project Collection

National Archives and Records Administration
- Record Group 26: Records of the United States Coast Guard
  - Series: Marine Board Case Files
  - Series: Vessel Documentation Case Files
  - Series: Official Logbooks of Merchant Vessels, 1942–1981
- Record Group 64: Records of the National Archives and Records Administration
  - Series: Morning Reports, 1940–1946
- Record Group 92: Records of the Office of the Quartermaster General
  - Series: Correspondence, Reports, Telegrams, Applications, and Other Papers Relating to Burials of Service Personnel
  - Series: Individual Deceased Personnel Files, 1939–1953
  - Series: Missing Air Crew Reports
- Record Group 111: Records of the Office of the Chief Signal Officer
  - Series: Historical Films
  - Series: Index to Personalities in the U.S. Army Signal Corps Photographic Files, 1940–1954
  - Series: Moving Images Relating to Military Activities
- Record Group 178: Records of the U.S. Maritime Commission
  - Series: Central Correspondence Files, 1936–1950

Record Group 242: National Archives Collection of Foreign Records Seized
Series: Downed Allied Aircraft Reports
Record Group 247: Records of the Office of the Chief of Chaplains
Series: Monthly Reports and Personnel Records
Record Group 319: Records of the Army Staff
Series: Official Military Personnel Files, 1912–1998

United States Army Heritage and Education Center
American Graves Registration Papers
Robert M. Littlejohn Papers

AUTHOR INTERVIEWS

Alzmann, Henry, 337th Quartermaster Battalion
Clarke, Judith A., daughter of Delbert Trueman
Davis, Robert A., 450th Bomb Group
Garbarini, Peter, 450th Bomb Group
Hayashida, Michihiko, 612th Quartermaster Graves Registration Company
House, Margaret, Clerk, American Graves Registration Command
Kasca, Karl K., Embalmer, American Graves Registration Command
Kitzman, Richard, 450th Bomb Group
Marallo, Joseph J., 450th Bomb Group
Messner, Robert M., 450th Bomb Group
Perkins, Floyd, 450th Bomb Group
Pinardi, Richard J., 450th Bomb Group
Smalley, Virginia A., wife of Delbert Trueman
Ward, Charles, 450th Bomb Group
White, Bess, widow of Lloyd White, 450th Bomb Group

WEBSITES

25th Infantry Wreckers: darowski.com/wreckers
450th Bomb Group Memorial Association: 450thbg.com
Ancestry: ancestry.com
Arlington National Cemetery: arlingtoncemetery.mil
Austrian National Library: anno.onb.ac.at
Fold3: fold3.com
Library of Congress Veterans History Collection Project: loc.gov/collections/veterans-history-project-collection
Newspapers.com: newspapers.com
ProQuest Congressional: congressional.proquest.com
Speaking of Kansas City Regional Oral History Collection: speakingkc.org
State Historical Society of Missouri: digital.shsmo.org/digital/collection/wwii
The U.S. Airborne During World War II: ww2-airborne.us
WWII Research & Writing Center: wwiiresearchandwritingcenter.com

Other Records

Davis, Robert: written account of 42-51566 downing
Kasca, Karl: family correspondence
Trueman, Dale: family correspondence
Trueman, Delbert: family correspondence, high school scrapbooks, high school yearbooks, military records, and photographs
White, Lloyd: World War II diary

www.ingramcontent.com/pod-product-compliance
Ingram Content Group UK Ltd.
Pitfield, Milton Keynes, MK11 3LW, UK
UKHW011933180826
8007IPUK00002B/4

9 780811 777667